Shakespeare's
Military
World

PAUL A. JORGENSEN

Shakespeare's Military World

UNIVERSITY OF CALIFORNIA PRESS
BERKELEY, LOS ANGELES, LONDON

University of California Press

Berkeley and Los Angeles, California

University of California Press, Ltd., London, England

Copyright 1956 by The Regents of the University of California

California Library Reprint Series Edition, 1973

ISBN: 0-520-02519-9

Library of Congress Catalogue Card No.: 73-87550

Printed in the United States of America

Designed by A. R. Tommasini

To
My Wife

Preface

For its size, if for no other reason, Shakespeare's military world commands the respectful attention of all who seek a better knowledge of his plays and ideas generally. Within its bounds are the battles which occur incessantly throughout the histories and which make themselves loudly heard in the most sedate of the tragedies; the armies which march across the stage even in plays where there is no warfare, or which straggle and limp across the stage if they are captained by a Falstaff; the soldiers who range from reluctant recruits to generals, and comprise at once the noblest and the most disreputable of Shakespeare's characters; and, finally, the ideas which govern warfare and armies, and the role of war in society. No one book, surely, can bring this entire domain within view. Shakespeare himself took many plays for the task, and even his vision was often fragmentary. He recognized that war is not a steady segment of human experience, that its presence may be felt without clashing armies, and that "peace" may be only an imperfectly identified stage of war.

Thus aware of the unsteady nature of my subject, I have tried to bring at least momentarily within view several aspects of Shakespeare's military world, and its population, which were manifestly of real interest to him and to his audience. I have sought the recurrent, the deliberate, in his point of view and artistry. Above all, I have tried to interpret his concept of war and his military personnel in Renaissance terms. Shakespeare's ideas about war were primarily those of his own day; and he altered even classical history to agree with contemporary doctrine. I would not, however, make of him a journalistic reporter of Elizabethan warfare. In the first chapter I suggest reasons why he resisted, for a large part of his dramatic career at least, a strongly detailed reproduction of current trends. He was not a professional, nor even a conscientious student of military science. Nevertheless, most of his military ideas would have been recognized as real, perhaps urgent, when they were first spoken from London stages. And to place ourselves in the position of his audience, we must refer to the printed sources of those military ideas: the numerous military treatises and newsbooks published during Shakespeare's lifetime. Only a sympathetic reading of these battered volumes—verbose, malprinted, and grimly didactic as they are—can prevent our seeing quaintness in the paltry armies and weapons which inspired Shakespeare's notion of "glorious war" and "the big wars." Whether or not he read more than one or two of these works is immaterial. What is important is that the ideas and controversies expressed in them were probably circulating in less exact—though not less confident—form in civilian conversation.

Some of the related Renaissance military interests which I touch upon have been the concern of other students. The scientific background of warfare, certainly one of the most difficult subjects ever to confront literary scholars, has been ably explored by others before me—notably Maurice J. D. Cockle, C. G. Cruickshank, John W. Draper, Francis R. Johnson, Paul H. Kocher, Sir Charles Oman, and Henry J. Webb, who compiled a full-length study of Renaissance military literature published as *Elizabethan Military Science: The Books and the Practice* (Madison, Milwaukee, & London, 1965). Related studies of war and peace in Shakespeare's day and in the early Tudor period have been undertaken by Robert P. Adams, G. G. Langsam, and G. R. Waggoner. And the important role of the *miles gloriosus* has finally, at the hands of Daniel C. Boughner, received worthy treatment. Other subjects only partially dealt with in the following pages—including naval warfare—I hope will prove stimulating to those more competent than I to say something new about them.

Besides help from these authors, I have received advice, encouragement, and criticism from scholars too numerous to mention here. I should, however, like to express particular gratitude to Professors Willard Farnham and Walter Morris Hart, who patiently guided me toward scholarly expression during my graduate days; to Professor Lily B. Campbell, from whose pioneering work I have taken many ideas and who read much of the manuscript with kindly vigilance; to Professors Hugh G. Dick and James E. Phillips, whose well-informed interest in the project, and unfailing help with the more difficult Renaissance questions, gave me much needed encouragement; and to Professors R. C. Bald, Thomas M. Cranfill, Godfrey Davies, and French Fogle, who have read portions of the manuscript which appeared as articles. For editorial assistance I am much indebted to Susan J. Haverstick and Kathleen Leidich, and, for help with the index, to Mildred Jordan. Perhaps my most pleasant memory of help abundantly received derives from my years of study at the Henry E. Huntington Library. Had it not been for this institution, and the scholars whom it attracts, I certainly could not have written this book.

P. A. J.

Los Angeles, California
September, 1955

Contents

CHAPTER I

"A Fearful Battle Rend'red You in Music"

The field of battle is not the most important or interesting part of Shakespeare's military world. It is perhaps significant that of the increasingly numerous and expert writers on army matters in Shakespeare,[1] none gives primary attention to his description or enactment of battles. Most are concerned with army life and theories of war, and they lose interest upon the sounding of the first alarum. But unlike Corporal Nym, they do not lose interest because "the knocks are too hot."[2] On the contrary, they find that the knocks tend to be anything but hot and that the liveliest hostilities occur among soldiers during peacetime or just before an engagement. As a result Shakespearean battles now enjoy the doubtful distinction of being perhaps the only weakness in his artistry that has not been ably defended.

---

[1] For notes to chapter i, see pages 315–318.

1

Would-be defenders have encountered a singularly unlucky difficulty: Shakespeare's own adverse pronouncement on the matter in *Henry V*. His famous remarks deprecating the staging of Harfleur and Agincourt suggest that his own interests lay elsewhere; and students have followed, on the whole wisely, his advice and example. Their acquiescence is wise in that Shakespeare, unlike certain of his more spectacular fellows, did not emphasize the physical staging of warfare. If, however, he scorned stage realism, it was not simply because he could not have it. The difficulties of staging the epic of Agincourt were extraordinary ones, and Shakespeare's comments upon them do not necessarily apply to his battles elsewhere. Other dramatists had found the martial resources of the stage quite adequate. Cannon and other instruments of violence for raising sieges had been put to vigorous use well before Shakespeare's first plays. In 1574, civilian casualties were reported in a London proclamation calling attention to the "sundry slaughters and mayhemminge of the Quenes Subjectes [that] have happened by ruines of Skaffoldes, Frames and Stages, and by engynes, weapons and powders used in plaies."[3] A moderate stock of such equipment was needed for the "good pretty fight" called for in storming a hold in *Captain Thomas Stukely*,[4] and for the assault in *Horestes* thus directed: "Go and make your lively battel and let it be longe eare you can win the Citie."[5] Actors and stage managers may well have extended certain of Shakespeare's battles in this impromptu manner—certainly there was good swordplay on the Elizabethan stage—but for these extensions Shakespeare was not accountable.

It would seem, then, that readers are wise in scorning— not in *Henry V* only but in the other warlike plays—the "four or five most vile and ragged foils, / Right ill-dispos'd in brawl ridiculous,"⁶ but are not right in assuming that Shakespeare's meager staging of battle was due simply to limited properties. (Even in *Henry V* a cannon makes a brief appearance, and might have been more prominently used.) That a more deliberate artistry lay behind Shakespeare's restricted battle display is suggested in the positive portion of the advice which he gives in *Henry V*. This is to eke out the performance with our minds.⁷ In other words, his poetry is to form the basis for enacting battles in the theater of the mind. Unfortunately, the advice is neither easily nor frequently followed for any play other than *Henry V*.

We have failed, I believe, to eke out the performance with our minds because we rely too literally on our mind's eye. A visual reading of Shakespearean military dialogue can be successful only, as in *Henry V,* when the poet himself sees the scene; and for a large number of his battles he does not do so. To be sure, he occasionally asks us to augment the scene and imagine massive action through such devices as "excursions," in which a few men from either side symbolize the course of the battle. But devices of this sort do not constitute his major imaginative appeal to the mind.

It is my proposal in this chapter that Shakespeare more frequently and effectively enlarged his military theater through an appeal to the ear—either through actual sound or through a stylized, connotative rendering of it in dialogue. Shakespeare heard warfare, if he did not always see it, as the beautiful recording of subdued and varied camp music in the Chorus to Act IV of *Henry V* indicates. By seeking to free from scanty stage directions and occasional dialogue some of the sounds which he typically associated with battle, we may hope to restore to his warfare a feature which he, and probably the "gentles" in his audience, especially esteemed. Sound and music are not the only important aspects of Shakespearean warfare, but they are the aspects most easily overlooked by present-day readers. They are significant, moreover, in that they embody part of the principle of order and decorum which controls his serious depiction of battle generally.

II

It was not through accident nor a greater alertness of ear than eye that Shakespeare many times recorded mainly the sounds of battle. Three influences had virtually predetermined that, as a serious dramatist, he should do so. These were (1) the Renaissance concept of war as musical harmony, (2) a classical convention that translated the fearful actualities of warfare into an elevated, sonorous discourse, and (3) the important functional role of military music in contemporary fighting.

The first of these was based on the ideal of war as a harmoniously ordered institution in which armies move as in a dance. Machiavelli argued typically that just "as he that daunseth, proceadeth with the tyme of the Musick ..., even so an armie obeiyng, and movyng it self to the same sounde, doeth not disorder."[8] Sir John Davies lifted the concept from simile to metaphor when he pictured "well-ordered War" as armies dancing to the drum.[9] In the highly mannered *Histriomastix,* this metaphor appears in grotesque coloring:

> Weele steepe our sinewie feet in blood
> And daunce unto the Musicke of the field,
> Trumpets for trebbles, bases, bellowing drummes.[10]

Perhaps the closest that Shakespeare comes to such an absurdity is in the pretentious rhetoric of *King John* when the newly betrothed Blanch asks if "braying trumpets and loud churlish drums" must serve as "measures" to her marriage pomp (III.i.303–304). But the apparent absence of this metaphor elsewhere in Shakespeare does not mean that it did not, at least indirectly, influence his concept of battle. It was an easy step from the notion of warfare as a musically guided dance to the more imaginative perception that it was itself a music. The quality of this music could be easily adapted by the playwright to dramatic context. It might be "warres cheerfull harmony"[11] or, more frequently, "warres sad harmony."[12] It is seldom casual sound, almost never silent.

Most of all, of course, the concept of war as music was encouraged by the Elizabethan habit of picturing the universe, man, and man's offices in a musical frame.[13] The problem is to determine what were the typical forms taken by warfare within this frame and, if possible, how they were come by. Here, I believe, the classical discourse of war offers substantial help, particularly for the Elizabethan drama. It not only underlies most of the rhetorical orchestration of war in dialogue, but influences the dramatic role played by the musical instruments themselves.

The quality which Shakespeare seems to admire in military discourse is stated by Canterbury as one of the three learned arts mastered by the mature Henry V (*Henry V* I.i.43):

> List his discourse of war, and you shall hear
> A fearful battle rend'red you in music.

The invitation is unluckily a hollow one for the reader, since Henry never has occasion to narrate a fearful battle. He does, however, tell how to behave during such a battle, in his "Once more unto the breach," and this speech, of an orotundity untypical of the King, may be indicative of the sort of rhetoric that was needed to dignify with "music" the ugliness and realistic disorder of war. A similar clue is given by a passage in the anonymous play *Edward III;* when, we are told, the Countess of Salisbury talked of war,

> It wakened Caesar from his Romane grave,
> To heare warre beautified by her discourse.[14]

A more detailed clue to the meaning of the "musical" discourse occurs in *The Noble Spanish Soldier,* a play written after this form of discourse had passed the flowering of its fashion.[15] Although in this instance, and in other later plays, the discourse is parodied, certain pretentious aspects are thereby brought helpfully into bold relief. Baltazar, a soldier fresh from battle, is courteously invited by the King to tell of his victory:

> And now Ænaes-like let thine own Trumpet
> Sound forth his battell with those slavish Moores.[16]

After Baltazar has described the "maine Battalia,...the Vaw...the wings"—technical features such as formed the basis of contemporary military journalism—the King is imperfectly pleased:

> This satisfies mine eye, but now mine eare
> Must have his musicke too.

Baltazar's ensuing "musicke" stresses the clamor of battle: "To that heat we came, our Drums beat, Pikes were shaken and shiver'd, swords and Targets clash'd and clatter'd, Muskets rattled, Cannons roar'd." In general it is a grandiloquent reporting of battle sound and atmosphere, and totally valueless as a narration of event. It has, in absurd form, all the grimace of Henry's "Once more unto the breach," but it is even closer to the Bleeding Sergeant's narrative in *Macbeth,* the manner of which is commended by King Duncan, who apparently felt that his ear had "his musicke too" (I.ii.43): "So well thy words become thee as thy wounds."

In defending Shakespeare's authorship of this controversial speech, Kittredge suggests that its language of "bombast and grotesque bluntness accords perfectly with what was expected of a stage soldier."[17] A fuller plea for its legitimacy is made by J. M. Nosworthy, who notes that its inflation resembles Hamlet's favorite recitation of the fall of Troy, which in turn is closely modeled on Aeneas' long narration in Marlowe's *The Tragedy of Dido, Queen of Carthage.*[18] If this is so, the speech of both Baltazar and Shakespeare's Sergeant points to Aeneas as the ultimate inspiration for this sort of martial narrative; and doubtless epic tradition was responsible for its elevated tone and much of its sonority. Virgil's Aeneas, to be sure, describes a massacre within a palace rather than an engagement on the field, and there are relatively few passages in the *Aeneid* which provide a deliberate orchestration of battle sounds. But these few passages may have had a disproportionate appeal to Elizabethans, whose taste is suggested by the heightening of Virgil's appeal to the ear in sixteenth-century translations. In Thomas Phaer's repeatedly published translation are to be found verses like the following:

> But brightbras troupe from far, his fearfull shivring
>   sounds expels,
> Thick, thick, and thereupon men shout, that hie heaven
>   yelping yels.[19]

Here was both "music" and the rhetorical amplification of detail that we shall find in the battle music of sixteenth-century drama. Again, in Book II, which Elizabethans apparently considered a model for warlike discourse, occur these lines:

> But the inner lodging all with noise and woful wailing
> soundes,
> With bounsing thick and larums lowd the buildings all
> rebounds
> And howling women shoutes, and cries the golden stars do
> smite.[20]

This passage is specially pointed out by the translator as "a wonderful breefe description of a city invaded." This stylized version of a "fearful battle" is found frequently in Renaissance literature.[21] Shakespeare uses it in Henry V's ceremoniously phrased threat to the Governor of Harfleur, describing the imminent sack of his city if it does not yield (*Henry V* III.iii.33):

>   in a moment look to see
> The blind and bloody soldier with foul hand
> Defile the locks of your shrill-shrieking daughters;
> . . . .
> Your naked infants spitted upon pikes,
> Whiles the mad mothers with their howls confus'd
> Do break the clouds.

But probably the authority of the *Aeneid* extended more to the general temper of battle narrative than to details. For the conventional rhetoric of the discourse, fully developed, we must turn to the English classical drama. How, aside from epic influence, this drama acquired its special form of battle rhetoric is uncertain, but Seneca's authority is, of course, the most likely. Though there is scarcely any sustained narrative of warfare in the Senecan plays, his stately use of the Nuncius, his rhetorical amplification, and the "thumping" energy of his verse in translations are all to be found in the English classical drama. The ways in which these traits were applied to the clamor-producing instruments of battle may well have been the peculiar achievement of the English classical dramatists themselves.

In the English classical plays, the narrative passes typically from a cursory view of battle formation ("This satisfies mine eye") to a vigorous recording of sound ("mine ear / Must have his musicke too"). When the King in *The Spanish Tragedy* asks his general to "unfolde in briefe discourse" his "forme of battell" and "warres successe," the general describes first the "proud aray," "daring showes," and colors of the armies, and then proceeds to uneventful sonority:

> Both [armies] cheerly sounding trumpets, drums, and fifes,
> Both raising dreadfull clamors to the skies,
> That vallies, hills, and rivers made rebound,
> And heaven it selfe was frighted with the sound.[22]

And the King, like Shakespeare's Duncan, applauds his soldier's discourse (I.ii.95): "These words, these deeds, become thy person well." In *The Misfortunes of Arthur* the Nuncius is characterized with perfunctory attempt at realism as "a Souldier sweating from the Camps," but the battle he relates has only one or two clearly discernible events; the rest is music:

> Hereat the Aire with uprore lowde resoundes,
> Which efts on mountains rough rebounding reares.
> The Trumpets hoarce their trembling tunes doe teare:
> And thundring Dummes their dreadfull Larums ring.

. . . .
From every side these fatall signes are sent:
And boystrous bangs with thumping thwacks fall thicke.[23]

So uneventful, so unconsecutive, indeed, proves the battle—
if we overlook the thundering, the bangs, and the thwacks—
that the Nuncius is finally moved to explain why his discourse
does not really tell what has happened (IV.ii.176):

> A vaine discourse it were to paint at large
> The severall Fates, and foiles of either side.
> . . . .
> Who oftnest strooke: who best bestowde his blade:
> Who ventred most: who stoode: who fell: who failde:
> Th' effect declares it all: thus far'd the field.

The "vaine discourse" deprecated by the Nuncius was, of
course, precisely the kind that within a few decades the Elizabethans would be devouring wholesale in the form of military
newsletters and journals.[24] Yet even in 1597 these books were
still, with their precise, technical language, suspect enough to
be ridiculed in Hotspur's "tales of iron wars" which Kate
has heard him murmur in his faint slumbers (*1 Henry IV*
II.iii.53):

> And thou hast talk'd
> Of sallies and retires, of trenches, tents,
> Of palisadoes, frontiers, parapets,
> Of basilisks, of cannon, culverin,
> Of prisoners' ransom, and of soldiers slain,
> And all the currents of a heady fight.[25]

And this was the type of discourse, "horribly stuff'd with
epithets of war" (*Othello* I.i.14), of which Iago maliciously
accuses Othello. The kind of narrative which made the gentle
Desdemona, as the Moor affirms (I.iii.149–150), "with a

greedy ear / Devour up my discourse," was doubtless closer to the dignity and music of his great "Farewell" speech.

Shakespeare was not, of course, so limited as the classical imitators in adherence to the rhetorical discourse. In practice, if not in conscious theory, he gradually repudiated the dead, meaningless sounds and rhetoric of the older narrative in favor of the realistic warfare which Henry V enacts, even though it does not get into his more posed speeches. But while generally renouncing the messenger, with his stylized report of battle, Shakespeare retained from the discourse its most valued features: its dignity, connotativeness, and above all its concentration on the sounds of battle.

When Calphurnia, in *Julius Caesar* (II.ii.19), envisions an ominous battle over the Capitol, she reports it as the classical messenger would do, passing swiftly from a statement of formations to the "noise of battle":

> Fierce fiery warriors fought upon the clouds
> In ranks and squadrons and right form of war,
> Which drizzled blood upon the Capitol.
> The noise of battle hurtled in the air,
> Horses did neigh, and dying men did groan.

It was appropriate that she should use this formal pattern, not only because of the classical context, but because the dramatic emphasis is on mood. In the earlier plays, however, it is natural to find the conventional clamor less discriminately used.

Typical of the warlike language of the early histories is Warwick's description of an actual engagement (*2 Henry VI* V.ii.3):

> Now, when the angry trumpet sounds alarum
> And dead men's cries do fill the empty air.

Although he reports the trumpet as sounding a functional signal, it is stereotyped as "angry," and the cries of the dying lose their realistic impact by a rhetorical amplification. In *Richard II,* however, Shakespeare is conscious of the reflection which such language casts on the speaker, for it is given to the rhetorically self-conscious King as he pictures the quality of warfare (I.iii.134):

> with boist'rous untun'd drums,
> With harsh-resounding trumpets' dreadful bray
> And grating shock of wrathful iron arms,

a speech, incidentally, which resembles the Messenger's report in Kyd's *Cornelia* (V.v.151):

> The clattring Armour, buskling as they paced,
> Ronge through the Forrests with a frightfull noyse,
> And every Eccho tooke the Trompets clange.

The stereotyped "boisterous" drum is absurdly elaborated in another early play, but with a humor and appropriateness to speaker that again suggests Shakespeare's condescending use of the conventional sounds. The Bastard Faulconbridge defies the Dauphin with words more thumping than the subsequent drum itself (*King John* V.ii.167):

> Do but start
> An echo with the clamour of thy drum,
> And even at hand a drum is ready brac'd
> That shall reverberate all, as loud as thine.
> Sound but another, and another shall,
> As loud as thine, rattle the welkin's ear
> And mock the deep-mouth'd thunder.

As one of Shakespeare's first and most vigorous satirists, the Bastard is outthumping even the noisiest of rhetorical drums, of which the following from *Caesar's Revenge* is typical:

Drums, let your fearefull mazing thunder playe,
And with their sound peirce Heavens brazen Towers,
And all the earth fill with like fearefull noyse.[26]

III

Although Shakespeare's attitude toward such tonal stereotypes grew more critical, they apparently impressed upon him
permanently not only the sense of warfare as auditory but
even the set pattern of instruments used in its orchestration.
These instruments all sound in Petruchio's memory of battle
(*The Taming of the Shrew* I.ii.204):

Have I not heard great ordnance in the field,
And heaven's artillery thunder in the skies?
Have I not in a pitched battle heard
Loud 'larums, neighing steeds, and trumpets' clang?

Even in Othello's memory of "glorious war," profoundly
sincere as it is, the stock instruments exclusively are used, and
used with some of the conventional rhetoric. Here are the
neighing steed, the ear-piercing fife, the spirit-stirring drum,
and, finally, the "dread clamours" of great ordnance (III.iii.-
351–356). The musical harmony of the speech is, however,
consummately appropriate, for in his farewell to harmonious
war Othello is expressing also a farewell to purposeful, orderly
life. Shakespeare has indeed given the "ear his musicke too,"
but in the intensity of both dramatic situation and verse the
formal design to do so is obscured.

In the rhetorical music of war, the "rude throats" of artillery are the most surprising performers. "My musicke is a
Canon," avows Baltazar,[27] and so it is, in part, in both Petruchio's and Othello's memories of battle. The fate which—at
least for serious dramatic purposes—confined these grim addi-

tions to modern warfare to the role of musical instruments, and refused them strategic importance in stage warfare, was a curious one and possibly influenced the character of artillery in the drama for years to come. It was a fate, moreover, that helps explain many of the nonstrategic uses of the authentic musical instruments—fife, trumpet, and drum.

In an age which had had some time to contemplate the ugly impact of gunpowder on the art of war, and which had done so realistically in military treatises,[28] one would expect to find a less melodious and stylized handling of cannon in the drama. A thoughtful literary depiction occurred only in a minority of cases, and those, paradoxically, comic ones. Shakespeare was better informed than the average playwright concerning the new engines of destruction, and had he chosen he could, without untypical anachronism, have presented a troubling study of their effect on strategy and morale. Except for peripheral episodes and commentary, he did not so choose. Instead, his characteristic references to great ordnance, such as those made by Petruchio and Othello, are sonorous rather than critical. Shakespeare seems to have been impressed mainly by the sound of artillery. He hears the "thunder" of cannon (*King John* I.i.26), their "roaring" (*1 Henry VI* III.iii.79), "their soul-fearing clamours" (*King John* II.i.383). If anachronism was a serious concern, Shakespeare need not have used their music so frequently in *Hamlet,* where their utterance carries to the clouds and back again, "re-speaking earthly thunder" (I.ii.126–128); nor need Coriolanus have imitated "the graces of the gods, / To tear with thunder the wide cheeks o' th' air" (V.iii.150–151).

In part, Shakespeare's practice was realistic in that artillery at first was valued especially for frightening by mere noise;

and at Harfleur—although Shakespeare characteristically does not note this strategic consideration—the thunder of cannon made an effectively terrifying impression on the besieged.[29] But the sound of cannon as heard by Shakespeare is not simply terrifying noise; it is "music," a part of the total orchestration of war.

Again, Shakespeare's musical reaction may be explained as the lyrical response of a poetic temperament to one of the most dramatic of human achievements. Even poets who set out to denounce artillery were likely to react first with wonder and only secondarily with thoughtful criticism. In a sonnet addressed "To all Instruments of warre," Jean Du Nesme cannot prevent lyrical awe from dominating his denunciation of these great weapons:

> Engines of Vulcan, heav'n affrighting wonders,
> Like brittle glasse the Rocks to cynders breaking;
> Deafning the winds, dumbing the loudest thunders;
> May ye be bound a thousand yeres from speaking.[30]

Certainly, when Shakespeare similarly apostrophizes the destructiveness or menace of artillery, the sonority of his verse is more impressive than any purposeful idea it may contain. This is true of Arcite's great prayer to Mars in *The Two Noble Kinsmen* (V.i.53), and true of Helena's plea to the deadly missiles that they spare her Bertram (*All's Well* III.ii.111).

Mainly, however, a more studied reaction, based on the classical discourse, seems to have been responsible for this general tendency. Effective models for Shakespeare's dignifying of cannon for serious drama had been offered him by earlier playwrights; these had already demonstrated how the "fearful battle" aspects of gunpowder could be translated into music. The General's narration in *The Spanish Tragedy* gives a conspicuous place to cannon, but only in clamor and atmosphere, not in a precise influence on the battle. The violent shot, he reports, resembled the ocean's rage,

> When, roaring lowde, and with a swelling tide,
> It beats upon the rampiers of huge rocks,
> And gapes to swallow neighbour bounding landes.[31]

When in *Edward III* Salisbury appears in the role of Nuncius to "sing of doleful accidents," he harmonizes with cannon and trumpets the way "the death procuring knell begins":

> Off goe the Cannons, that with trembling noyse
> Did shake the very Mountayne where they stood;
> Then sound the Trumpets clangor in the aire.[32]

In Peele's *The Battle of Alcazar,* the cannon music serves as both rhetorical and actual part of the battle atmosphere. "Give ear," says the Presenter, "and hear how war begins his song with dreadful clamours, noise, and trumpets' sound"; and this rhetorical prelude is rudely amplified by the ear-splitting music of actual cannon offstage: "Alarums within; let the chambers be discharged."[33] The technique was a good one for the public theaters, since it made an effective compromise between classical austerity and popular desire for "great noises that fill the ear," a trait that a foreign observer noted in the English.[34] Shakespeare follows Peele's example in the beginning of Act III of *Henry V*. The Chorus, filling the role of Peele's Presenter, suddenly animates the verbal portrait of the siege:

> and the nimble gunner
> With linstock now the devilish cannon touches,
>   *Alarum, and chambers go off.*
> And down goes all before them.

Mainly, however, Shakespeare's cannon sound only in the controlled rhetoric of his dialogue and choruses, and rarely intrude, even symbolically, into the decisive business of his warfare.

When, therefore, Shakespeare placed the sound of cannon within the musical discourse, he was not making an original addition, nor was he necessarily ignorant of the strategic function of artillery. He was following, rather, the approved manner of his more decorous predecessors, who thought that by confining cannon to a stylized verbal commentary they could suggest some of its atmosphere and power and still not impair the dignity of their drama. When Shakespeare does talk accurately of gunpowder and its effect, he is usually careful to choose a context wherein he cannot be accused of an indecorum. Hotspur's technical discussion of "basilisks, ... cannon, culverin" is playfully reported, as is the dandy's prescription for gunpowder wounds in the same play. In a class by themselves, of course, are Falstaff's grimly comic reflections on "shot" and "grinning honour"—reflections that come perilously close to overreaching their proper stratum in the play.

IV

Of the battle music which literally sounded on the Shakespearean stage, by far the largest part was played by drum, trumpet, and fife. Though on occasion these instruments owe their dramatic coloring to an accompanying rhetorical commentary, and though the full vigor of their military use is often, as with artillery, muted by classical tradition, they tend to be more functional than cannon. Of all nonverbal sounds, they are Shakespeare's most articulate clues to the course of battle; and for connotative value they are sometimes more effective than even the poet's words. In the simple but crucial battle scene (V.ii) from *Lear,* for example, the conflict, except for the slight appearance of marching armies, is fought and decided entirely "within." Battle sounds are therefore of real importance. In this case, the only clues to what is happening are two musical signals, "Alarum and retreat within." The audience must have understood these signals; they were not fanfare. On the other hand, music, however simple it may be, inevitably conveys mood. "Alarum," in particular, was characteristically used with deliberate concern for its emotional value. A study of Shakespeare's military music must therefore pay attention to both its informative and its emotional functions; and it must also recognize that the two are often scarcely separable, especially in an age which considered music to be an extremely precise orator to human passions.[35]

In attempting to distinguish between music which carries primarily a military meaning and that which serves primarily as orchestral background for a dramatic mood, our best criterion is the account of military music given in martial treatises. These treatises, in contrast with the rhetorical models supplied by the English classical drama, esteem music mainly for its utility on the field. Since, however, military utility sometimes includes evoking of a purposeful emotion, the distinction is not perfect, and in a few cases it is impossible to say whether Shakespeare was closer to military manual or to rhetorical discourse. Occasionally, for example, his battle music has no purpose other than that of cheering the troops (*Richard III* V.iii.270; *1 Henry IV* V.ii.98) or of celebrating a victory (*Anthony and Cleopatra* IV.viii.36; *Coriolanus* I.ix.65). Both practices are in accord with the precepts of treatises which Shakespeare may have read. Purlilia, writing from classical precedents "Of trompettes and other clamours in an hoste," recommends in an attack that "the trompets blowe up alarum, al the host to make an outcrye, and brefely to fyll heaven and earth with the noyse and sound of trompettes, and make all on a rore, wherewith thyne enemyes be afrayed, & thy frendes gladdened." Proof of this precept was to be found in Pompey's disaster when he ordered his soldiers to move secretly "without any brute or noysemaking."[36] That Shakespeare may have read either Purlilia's recommendation or a similar one elsewhere is suggested by one of Fluellen's typically bungled bits of erudition: sternly rebuking his fellow captain for talking above a whisper, he prescribes for his friend a careful study of "the wars of Pompey the Great" (*Henry V* IV.i.65–75). On the other hand, English classical dramatists had taken full advantage of the mood available in clamorous music, and like Shakespeare had used it mainly in dialogue rather than stage directions, with rhetorical amplification and with stock epithets. In *The Spanish Tragedy* both armies advance "menacing,"

> Both cheerly sounding trumpets, drums, and fifes,
> Both raising dreadful clamors to the skie.[37]

Here seems to be ample precedent for Richmond's direction in *Richard III* (V.iii.270): "Sound drums and trumpets boldly and cheerfully," and for Antony's vaunting command to the trumpeters (*Antony and Cleopatra* IV.viii.36):

> With brazen din blast you the city's ear;
> Make mingle with our rattling tabourines,
> That heaven and earth may strike their sounds together.

With musical signaling, however, Shakespeare's agreement with the functional directions of the handbooks is closer, though again the agreement is likely to be found in the bare orders of stage directions rather than in their rhetorically colored counterparts in the dialogue. His principal divergence from contemporary manuals is usually in an absence of technical detail, not in the frequency or importance with which the signals are used. With even a minimum knowledge of military science, he could not have been ignorant of the prestige and high salaries of able army musicians, and of the professional skill in sounding and interpreting commands which made them merit the prestige. And although he need not, for his dramatic purposes, have been technically expert in the great variety of music demanded of each instrument, he knew enough about the military utility of the three major instruments to make fairly distinct demands upon each. Certainly one cannot question his well-informed interest in music generally.

Of the three instruments mentioned by Othello, the "ear-piercing fife" had the least value in giving orders. Francis Markham, principal Elizabethan authority for army music, considered it useful only for the march and for entertainment. Although he joins the drum and fife in one discussion, he urges a careful distinction between the two, for "the Phiphe is but onely an Instrument of pleasure, not of necessitie, and it is to the voice of the Drum the Souldier should wholly attend, and not to the aire of the whistle; for the one (which is the Drumme) speakes plainely and distinctly; the other speakes loud and shrill, but yet curiously and confusedly."[38] That the fife was esteemed more for enlivening the music than for carrying directions is further evidenced by Tabourot's instructions to fife players: They were to perform as they chose, being careful only to keep time with the drum.[39] Shakespeare's practice reflects the limited utility of the fife. While recognizing "the drum and the fife" as authentic military instruments in contrast with "the tabor and the pipe" (*Much Ado* II.iii.13), he specifies the fife only for the march, and that rarely (in *Timon of Athens* IV.iii.47, and in Falstaff's "playing upon his truncheon like a fife"). Most of Shakespeare's marches call, rather strangely, for the drum alone, despite the common use of the fife in Elizabethan armies.[40] If, however, the "whistle" used in naval commands was related to the fife (both were often indiscriminately referred to as "whistle"),[41] Shakespeare correctly understood the value of this instrument at sea. "Mariners," according to Le Roy, "know what they are to do by the only whistle of the Master."[42] And Shakespeare's Chorus in *Henry V* (III.9) asks the audience to hear "the shrill whistle, which doth order give / To sounds confus'd." But similar reference is never made to land warfare.

In distinguishing between the functions of the trumpet and the drum in Shakespeare's usage, we shall find the military handbooks of greater, though still not adequate, help. It is important to learn from the handbooks that the trumpet was preferred for cavalry signaling.[43] Of less importance dramatically were the precise cavalry signals used: *"Butte sella,* Clap on your saddles; *Mounte Cavallo,* mount on horseback; *Tucquet,* march; *Carga, carga,* an Alarme to charge; *Ala Standardo,* a retrait or retire to your Colours; *Auquet,* to the watch, or a discharge for the watch, besides other points, as Proclamations, Cals, Summons."[44] Although Markham regarded these as important for all soldiers to learn, Shakespeare could

obviously make small use of them on a stage where a kingdom might be vainly offered for a horse. Moreover, they were
still, like the language of fencing, imperfectly naturalized and
therefore unsuited for patriotic English usage. It is appropriate that his most technical cavalry command should be
given by the French nobility at Agincourt, since their warfare
is ridiculously dependent on horses. In the Constable's command, preparatory to the charge (*Henry V* IV.ii.34),

> Then let the trumpets sound
> The tucket sonance and the note to mount,

we find curiously reversed the second and third signals listed
by Markham: *Mounte Cavallo* and *Tucquet*. Although
Shakespeare's knowledge of cavalry action does not seem convincingly professional in this instance, he had a better understanding of cavalry organization than did one of our best
students of Elizabethan music, in that he recognized two distinct meanings of *cornet*. Commenting upon the passage in
1 Henry VI (IV.iii.25) where York accuses Somerset of
treachery and exclaims "He doth stop my cornets," E. W.
Naylor remarks that it "simply means 'prevents the victory
being mine.' 'Cornets' meant what a 'brass band' means to
us."[45] To Naylor, "stop my cornets" was identical to "stop my
music." Actually, the cornets referred to by York are his
standard-bearers (or perhaps the standards themselves), cavalry officers equivalent to the infantry's ensigns and having
no connection with music.

Of the other cavalry commands for trumpet listed by Markham, only the alarum (*Carga, carga*) and the retreat (*Ala
Standardo*) are used significantly by Shakespeare. But few of
the instances are explicitly assigned to the trumpet, and the

alarum is seldom identified clearly with the charge.[46] It is also seldom possible to decide whether or not the commands are intended for horsemen. The summons, or call for parley, for example, although listed by Markham as a cavalry command by trumpet, seems to be merely a general military function in Shakespeare. When Macduff approaches Dunsinane and orders his trumpets to speak defiance, it would be farfetched to assume that the choice of trumpet rather than drum implied a cavalry approach.[47] A better case might be made for the discriminate use of trumpet in *Timon of Athens* when it announces (I.i.249) the arrival of "Alcibiades and some twenty horse"; for later in the play (IV.iii), when Alcibiades is proceeding on foot "in warlike manner," he is attended only by the infantry instruments of drum and fife.

Whether or not they are invariably intended for horsemen, the trumpet calls (occasionally named "sennet" or "tucket") announcing the approach of armies are of some dramatic importance.[48] These calls, basically medieval and courtly, are often ceremonious only. Nevertheless, dramatists valued them for offstage music which could accurately indicate the identity and movement of armies without the necessity for bringing these onstage. Kings and ranking military officers had their specially identifying trumpet music. Thus, Iago is the first to recognize the arrival of Othello in Cyprus because he knows the Moor's "trumpet" (II.i.179). In *All's Well,* Lafew recognized that the King is coming (V.ii.55): "I know by his trumpets." And again in the same play, both the identity and direction of an army are revealed by their trumpets (III.v.8): "they are gone a contrary way. Hark! you may know by their trumpets." The identifying quality of these trumpets was in the notes played and not in such rhetorical features as the "lusty trumpet" which announces the Bastard in *King John* (V.ii.117).

The drum, rather curiously in view of modern standards, was a more precise as well as a more connotative military instrument than the trumpet; and Shakespeare correctly understood it to be of vital military importance. As "the tongue of war" (*King John* V.ii.164), it spoke distinctly a considerable variety of orders. In Shakespeare's only juxtaposed contrast between it and the trumpet—"A flourish, trumpets! Strike alarum, drums!" (*Richard III* IV.iv.149)—the trumpet's message is ornamental only, whereas the drum is assigned a functional command.

There was good reason in Renaissance warfare why Shakespeare's Bertram should refer to the drum as "this instrument of honour" (*All's Well* III.vi.69), and why Parolles should affect implacable grief at the loss of one. Drummers were entrusted with secret information and, Ralph Smith warns, if they should fall into enemy hands "noe guifte nor force should cause them to disclose any secrettes that they knowe."[49] In battle the drummer was the center of activity and communication. "Ever at his Captaines heeles," writes Markham, "it is he that brings the Battels to joyne, hee stands in the middest when Swords flie on all sides; hee brings them to pell, mell, and the furie of execution; and it is he that brings them both on and off, when they are either fortunate, or abandoned and forsaken."[50] But the drummer's most professional skill was in signaling, and the drum major had to know not only the beatings for his own army but the meaning of sounds heard in the enemy's camp. It was also desirable that commanding officers know the enemy signals. Bayard was able to escape during a night surprise because he recog-

nized that the drums heard behind him were those of the
Spanish infantry "beating the alert" and could be nothing
else.[51]

Just how many drum commands for infantry were actively
used in Shakespeare's day it is hard to determine. Probably
the theorists—like Captain Hindar, who had written a notoriously exacting book on the drum—were well ahead of practice. Moreover, the fullest accounts of drum commands date
from the 1630's and record elaborate signals not present in
the Elizabethan period either in drama or in military journalism.[52] The total impression gained from these sources is of a
considerable body of signals which were available to English
armies but which, because of their foreign origin and different periods of adoption, were far from uniform in Shakespeare's day. Few of these would have recommended themselves to a dramatist who had to rely upon the familiar and
established if he wished his audience to understand him.

Apparently the basic drum commands paralleled for infantry the trumpet commands for cavalry, but with more
variations within each command. Shakespeare did not technically exploit this full variety, but some indication of his
expert use of the drum can be gleaned from the two functions—the march and the alarum—which he uses to greatest
dramatic advantage and seldom confuses with corresponding
trumpet calls.

At Mile End, where citizen soldiers drilled on holidays,
Londoners could readily become familiar with the uses of the
drum for the march, and particularly with the prominence of
this instrument in the basic drills. Beaumont and Fletcher
have parodied the awesome impression made on the populace
by the drummer. Foremost among the experiences at Mile

End, the Citizen in *The Knight of the Burning Pestle* recalls the commanding eloquence of one "drum-Ned": "Ran, tan; tan, tan, ran, tan: Oh wench an thou hadst but seen little Ned of Aldgate, drum-Ned, how he made it roar again, and laid on like a tyrant: and then struck softly till the Ward came up, and then thundred again, and together we go!"[53] That Shakespeare, too, was well acquainted with Mile End is shown by Shallow's memories of the sounds of a gun drill there, and the stirring music of the drum accompaniment (*2 Henry IV* III.ii.298–306). The dramatist must also have seen many less exemplary bodies of conscripts marching through the counties, to a sparser, grimmer music, like the ex-prisoners in Falstaff's wretched company who "march wide betwixt the legs" (*1 Henry IV* IV.ii.42).

It was probably from the more formal occasions that Shakespeare gained his knowledge of the "English march" which—after "Drum sounds afar off"—he calls for in *1 Henry VI* (III.iii.30), followed by the description of Talbot marching "with his colours spread, / And all the troops of English after him." The English march was one of "gravity and majestie," as Charles I characterized it in a royal warrant calling for its revival after long neglect, and it had been by the "approbation of strangers confest and acknowledged the best of all marches."[54]

Charles's warrant also emphasizes another fact of importance in Shakespeare's use of the march: that "the ancient custome of nations hath ever bene to use one certaine and constant forme of March in the warres, whereby to be distinguished one from another." That the drum helped communicate this distinction is apparent from Fynes Moryson's complaint that "a man can hardly distinguish betweene the beating of the drums of the Sweitzers, and Germans, save that the former march is more grave and slow, and not so tumultuous as that of the Germans."[55] William Barriffe's ceremonious program for the trainees in Merchant-Taylors Hall contrasts the march of the Saracens with that of the English by their drum music: the former guided by "a Turky Drumme, and a hideous noise making pipe" and the latter by "Drums beating a lofty English march."[56] The performance of the English march in *1 Henry VI* is contrasted with the playing of the French march immediately afterward, heralding the arrival of Burgundy and his troops. Although a token segment of each army may actually have marched across the stage, nothing in either stage directions or dialogue demands that the contrasting marches be communicated in any way but through drum music and the comments of Pucelle. And when modern editors almost invariably augment Shakespeare's directions by bringing troops on stage (Kittredge is typical in supplying: "Enter, and pass over at a distance, Talbot and his Troops"), they put too little trust in Shakespeare's music. The patriotic mood conveyed by contrasting drums must have been intense, and the appearance of a few soldiers would have been prosaic by comparison. Little of this mood, to be sure, is suggested by the meager directions which Shakespeare himself supplied: "Drum sounds afar off," "Here sound an English march," and "French march." Our problem, here and elsewhere, is to read as "spirit-stirring" music what appear to be only nonmusical directions.[57]

In still other ways Shakespeare depicts the contemporary importance attached to identifying the army and its direction by the sound of drum. It is one of Pucelle's less supernatural perceptions that she can identify both the English army and its direction by the distant sound of its drum (*1 Henry VI* III.iii.29):

> Hark! by the sound of drum you may perceive
> Their powers are marching unto Paris-ward.

Fluellen, that irreproachable militarist, is able upon hearing Henry V's drum to recognize the approach of his sovereign (*Henry V* III.vi.90); and here it is interesting to observe the use of the drummer as musician for the English general, in contrast with the trumpets already noticed in connection with the French horsemen. In *3 Henry VI* (V.i.8 ff.) occurs an instance of strategic importance, involving a critical misunderstanding of drum identity. Warwick, awaiting the expected support of Clarence and his forces, hears a drum that he takes to be that of his ally. Somervile, however, objects that it could not be Clarence's, since this drum indicates a march from the opposite direction; whereupon Warwick assumes that it must be "unlook'd-for friends." While they are thus speculating, Edward's hostile army arrives as a grim clarification of the mystery.

The knowledge of military practice which Shakespeare reveals in these instances is less impressive than his realization of the connotative value of music for the march. Some of this effect is dependent upon dialogue; but in more instances than can be found for the trumpet, the drum is allowed to speak for itself. In the dead march, notably, Shakespeare found the muffled beat of the drum eloquent beyond words. The simple military function of the dead march was, as Markham defines it, "when any dies, the Drumme with a sad solemnitie must bring him to his grave, for it is the only mourner for the lost, and the greatest honor of Funerals."[58] This, amplified by the peal of ordnance, is the "soldiers' music" which speaks loudly upon the death of Hamlet; and it is especially impressive as the final utterance of a play in which words have previously said everything possible about the human predicament. The dead march is also the final action and utterance in *Coriolanus,* another play in which the silencing of grim human struggle can best be expressed not by voices but by the somber, impersonal music of drums. "Beat thou the drum, that it speak mournfully," commands Aufidius (V.vi.151), and the order is made specific by the last stage direction: "A dead march sounded."[59] The subdued atmosphere evoked by this kind of march was also well suited for covert military advances, as when in *1 Henry VI* Talbot marches to surprise and scale Orleans, his "Drums beating a dead march" (II.i.7). The menacing mood conveyed by the drum on such an occasion is suggested by Bolingbroke's politic decision not to use this music upon approaching the beleaguered Richard (*Richard II* III.iii.51): "Let's march," he commands, "without the noise of threatening drums." In *Timon of Athens,* on the other hand, Alcibiades marches into chastened Athens to the rumble of drums, probably restrained like his conquest of the city. "Let our drums strike," is the last line of the play, and is as appropriate as the similar endings of *Hamlet* and *Coriolanus.*

In the other major dramatic function of the drum, that of beating the alarum, there is inherent an even greater ominous power; and it is not surprising that many of Shakespeare's drum calls to battle betray the influence of English classical drama, with its emphasis on stylized emotion. The military handbooks offered him few technical details about the alarum—so few, in fact, that he must have felt licensed to use the direction whenever he needed sounds to announce present or imminent battle.[60] Moreover, several instances which Shakespeare labels "alarum" are indistinguishable from the marches of approaching armies, and though the notation for the two functions certainly differed, their dramatic effect was similar. Both provided a persistent and usually rising accompaniment for battle scenes.

The atmospheric value of the drum alarum was enhanced, as it was with the march, by the variety of music available. "Short alarums" apparently announced sudden or brief onslaughts (*1 Henry VI* I.v.14 and I.v.26; *Henry V* IV.v.5). "Low alarums" (*Julius Caesar* V.iii.96) could suggest a sinister or subdued threat in the offing, and usually were meant to give the impression of remoteness. Drummers off stage probably sounded them from as great a distance as possible. Persistent alarums, sometimes underlined by "Alarum still," suggested a monotonous urgency or implied that the battle was still raging on other fronts despite a cessation locally. Thus in *Coriolanus* (I.v.4), the direction "Alarum continues still afar off" emphasizes the disorder and selfishness of the common soldiers, who are engrossed in petty pillage while the battle is still very much alive. The alarums which sounded for on-stage battles were doubtless loud. Only rarely does Shakespeare specially label such alarums,[61] but their customary volume may be inferred from the necessity of defining exceptional alarums as "low." Military practice demanded that the drum signals be clearly heard above the din of battle. A curiously specific indication in *Coriolanus* would place the carrying range of alarums at approximately a mile and a half. When Coriolanus is told that the armies are fighting at this distance from him, he predicts, with a clear reference to the drum (I.iv.9): "Then shall we hear their 'larum, and they ours"; and his prediction is promptly verified.

The effect which Shakespeare achieved through distant and approaching drums constitutes his finest dramatic use of martial instruments, and represents a skillful combination of rhetorical and functional music. In *1 Henry VI*, the stage direction for "Drum afar off" is enriched by the rhetorical identification of the drum which a French officer gives the threatened Talbot (IV.ii.39):

> Hark! hark! The Dauphin's drum, a warning bell,
> Sings heavy music to thy timorous soul;

and his own drum, he assures Talbot, "shall ring thy dire departure out." The assurance carries a double meaning, for it implies not only the alarum to mortal battle, but the grim promise of a dead march for Talbot's funeral. In the same play, the atmospheric quality of an unidentified alarum is heightened first by thunder and lightning and then by Talbot's equally Senecan question (I.iv.98):

> What stir is this? What tumult's in the heavens?
> Whence cometh this alarum and the noise?

The ominous suggestiveness of the occurrence is not dispersed by the messenger's matter-of-fact explanation—that the French have gathered head under Pucelle—for the influence of Joan is supernatural. The same combination of the atmospheric and the purely military drum that forebodes the death of Talbot recurs many years later, with less rhetoric, in *Antony and Cleopatra*. When Enobarbus is discovered dying and "Drums afar off" are heard, Caesar's sentinel observes

(IV.ix.30): "Hark! The drums / Demurely wake the sleepers." The signal referred to is only the prosaic one described
by Markham as follows: "in the morning the discharge or
breaking up of the Watch."[62] But the "demure" music here
has the overtones of Nemesis overtaking a renegade. "The
hand of death hath raught him," observes the sentinel, a truth
which the muffled drumbeat underscores.[63]

The fully Senecan employment of the alarum drum as
Nemesis is well illustrated in Peele's *The Battle of Alcazar,*
where a Presenter interprets the signal more formally than
Shakespeare usually does in his dialogue:

> Now Nemesis upon her doubling drum,
> Moved with this ghastly moan, this sad complaint,
> 'Larums loud into Alecto's ears.[64]

In *Julius Caesar* Shakespeare uses persistent "Low alarums"
as musical accompaniment for Caesar's Nemesis-like pursuit
of Brutus—but with an ultimate clarification in terms of
military function. Finding Cassius dead, Brutus exclaims
(V.iii.94):

> O Julius Caesar, thou art mighty yet!
> Thy spirit walks abroad and turns our swords
> In our own proper entrails;

and the premonition is underscored by "Low alarums."
When, subsequently, Brutus has twice seen Caesar's Ghost
and been beaten "to the pit," the alarums, still low, accompany his request that Volumnius kill him (V.v.23). Then,
with "Alarum still," the sense of hastening doom is emphasized as Clitus cries, "Fly, fly my lord! There is no tarrying
here" (V.v.29–30). And finally, after the stage direction
"Alarum. Cry within: Fly, fly, fly!" (V.v.42), the identity of

the Nemesis becomes prosaically clear with the arrival of the victorious enemy, whose presence on stage is far less impressive than the suggestiveness of their distant drums.

When, some eight years later, Shakespeare wished to provide a similar tension for the closing scenes of *Macbeth,* he turned naturally to the same atmospheric uses for martial music, but without the more obvious Senecan identification of an avenging spirit. Most of the fifth act of *Macbeth,* from the second scene through the eighth, is drawn tensely together by the now intermittent, now steady, beating of drums. "Drum and colours" appear prominently in most of these scenes, announcing the approach of army after army to the place of Macbeth's last stand. Just as Brutus had been told, "There is no tarrying here," so Macbeth comes to the deeper realization that "There is no flying hence nor tarrying here" (V.v.48). But from a reading edition of the play, with its constant scene division, one has no awareness of the drum music which beats this truth home; for the scene ends within some four lines, and the reader is not likely to anticipate the approaching music announced at the beginning of the next scene (the sixth): "Drums and Colours. Enter Malcolm, Siward, Macduff, and their Army with boughs." Actually, of course, these scenes were continuous on the stage, and their continuity was strengthened by the cumulative effect of drums beating first an approaching march and finally alarums. Only with concentration will the reader notice how the inconspicuous directions for alarums increase near the end. Within the thirty-nine lines which comprise scenes six and seven, are the following musical directions: "Drums and Colours," "Alarums continued," "Alarums," "Alarums," and "Alarum." Macduff, like Octavius Caesar, may be a prosaic instrument of Nemesis, but not so the relentless music with which—in more than a military sense—he encompasses his victim.

With his actual military music, then, as well as with his rhetorical "music" of the classical discourse, Shakespeare's most effective and most consciously sought technique lies in transporting his audience from the immediate experience of battle—in which sounds, cannon, and blows have a precise, uncolored meaning—to a superior level of imaginative participation. On this level, not the mind's eye but the mind's ear is appealed to principally as a substitute for a full stage display of warfare. Remoteness, inherited partially from the classical messenger, is an essential quality of both the martial discourse and the martial music. And the ear, more susceptible than the eye to the suggestiveness of distant and imminent events, is impressed both by the "sad harmony" of rhetoric and by a skillfully connotative use of drum and trumpet.

CHAPTER II

Major Discords

The concept of war as musical harmony, which led Shakespeare to elaborate connotatively upon the sounds of battle, also influenced his interpretation of success and failure in warfare. He did not give decisive importance to such realistic agents of battle as cannon. Instead he traced the disastrous or imperfect outcomes of engagements to causes within the jurisdiction of the laws of nature. These causes tended to be discords violating the ideal harmony of war and of the macrocosm of which it was a part. Moreover, they were major discords, of a significance well beyond the casual strokes of physical battle.

War was one of the most precariously ordered and civilized of human enterprises; far more seriously than peace-inspired institutions like civil government and marriage, it threatened to revert to chaos. No wonder writers so anxiously insisted upon its ideal orderliness, for the violation of this orderliness in so potentially barbarous an institution might well have resulted in more than military defeat. The ultimate consequence was ominously described by one military writer as follows: "The olde Chaos will returne, and vertue die at the feete of confusion."[1]

II

Of the discords within Shakespeare's military world, the most rudimentary was lack of order in battle array and movements. In *Cymbeline* he commends the British as men much improved in martial order since the time of Caesar (II.iv.20):

> Our countrymen
> Are men more order'd than when Julius Caesar
> Smil'd at their lack of skill but found their courage
> Worthy his frowning at. Their discipline
> (Now wing-led with their courages) will make known
> To their approvers they are people such
> That mend upon the world.

The praise was not only anachronistic for the time of Cymbeline but doubtfully deserved early in the seventeenth century. Not until late in Elizabeth's reign would the English even have taken any special pride in being commended for discipline as well as courage. The sturdy attitude which had prevailed since Agincourt is stirringly expressed in Heywood's *Edward IV*:

> We have no trickes nor policies of warre,
> But by the antient custom of our fathers
> We'll soundly lay it on.[2]

Only the persistent efforts of soldier authors had been able to transplant the lessons of alien military procedures into England. These reformers translated older authors, like Frontinus

---

[1] For notes to chapter ii, see pages 318–320.

and Vegetius, and early Renaissance spokesmen for order, like Machiavelli. But even the lessons of the foreign masters were not enough. The English might read about, but they could not easily be brought to respect or practice, what Captain Fluellen calls "the disciplines of the pristine wars of the Romans" (*Henry V* III.ii.87–88)—or any disciplines, for that matter. No doubt the irregular conditions of sixteenth-century wars were partly responsible. In the "Proeme Dedicatorie" to that most melancholy of military treatises, *Certain Discourses* (1590), Sir John Smythe claims that it has been impossible for Englishmen "to learne any Art or Science Militarie in the civill warres of France, nor in the disordred warres of the Lowe Countries under the States, but rather the contrarie, that is, disorder and confusion."

Whatever the reason for this sad condition, Shakespeare was justified in picturing disorderly fighting, particularly in retreats, as an important cause of disaster. And although he showed little interest in the mechanics of ideal battle array, he had a lively idea of its opposite. The seriousness of failing to maintain order during battle is sententiously expressed in one of his earliest works. In *Venus and Adonis* the mounting panic felt by Venus is translated into a military simile (lines 893–894):

> Like soldiers when their captain once doth yield,
> They basely fly and dare not stay the field.

This martial commonplace is dramatized, though perfunctorily, in 2 *Henry VI,* when Clifford uses it to account for the defeat of his army (V.ii.31):

> Shame and confusion! All is on the rout.
> Fear frames disorder, and disorder wounds
> Where it should guard.

In *Henry V* disorderly fighting becomes more impressively a part of the play; becomes, indeed, the only strategic explanation for the French defeat. The Constable calls desperately upon disorder, "that hath spoil'd us," to "friend us now" (IV.v.17). Orleans hopes yet for some order so that the immense numerical superiority of the French can be felt. But Bourbon, like the Constable, offers the desperate advice which the French leaders disastrously follow (IV.v.22): "The devil take order now! I'll to the throng." In *Cymbeline* the reverse of this situation is illustrated, as three Britons, taking a firm stand, convert a rout for the British into a headlong, bloody flight for the Romans. This miracle, though attributed to "the heavens" (V.iii.4), is remarkable as Shakespeare's longest strategic explanation of an engagement.

Although Shakespeare thus acknowledges the importance of disciplined fighting, the acknowledgment does not go much beyond perfunctory or commonplace statement. It does not represent any thoughtful interest in the subject; it does not lead him, except perhaps in *Cymbeline,* to rearrange or reinterpret his historical source in its favor; and it never attaches itself to characterization or to any thematic issues in the play.

III

For more pervasive discords, consciously created, we must turn to dissensions among Shakespeare's military personnel. There are many such scattered throughout the plays, and some of these must be studied in more limited contexts. In the following chapter, for example, will be found clashes which become most significant in terms of special offices; and in the next, discords involving common soldiers. The two

chosen for consideration here are of general rather than limited interest; they often form Shakespeare's major commentary on battles; and they best illustrate the theoretical aspects
of discord. They are sententiously stated by Sir Robert Dallington in one of his military aphorisms:

Scilurus shafts, while they were close bound in a bundle, could
neither be broken nor bowed: but taken one by one, they were
easily snapped in sunder. So fareth it with the forces of an armie,
whose safetie depends upon the unitie and mutuall conjunction of
the inferiors with the superiors, and of these one with another.
Wherfore, nothing is more dangerous in the services of warre or
peace, then discord and faction among the great ones.[3]

As dramatized by Shakespeare, the two kinds of dissension
may be more precisely expressed as (1) friction between two
or more heads of an army and (2) insubordination resulting
from a pervasive neglect of rank and degree.

The first of these, resulting usually from joint command,
occurs so prominently in plays featuring battle that it seems
to have been one of Shakespeare's basic military interests. It
occurs regardless of source authority and regardless of whether
the battle is English or Roman. We shall find it in *1 Henry
VI, 1 Henry IV, Julius Caesar,* and *Coriolanus;* and its absence in *Henry V* is as meaningful as its presence in other
plays, for here Shakespeare fully demonstrates the virtue of
single, undivided command. We shall find, moreover, that
Shakespeare not only tends to give his armies two generals
rather than one; with the exception of *1 Henry VI,* he moti-
vates dissension between them by seeing to it that one of the
generals is impetuous and usually young, whereas the other
is astute or crafty, and usually mature.

Probably Shakespeare's interest in the dissensions of joint

command paralleled that of other Renaissance thinkers in that it derived from classical instances. He might, like Machiavelli, have found abundant provocative material in Livy. But there was a still better source. In Plutarch, more than in any other historian, Shakespeare encountered an impressive and insistent interpretation of Roman warfare during the Republic as a series of tensions between incompatible generals. Here, for the dramatist, was a congenial view of military history that sought out what Plutarch called "the signes and tokens of the minde only."[4] Plutarch, of course, gave far more strategic details of battles than did Shakespeare, but in the strained co-working of minds like those of Fabius and Minucius, Fabius and Marcellus, Aemilius and Varro, and Cassius and Brutus, obviously lay his real interest. The historian never tires, and never permits his reader to tire, of the clash between an older, cautious general and the hot-blooded youth with whom he is unhappily joined. The almost unvarying pattern is illustrated in Plutarch's "Aemilius." When Scipio Nasica insists upon giving battle instantly, Aemilius answers: "So would I doe, if I were as young as thou. But the sundry victories I have wonne heretofore, having taught me by experience the faultes the vanquished doe commit: doe forbid me to goe so whottely to worke (before my souldiers have rested, which dyd returne but now) to assault an armie set in suche order of battell."[5]

But though he furnished sharply pointed narratives illustrating the problems of joint command, Plutarch's military judgment upon this practice was not that of the Renaissance. On the whole he accepted it, like the Romans themselves, as a purposeful, if not unmixed, blessing. He seems, for example, to endorse the opinion of Posidonius concerning the strategic worth of employing Fabius jointly with Marcellus: "that Fabius constancie and resolutnes in warres to fight with securitie, and to commit nothing to hazard & daunger, being mingled with Marcellus heate and furie: was that only, which preserved the Romaines empire."[6]

When, in the Renaissance, a widespread debate arose over the desirability of joint command, the same Roman examples were used, but from a more critical point of view. Only a few political and military theorists recommended the use of two generals, and these authorities tended, like Plutarch, to interpret Roman precedents favorably. Thus Procter, under a heading often used for the dispute, "Whether it be more expedient to have one Generall, or manye," recalls that "Fabius and Minutius, were thought to be well matched together against Hanniball: the one grave, and somewhat slowe by his age, the other hott, quicke, and lusty."[7] And Bodin, although acknowledging that "the dissension which is commonly betwixt them which are in power equall, is sometimes an hinderance," nevertheless accepts the Roman point of view that a commonwealth led by two generals is "not so subject to be turned into a Monarchie."[8]

The majority opinion regarded this segment of Roman history more pessimistically. Ralegh, telling the story of Aemilius and Varro in his *History of the World,* points the moral for his Renaissance readers: "Thus, while the Romans think themselves to have the better of their enemies, they fall into an inconvenience, than which few are more dangerous; dissension of their chiefe commanders."[9] Hurault, likewise, affirming that "there behoveth no mo but one to commaund an armie," cites Aemilius and Varro ("the one was too slow, and the other too quicke") as causing a confusion, "the harme whereof the Romans felt a long time after."[10] Even Caesar's *Commentaries* were pillaged for whatever evidence they would yield against joint command. Both Clement Edmonds and Henri, Duc de Rohan, wrote observations on the *Commentaries,* and both included a section, forcibly interpolated in each case, advertising the fatal effects of two or more generals.[11]

What, more specific than abhorrence of discord, lay behind this Renaissance interest in the subject, and, in particular, the partisan form it took? One possibility immediately suggests itself: the sixteenth-century insistence on the "specialty of rule." And, in fact, military theorists used the same analogical arguments for one general as did the political theorists on behalf of one ruler. To Sutcliffe it seemed no more unnatural for a body to have two heads than "for an army to be encumbered with divers heads of contrary disposition."[12] And authorities as diverse as Guevara and Barnaby Rich piously extended the analogy to its ultimate expression in divine government.[13]

Did not, however, something more urgent than theory influence the Renaissance attitude? On the Continent there is little doubt that immediate military crises were involved. Hurault was attracted to classical precedents less for their theoretical interest than for the light they shed on current French disasters. In the civil wars of his own country he attributed the defeats to the jealousy of princes in joint command.[14] For Machiavelli's attitude, there is even less question of motivation, since a split generalship epitomized for him the division of Italy and its humiliating military weakness. Multiple command, he writes, creates "much confusion." If, in fact, "the occasion were inquired after, why the Italian and French Armyes are now adayes ruined, we should find this had been the principall."[15]

In England the urgency of current military mishaps was less acute, but still sufficient to maintain lively interest in the subject. Indeed, if one is at all addicted to topical identification, the present subject is likely to prove dangerously tonic. Shortly before Shakespeare wrote *1 Henry IV*, Essex and the Lord Admiral were sent as joint commanders on the Cadiz expedition. Essex was troublesomely young and zealous; Howard was stubbornly old and cautious. All eyes were on the enterprise, and especially upon Essex. Addressing him as a general, Sutcliffe had written, "God hath placed your Lordship as it were on a high stage in this estate."[16] And on this high stage Essex and Howard apparently proceeded to re-enact the timeless Roman stories. Reading of the voyage in Camden, one encounters repeated crises like the following: "Essex, full of courage and youthfull heate, was of opinion that the Forces were presently to be landed. Raleigh, and especially the Lord Admirall were of a contrary minde, which Lord never approved rash counsailes."[17] And commenting upon the imperfect success of the expedition, Camden writes: "If there were an error it seemed to be in this, for that matters were not managed by the command of one."[18] Unfortunately, the same instructive telling of the story is not conspicuous in narratives of the expedition written by eye-witnesses. These writers may mention occasional friction, but their accounts are not dominated by the pattern, nor do they pronounce a critical judgment upon it.[19] Camden is a historian, viewing the event in a larger context, and he achieves both form and meaning for his narrative by following the pattern of Renaissance commentators upon classical history.

Shakespeare's method is in some respects very similar. Valuing Plutarch's historical formula for its dramatic worth, he applies it to all kinds of battles, including those in which the Greek historian missed an opportunity to do so. But writing as a man of the Renaissance, he tends to highlight the dissension—most often in the losing army—so as to make the co-generals seem specially incompatible. He does, in short, precisely what a critic accused playwrights of doing: "If they write of histories that are knowen, as the life of Pompeie; the martial affaires of Caesar, and other worthies, they give them a newe face, and turne them out like counterfeites to show themselves on the stage."[20]

In *1 Henry VI* Shakespeare is solely responsible for the pivotal scenes (IV.iii and IV.iv) exposing the dissension between York and Somerset, "great commanders" of the English forces in France. In fact, Shakespeare risks monotony by repeating substantially the same pattern in successive scenes. Seeking prompt aid for Talbot, Sir William Lucy appeals in turn to each general, begs him not to let "private discord" prevent action, and, failing in his appeal, moralizes the effect of "worthless emulation" on the English cause. Lucy's comment upon York's stubbornness best expresses the military import of these scenes (IV.iii.47):

> Thus, while the vulture of sedition
> Feeds in the bosom of such great commanders,
> Sleeping neglection doth betray to loss
> The conquest of our scarce-cold conqueror,
> That ever-living man of memory,
> Henry the Fifth. Whiles they each other cross,
> Lives, honours, lands, and all hurry to loss.

Besides the doggedness with which this theme is insisted upon, the play is remarkable for an unusually tangible connection between the theme and the actual cause of defeat. Shakespeare makes it perfectly clear that Talbot loses because support does not reach his isolated band of men.

On the other hand, the play is also remarkable in not fully utilizing what was to become Shakespeare's favorite explanation for incompatiblity between generals: the classical difference in age and temperament. To be sure, there is a hint of a temperamental clash. Somerset justifies his refusal to act by describing the expedition as "too rashly plotted" by York and Talbot, and as an "unheedful, desperate, wild adventure" (IV.iv.2–7). But whatever rashness York may have, it is scarcely enough to make a Minucius or a Varro of him.

It is not until *1 Henry IV* that the classical pattern of one impulsive and one conservative general makes its presence unmistakably felt. Here Shakespeare not only began its central use, but enforced it, as he was to do on later occasions, by showing it in two relationships within the play. Both relationships are unhistorical. From the first of these, that between Hotspur and Glendower, Shakespeare constructed one of the play's best scenes. Young Percy finds his older ally "as tedious as a tired horse" (III.i.159), and threatens by his unruly temper to terminate the conspiracy before it is well begun. Except, however, for the faint possibility that the "crossings" he has received may have helped persuade Glendower not to appear at Shrewsbury, the argument has no immediate influence on the battle. Its principal military significance is in foreboding Hotspur's inability to command jointly with any person emotionally more mature than a Douglas.

We are thus prepared for the more important teaming of Hotspur with his uncle Worcester at Shrewsbury. Here, more decisively than in the former relationship, we find the irresponsible youth paired with a cautious older man. Worcester dourly regards his co-general as a warrior dominated by "youth and the heat of blood," "A hare-brain'd Hotspur, govern'd by a spleen" (V.ii.17–19). Early in the play he had gained a disconcerting foretaste of his nephew's military philosophy. Having spent a wearing quarter-hour trying to instruct the "wasp-stung and impatient fool" (I.iii.236) in a methodical preparation for war against the King, he must have listened with grim misgivings to Hotspur's boyish enthusiasm ringing out at the end of the indoctrination (I.iii.301):

> Uncle, adieu. O, let the hours be short
> Till fields and blows and groans applaud our sport!

The contrasting temperaments of uncle and nephew come closer to friction as Northumberland defaults and the management of the rebel army falls principally upon the two of them. It is in debating the seriousness of Northumberland's absence that the two generals most interestingly reveal their diametrically opposed natures. Worcester correctly sees the Earl's default as "a maim to us" (IV.i.42), a division apt to "breed a kind of question in our cause" (IV.i.68). Hotspur is at first angry at his father's failure to appear, but upon hearing Worcester's opinion, he adopts a strenuous optimism and insists that Northumberland's absence adds "a lustre and more great opinion, / A larger dare to our great enterprise" (IV.i.77). The pattern is repeated upon word of Glendower's

default. To Worcester, "that bears a frosty sound" (IV.i.128);
to Hotspur it is a spur to action (IV.i.131):

> My father and Glendower being both away,
> The powers of us may serve so great a day.

And his final words in this episode, "Doomsday is near. Die
all, die merrily," ring out like those in the earlier scene, prevailing over the gloomy reasonableness of his uncle.

But it is in the immediate preparation for fighting that the
incompatibility of the two rebels has the most serious possibilities. Hotspur is for instant battle (IV.iii.1): "We'll fight
with him tonight." Worcester demurs: "It may not be." Then
the dissension between the leaders spreads to Douglas and
Vernon, and threatens to split the rebellion into still smaller
elements. In pleading for immediate battle, Hotspur is obviously ill-advised. Few of the rebels' horse have arrived;
Worcester's came only recently and are still tired; and the
King's horse have a temporary numerical advantage. On the
basis of these facts, Shakespeare seems to endorse Worcester's
solemn plea (IV.iii.29): "For God's sake, cousin, stay till all
come in." In making this endorsement, the playwright is
forced not only to ignore but to reverse the historical interpretation of the battle, for speed was of the utmost importance at Shrewsbury, and both the King and the rebels were
praised for it.

To what extent did Shakespeare intend the prebattle dissension to be responsible for the rebels' defeat? From what
actually happens at Shrewsbury, one must answer: Not at all.
The warfare is a series of individual encounters, without
pressure of time and without horse, culminating in the

Prince's slaying of Hotspur. Nevertheless, I believe it unlikely that Shakespeare, having so carefully redesigned the facts of history for a more thoughtful interpretation of the battle, meant us to displace this interpretation in favor of the casual fighting which follows. The two are distinct and equally necessary. Hal's slaying of Hotspur supplies the physical excitement of combat (within the limits of the stage) and climaxes the personal rivalry of the two youths. But the friction between Hotspur and his senior commanders is equally important in exposing the psychological weakness of the rebellion and in preparing a Renaissance audience to expect—even in a conventional and limited battle scene—its ready defeat.

The rivalry between Hotspur and Hal is, of course, just as important as critics have declared it to be. But it has undeservedly received full credit for Shakespeare's boldest reshaping of history in the play: the reduction of Hotspur in point of age from a mature warrior, older than Hal's father, to a "Mars in swathling clothes, / This infant warrior" (III.ii.-112). The impressive scope of Shakespeare's design becomes apparent only if we recognize that the classical contrasts between Hotspur and his senior colleagues, resulting from the change, are too pervasive to have been casual afterthoughts.

In *Henry V* Shakespeare follows up his picture of confusion in *1 Henry IV* by pointedly demonstrating the virtues of single command. Dissensions among the English are limited to the limbs of the army, and are competently corrected by the single head. In contrast it is the three French heads—the Dauphin, the Constable, and Orleans—who bicker among themselves in the absence of the rightful head, the French King, and whose conflicting counsel during a crisis symbolizes the aimlessness of their cause.

A reversed sequence of pictures is implicit in *Julius Caesar*. Here, although we are not shown the triumphant period of Caesar's generalship, the image of this period persists almost as mightily as Caesar's Ghost as a background to the muddled generalship of the conspirators, and even of the two victorious generals.

The focus of Shakespeare's military interest in this play is, of course, on the joint command of Brutus and Cassius. Plutarch had already contrasted the two men in both age and temperament, but not with the clarity which we find in Shakespeare's great prebattle scenes. These scenes owe much of their animation and military import to a reinterpretation in terms of Renaissance views of joint command. The principal change is made at the expense of Brutus. Shakespeare seems to have repeated, though less drastically, the procedure used with Hotspur. Brutus acquires an impetuous desire for prompt fighting instead of the loftier, more thoughtful motive for action found in Plutarch: "to the end he might either quickly restore his country to her former liberty, or rid him forthwith of this miserable world."[21] In Plutarch, moreover. the issue is not whether there shall be immediate battle but whether a war shall be risked now at all.

To a certain extent the pattern of conflict between Shakespeare's two conspirators is reminiscent of *1 Henry IV*. After two episodes (IV.ii and IV.iii) of general argument between the two leaders, with demoralizing effect on the army, there occurs the following difference of opinion concerning strategy. Like Hotspur, Brutus asks (IV.iii.196): "What do you think / Of marching to Philippi presently?" and like Worcester, Cassius demurs: "I do not think it good." But despite these similarities, there is a marked improvement upon the situation at Shrewsbury. Shakespeare now carries the unlucky aspects of the dissension into the actual battle scenes. To a certain extent Plutarch helped him here, where Holinshed had not, since the Greek historian stressed the imperfect coördination resulting from two commanders. But where Plutarch attributes Brutus' premature charge to the impatience of the troops, Shakespeare blames it upon Brutus' overeagerness in giving the word too early.[22] The dramatist is also solely responsible for assigning tactical consequences to Brutus' insistence on taking the initiative; both Octavius and Antony comment upon the advantage in position it gives them (V.i).

Although Octavius and Antony are victors at Philippi, Shakespeare has no intention of giving them, as co-generals, credit for the triumph. The battle is lost by confusion rather than won by strategy. The two victorious generals are scarcely more capable together than the losers. Like Cassius, Antony pleads his superior age, in bickering with his co-general (IV.i.18). And to stress the friction between the two, Shakespeare transfers to them a dispute which Plutarch assigns the conspirators, concerning who is to lead the right wing.[23] Possibly by his dark picture of the early alliance of Antony and Octavius, the dramatist was glancing ahead to their more troubled relationship in *Antony and Cleopatra*. In any event, their joint command in *Julius Caesar* leaves upon the reader an impression more of ominous discord than of concerted achievement. It is the still potent spirit of Caesar that triumphs through these fragments of his former power.

Coriolanus is the last work in which Shakespeare's interest in battles concentrates upon the clash of joint commanders; and yet the play is, paradoxically, second only to *Henry V*

in picturing the strength of a single leader. Though twice
teamed with another general, Coriolanus each time breaks
from the team and conquers prodigiously on his own. The
best that his co-general can do is let him have his way. As
one of them philosophically remarks, "yet dare I never /
Deny your asking" (I.vi.64).

Coriolanus is first matched, entirely without warrant from
Plutarch, with the elderly Cominius. Although the senior
general is supposedly in charge of the Volscian expedition,
young Marcius establishes himself at first as an equal and
later as a dominant commander. The result—possibly the
most interesting aspect of the campaign—is a series of contrasts between impetuosity and cautious tactics. Coriolanus
hotly charges; Cominius strategically retreats, and is rebuked
by Coriolanus for momentarily letting the battle rest. After
rebuking his senior general, Coriolanus demands of him, in
the manner of Hotspur and Brutus,

> that you not delay the present, but,
> Filling the air with swords advanc'd and darts,
> We prove this very hour.
>
> (I.vi.60)

In Plutarch it is the troops who are anxious to join battle.

The contrast which Shakespeare thus invented produced
no important discord in itself; and the dramatist doubtless
designed it with one eye on the forthcoming dissension with
Aufidius. Although Shakespeare had found this unlucky alliance in Plutarch, he did not find it as a clear instance of joint
command or as a contrast in temperaments resembling that
between Worcester and Hotspur. The historian's Aufidius
remains to guard the home territory, and the friction between

the two generals does not so clearly derive from the military relationship. In Shakespeare the relationship is steadily developed. Aufidius, in the first warmth of the alliance, offers the Roman "one half of my commission" (IV.v.143). Shakespeare's unpleasant intentions in the joint command become promptly apparent as the Volscian servingmen comment cynically upon it, agreeing that "our general is cut i' th' middle and but one half of what he was yesterday, for the other has half by the entreaty and grant of the whole table" (IV.v.208). As the battle gets under way, Coriolanus takes more than his half of the command, as he had done with Cominius; and it is appropriately Cominius who reports to the Romans the status of Coriolanus' new alliance (IV.vi.124):

> Tullus Aufidius,
> The second name of men, obeys his points
> As if he were his officer.

In order to emphasize Aufidius' growing discontent, Shakespeare invents a scene between him and a lieutenant, in which the "darkening" of the Volscian leader by Coriolanus' aggressiveness is grimly commented upon. Entirely Shakespeare's, and central to his interpretation of the Coriolanus-Aufidius alliance, is the moral which the lieutenant draws in his belated advice to Aufidius, that

> you had not
> Join'd in commission with him; but either
> Had borne the action of yourself, or else
> To him had left it solely.
>
> (IV.vii.13)

But this instance of joint command, however much it may irritate Aufidius and however fatal it may ultimately prove to Coriolanus, does not have a profound influence upon any battle. Once more Shakespeare was given no opportunity by the story he inherited to carry his favorite type of dissension into scenes of combat. The divided command serves, consequently, only as an ominous background to battle and forebodes Coriolanus' final and fatal clash with the more cunning Aufidius in a postwar situation. At most one can say that it would have been better for the Volscians, for Coriolanus, and for Aufidius if the lieutenant's advice had been followed and there had been no division of authority.

Because several of Shakespeare's most fully dramatized examples of joint command are marked by friction and confusion, it is tempting to conclude that he accepted the majority opinion of Renaissance writers on war and rewrote military history as a partisan of single command. Such a conclusion, however, meets the same difficulties as any other attempt to find a consistent point of view in Shakespeare. There are the inevitable exceptions. Shakespeare is quite capable of depicting joint command without picturing its defects or calling special attention to it. Prince John and Westmoreland, Macbeth and Banquo, serve together successfully and without friction. Here, as elsewhere, Shakespeare is more dependable as a master of dramatic situation and character than as a student of war. If his dramatic purpose does not call for dissension between generals, he does not supply it, even though history offered him the two generals.

But to deny Shakespeare a consistent and professional military attitude toward the subject is not to deny him an alert interest in it. A playwright, like any well-informed member of his audience, might recognize the dangerous possibilities of a certain military situation, without the reformer's insistence that it must always occur. It is sufficient for us to acknowledge that Shakespeare understood the theoretical aspects of joint command, as of divided rule in government, and that, when he chose to do so, he commented vigorously upon them, both by dramatic situations and by dialogue. He fully understood the chaotic disorder to which divided authority might lead a government or an army. Coriolanus is not speaking with excessive feeling when he says (III.i.108):

> my soul aches
> To know, when two authorities are up,
> Neither supreme, how soon confusion
> May enter 'twixt the gap of both and take
> The one by th' other.

IV

In turning from discords between the heads of an army to discords of insubordination, we find that the same general law of nature is being violated. For this law did not merely prescribe that a body should have no more than one head; it assigned, as James E. Phillips has shown, a proper and circumscribed function for every member of the body. A passage in Edward Forset's *A Comparative Discourse of the Bodies Natural and Politique* (1606), cited by Professor Phillips, is especially pertinent to the concept of degree within Shakespeare's armies: "Each part is to know and administer his owne proper worke, without intermising or entermeddling in the offices of an other. Shall the foot be permitted to partake in point of preeminence with the head? or were it seemlie for the head, leaving his state, to abuse himselfe to a toyle manibus pedibusq; in the trading business?"[24]

The Shakespeare play in which the violation of this law is

most instructively depicted is, of course, *Troilus and Cressida*.
A large part of this work—comprising its military thesis—is
devoted to exposing the weakness of an army in which individual members do not exercise their proper functions for
the good of the corporate enterprise. Although there is little
chance of saying anything original about a play which has
been so well studied by others,[25] it can scarcely be bypassed
in a discussion of major discords within Shakespeare's military world. It represents Shakespeare's most sustained and
formal statement on the subject of degree within an army.
As such, it is valuable not only in itself but as the dramatist's
own preface to his more detailed studies of rank, which will
be discussed in the next chapter.

In his famous speech on degree, Ulysses presents what is
doubtless Shakespeare's explanation of the Greek stalemate
in the Trojan campaign. When degree is "vizarded," Ulysses
states, there can be no distinction between the worthy and
the unworthy (I.iii.83–84). This "neglection of degree," instead of producing untrammeled progress, "goes backward
with a purpose / It hath to climb" (I.iii.127–129). Specifically,

> The general's disdain'd
> By him one step below, he by the next;
> That next by him beneath. So every step,
> Exampled by the first pace that is sick
> Of his superior, grows to an envious fever
> Of pale and bloodless emulation.
> And 'tis this fever that keeps Troy on foot,
> Not her own sinews.
>
> (I.iii.129)

The reason suggested by Ulysses for the "neglection of degree" is lack of inspiring and decisive command. As com-

mander in chief, Agamemnon has not exercised his ordained duty, which is "specialty of rule." Hector, who can afford to be more direct than Ulysses, says of Agamemnon (II.ii.211):

> I was advertis'd their great general slept
> Whilst emulation in the army crept.

Although the situation had, on its religious and political levels, benefited from wider and more expert analysis, military writers, too, gave it their serious attention, and in terms more pertinent to the specific situation in *Troilus and Cressida*. The ideal of military government which Agamemnon violates is pointedly stated by the Elizabethan soldier William Blandy: "As the Generall is, so are his Captaynes, Lieuetenauntes, officers and souldiars. For where the desire of true honor, and glory is in the Generall imprinted, there the Captaynes, officers, and souldiars, by a naturall love and inclination that the best mindes are stirred therewith, are much more set on fire and enkindeled."[26] It is absence of this central imperative in the Greek camp to which Ulysses alludes when, employing an analogy with bees, he asks (I.iii.81):

> When that the general is not like the hive,
> To whom the foragers shall all repair,
> What honey is expected?

Emphasizing the reality rather than the ideal, Matthew Sutcliffe answered Ulysses' question directly when he wrote: "Of the weakenesse of Generals, proceede contentions betwixt the chiefe commaunders, delayes, needelesse expenses, disorders, disgraces, and the overthrows of Armies and States."[27] Machiavelli had also predicted the insubordination to be expected from Agamemnon's negligent generalship. The Florentine might, in fact, almost have been describing the relationship between Shakespeare's "great general" and insolent subordinates like Achilles and Patroclus when he said that if the head of an army does not exercise firm control over his officers, the latter "becometh in everie condicion insolente." For, the general is warned, "thou becomest of small estimacion, where thou chaunsest not to bee able to maintaine the dignitie of thy degree, and not mainetainyng it, there foloweth of necessitee tumulte, and discorde, whiche is the ruine of an armie."[28]

If, in *Trolius and Cressida,* Shakespeare went beyond theory of this sort in seeking topical significance for his study in pervasive discord, it is impossible to confine him to any one of several English campaigns. In pretentiousness and in weak and dawdling leadership, the Irish expedition of 1599 was a likely candidate. On the other hand, the English failure was not due to a resultant insubordination. There were several prima donnas on the staff, but these were Essex's favorites and were devoted to him. There was more bickering from rank to rank at the conclusion of the much maligned voyage of 1589. Then, as one of its participants remarks, the "common sort" were far "from reverencing or regarding any persons of conduction"; indeed, "the base and common souldier hath been tollerated to speake against the Captaine, the souldier and Captaine against the generalls."[29] The situation interestingly parallels that in *Troilus and Cressida,* where

> The general's disdain'd
> By him one step below, he by the next;
> That next by him beneath.

But at Ostend in 1588 a similiar situation had been reported. Sir William Drury wrote to Burghley that not only was there "dissension between the Governor and captains, and between captains and soldiers," but there was no discipline of misconduct.[30]

Perhaps the most notorious instance of supposed insubordination was on the unlucky Islands voyage of 1597.[31] This voyage was also closer in date to the appearance of *Troilus and Cressida* than the two instances just mentioned, and its dissensions became a national scandal. The English forces were divided in allegiance between Essex, the commander in chief, and Ralegh, one of his two seconds-in-command. An ugly incident brought the jealousy between the two factions to a head. Ralegh, after impatiently awaiting the arrival of his superior, attacked Fayal on his own initiative. When, according to Camden, Essex arrived and found the town already taken, he was advised by one of his followers that Ralegh "had seyzed upon the town to no other end, but to prevent Essex of the glory." Still other Essex partisans urged him to call Ralegh to a military court-martial for having landed without authority.[32] But the problem of how far a subordinate might exceed his commission had become noteworthy in England well before the Islands voyage. Following the defeat of the Armada in 1588, for example, "martiall men warmly disputed the Case, whether Instructions were not religiously to be observed and kept to, whatsoever should fall out, lest through Neglect of Obedience all Authority and Command should be violated."[33] What is more, the type of insubordination exemplified on the Islands voyage involved a sin not of omission, as in *Troilus and Cressida,* but of commission. It more closely approximated the problem briefly posed in *Antony and Cleopatra* when Ventidius explains why he did not follow up his successes against the Parthians (III.i.11):

> O Silius, Silius,
> I have done enough. A lower place, note well,
> May make too great an act. For learn this, Silius:
> Better to leave undone than by our deed
> Acquire too high a fame when he we serve's away.
> . . . .
> Who does i' th' wars more than his captain can
> Becomes his captain's captain; and ambition,
> The soldier's virtue, rather makes choice of loss,
> Than gain which darkens him.

This utterance not only evidences the general nature of the problem of insubordination in Shakespeare's plays—suggesting that Shakespeare did not limit it to any one place or topical source—but discloses the paradoxical fact that the strength of the commander may ideally suppress rather than encourage individual action, however lucky the action may prove to be. To many readers Ventidius' doctrine has seemed an unpleasantly politic one, and it has even been cited by MacCallum as part of the cynical philosophy pervading the Roman world of *Antony and Cleopatra*.[34] Unfortunately, moreover, the unsavoriness of an idea is seldom helped even when Shakespeare goes out of his way to endorse it, as he does here in the approving words of Silius (III.i.27):

> Thou hast, Ventidius, that
> Without the which a soldier and his sword
> Grants scarce distinction.

But it is difficult to resist the more dramatic evidence that in none of his plays, English, Greek, or Roman, does Shakespeare present a favorable case for any soldier who fails to observe the confines of his office, either through willful action or through willful inaction. Conversely, within Shakespeare's ideal armies, like that of the Earl of Richmond or Henry V, each member knows his proper office and does not exceed it. This ideal is forcefully affirmed by Richmond in his preparations for battle (*Richard III* V.iii.23):

> Give me some ink and paper in my tent.
> I'll draw the form and model of our battle,
> *Limit each leader to his several charge,*
> And put in just proportion our small power.
> [*Italics mine.*]

Limiting each leader to his charge was a precaution of utmost importance in Elizabethan amphibious expeditions, apt as these were to be dominated, like the Greek army in *Troilus and Cressida,* by honor-hungry individuals. In preparing for the Cadiz voyage, Essex wrote: "I am busied in bringing all this chaos into order: in setting down every man's rank and degree, that those under me may not fall by the ears for precedence and place, as in other armies hath been. I am setting down the parts, and bounds, and limits of every man's office, that none may plead ignorance if he do not his duty, nor none encroach upon his fellows."[35] The necessity for laws designed to bring "chaos into order" was illustrated in 1597 when there were "open jarres" over precedence among Ralegh, Sir Conyers Clifford, and Sir Francis Vere. Clifford, as Vere claimed, was a man of haughty stomach; and "lest ignorance or will might mislead him in the execution of his office, and [in order] to give a rule to the rest of the high officers ... to the better directing of them in their duties," Vere "propounded to my Lord of Essex as a thing most necessary, the setting down in writing, what belonged properly to every office in the field; which motion his Lordship liked well."[36]

V

What, in Elizabethan armies, "belonged properly to every office," is a question of considerable importance in a study of Shakespeare's military world, since it was natural that a degree-conscious country should do its best to define the military hierarchy and thereby prevent the type of chaos dramatized in *Troilus and Cressida*. Most military books gave impressive space to the duties and honors pertaining to all ranks. In fact, many of these works were responsible for instituting in England the present-day concepts and vocabulary of rank. The title of Gyles Clayton's treatise, published in 1591, describes the contents of the sort of book which familiarized the English public with old and new military titles: *The Approved Order of Martiall Discipline, with Every Particuler Offycer His Offyce and Dutie*. Likewise, the first book of Thomas Styward's *The Pathwaie to Martiall Discipline* (1581) "Entreateth of the Offices from the highest to the lowest." Often, too, these manuals were organized on the basis of rank so that problems which today seem relevant to the army as a whole were assigned to appropriate offices.

Most of the Shakespeare soldiers so far studied have no clearly defined—certainly no Renaissance—rank. From Plutarch and other sources for classical history, or from Holinshed, Shakespeare inherited no titles for his heroes other than "general." In *Troilus and Cressida* the expression "great general" may be used to indicate commander in chief, but the prevailing vagueness of rank in the play is exemplified in the lines already quoted:

> The general's disdain'd
> By him one step below, he by the next;
> That next by him beneath.

But in his plays dealing with more recent history, Shakespeare not only used specific titles but reflected the Elizabethan practice of associating personality and action with rank. However interesting soldiers in these plays may be in other respects, their personalities as soldiers cannot be fully appreciated outside the context of their military office. It is therefore appropriate that we make a separate investigation of Shakespeare's officers who seem to be significantly connected with the rank they held. In so doing, we shall find that the presence of a defined and labeled military hierarchy is not in itself sufficient to bring "chaos into order," even though it lessens the kind of irresponsibility dramatized in *Troilus and Cressida*. Times have not changed in this respect. Consciousness of rank may serve only to define and clarify the emulation. Shakespeare thoroughly understood this fact and, as we shall see, made good drama from it.

Military Rank

Just how thoroughly Shakespeare knew military rank, and how he came by whatever knowledge he possessed, are still moot questions. J. W. Draper and Sir John Fortescue, pioneer authorities on the subject, credit the dramatist with only a slight knowledge of army titles, acquired mainly from conversation with returned soldiers or from drills at Mile End. On the other hand, Henry J. Webb has recently offered at least equally cogent evidence on behalf of Shakespeare's competent knowledge.[1] And Sir Duff Cooper has found Shakespeare's understanding of warfare, as seen from the lower ranks, so discerning that he assumes the dramatist to have served during his "dark years" as a noncommissioned officer; in fact it is to Cooper that we owe the startling notion of a "Sergeant Shakespeare." As sergeant, Cooper reasons, Shakespeare would have had no close contact with any officer higher than captain; hence, when the dramatist tries to depict

---

[1] For notes to chapter iii, see pages 320–324.

63

a general, "he relies upon his poetic imagination rather than his personal experience," with unrealistic results.² Cooper's theory is a pleasant one, but admittedly tentative. Indeed, none of the writers mentioned above makes any claim to finality and, except for Cooper, none has gone much beyond the situation in *Othello*.

The present survey will seek greater perspective by including several plays—specifically those using a Renaissance military hierarchy—and by looking beyond the mechanics of rank to the personalities through which Shakespeare gave it so various, if unreliable, an embodiment. A specially detailed study of Henry V as general is provided, for two reasons: to examine the truth of Cooper's important assertion that Shakespeare was ignorant of ranks above the captaincy, and to emphasize the difference between Shakespeare's portrait of an ideal commander in chief and his portraits of the contentious joint commanders studied in the last chapter.

II

In Shakespeare's English histories written before 1596 there is slight indication of rank below the general. As I have mentioned, the omission may merely have reflected the situation in Holinshed. Possibly, too, Shakespeare correctly recognized that English forces of the periods represented were organized on feudal lines. If so, it is hard to account for the sudden and anachronistic emergence in both parts of *Henry IV* of the splendidly authentic figure of Falstaff as Elizabethan captain, with almost a complete representation of a company of infantry. One can only surmise that Shakespeare, like many of his alert fellow countrymen, began to read military literature during this critical period in national defense, since even

Cooper does not place him in the army at this time. Whatever the reason, Shakespeare reveals in the years between *1 Henry IV* and *Othello* a special interest in the qualifications, problems, and psychology of army offices.

To be sure, the interest does not show itself most impressively in a technical accuracy. In the *Henry IV* plays the nomenclature of rank is used primarily for comic effect, often with satirical intent. Bardolph as corporal and Pistol as "ancient" (the early form of *ensign*) are singularly imperfect representatives of their ranks. Their titles, if not intended as gross misapplications of esteemed offices (for which Captain Falstaff is to blame), seem to be self-conferred honorifics and hence are easily changed to suit their present mood or sense of importance. Pistol, for example, enjoys a brief period as lieutenant at the end of *2 Henry IV,* and the Hostess labors under the impression that he is a captain; yet in *Henry V* he becomes, if anything official, an ensign once more, while the scoundrel Bardolph has leaped past him from corporal to lieutenant. The only military use of these irregular humorists in *Henry IV* occurs when Bardolph helps Falstaff with the infamous recruiting in *Part II.* We shall find them more specifically, but not more usefully, employed in the warfare of *Henry V.*

More perplexing in the lower hierarchy of *Henry IV* is the absence of a sergeant. Captain Falstaff avers that his "whole charge consists of ancients, corporals, lieutenants, gentlemen of companies" (*Part I,* IV.ii.25–26). The omission is strange for a dramatist supposed by Sir Duff Cooper to have held the rank himself. It is not, moreover, peculiar to *Henry IV.* Except for a perfunctory appearance of a French sergeant in *1 Henry VI* (II.i), the office does not occur anywhere in the plays. The bleeding sergeant in *Macbeth* (who is called "Captain" in the stage directions) is no more than the messenger of Senecan tragedy. His rank is as ill defined as is that of the general who serves as Nuncius in *The Spanish Tragedy*. Most of Shakespeare's sergeants are sergeants of the law.[3] His slighting of this military rank, unthinkable in a modern writer, is understandable in a writer of the Renaissance, since in sixteenth-century armies neither the sergeant nor the corporal was associated, as now, with a distinct and popularly recognizable personality.

What these offices lacked dramatically, the captaincy supplied with God's plenty.[4] No Elizabethan officer had greater notoriety. Shakespeare took full advantage of this fact by making Falstaff the most interesting military personality in *Henry IV*. And by placing him in the comic segments of the play, Shakespeare was justified in making him far more realistic and clearly defined as a soldier than any of the feudal lords to whom history had assigned the warfare.

In his nonmilitary capacity Falstaff is comic because his behavior so aptly contradicts what his years and public station demand of him. A white-haired man who should be brooding on mortality and offering staid counsel to the Prince, he is instead the most wantonly youthful of all Shakespeare's characters. Similarly his comic appeal as captain comes from just as brilliant a reversal of the ideals of this office. The Elizabethan captain, because of his immense influence in recruiting men, leading them into battle, and dispensing royal funds, was an officer of literally frightful importance. Soldiers, according to Barwick, should aspire to this responsible rank only on the basis of "valour, knowledge, and good behaviour."[5] And Sutcliffe demands that captains be "the most strong, valiant, discrete, and active souldiers" and "of body able to endure labour."[6] Of these qualities, Falstaff can lay claim only to a remarkable discretion. His greatest failing, of course, is in his gross disregard for the well-being of his newly levied company: "I have led my rag-of-muffins where they are pepper'd. There's not three of my hundred and fifty left alive; and they are for the town's end, to beg during life" (*1 Henry IV* V.iii.36–40). This confession achieves much of its hideous comedy—a comedy not without effect upon cannon fodder in the audience—through its reversal of the captain's most sacred trust; for the "deepe and principall consideration [which] ought to be in a Captayne," wrote William Blandy, is "that a charge of the lives of men is to him committed."[7]

In reversing certain key precepts of military conduct books and defining the rank of captain in terms of what this officer should not be, Shakespeare might seem to be independently responsible for the satire which results. Actually, he was able to take most of his satire with slight change from the conduct books. Whereas these works are solemnly idealistic in pre-scribing for other offices, they are sardonically disillusioned in discussing the captaincy. The writers were often captains themselves and had been obliged to watch their title becom-ing, as Doll Tearsheet put it, a "word as odious as the word 'occupy,' which was an excellent good word before it was ill sorted. Therefore captains had need look to't" (*2 Henry IV* II.iv.161–163). Did not even Parolles of *All's Well* prefix captain to his name before deciding that he could eat and sleep as well without it? Because of the resultant discredit to them personally and to their profession, the good captains followed Doll's advice and looked to it. They wrote with unusually vivid detail about the current malpractices that gave to the captaincy a criminal reputation. Gyles Clayton, in beginning his discussion of "The election of a Captayne, hys Office," has patience for only one sentence describing the ideal before launching a vigorous attack on the actuality.⁸ And Barnaby Rich, who survived the shame of his office to become the oldest captain in Her Majesty's service,⁹ had only this in 1587 to say of the appointment of a captain: "Wee never number his yeares, we neither consider his knowledge, we little regard his worthines, we lesse esteeme his experience, we scarce examine his honestye."¹⁰

General abuse of this sort was doubtless valuable to Shakespeare, and he found ample accommodation for it in his spacious conception of Falstaff. But more directly useful were specific instances of malpractices which the soldier authors related with journalistic detail.¹¹ Kindly critics, from Maurice Morgann to A. C. Bradley, have credited Falstaff with courage for leading his 150 into the thick of battle, with 147 casualties. The happy coincidence that Falstaff himself was one of the survivors calls for explanation, and this is readily forthcoming from the military books of the time. Sir John Smythe tells how certain captains, to cheat their soldiers of pay, "devised some verie daungerous enterprise to employ their bands and companies in, to make proofe how manie in such exploytes should leese their lives, that they might enrich themselves by their dead paies."¹² "Dead pays" were one of the outstanding army scandals in Elizabeth's reign. Since a captain could draw pay for a full company, even though it had been seriously depleted, it was to his advantage to lose men. And if he were required to keep a minimum number, he could "pad" the muster roll, a connivery recognized by the remark in *All's Well* (IV.iii.188): "The muster file, rotten and sound, upon my life, amounts not to fifteen thousand poll," and acknowledged by Falstaff when, in conscripting Shadow, he punningly expresses the need for "a number of shadows to fill up the muster book" (2 *Henry IV* III.ii.145–146). Falstaff's declaration of the "loss" of 147 men is to be taken, then, not as a regret but as a statement of no mean accomplishment.

But one might still insist that even with mercenary motives the old villain needed courage to lead his men into slaughter. Here again the handbooks are disillusioning. In arguing that captains of infantry should honorably go on foot themselves, Smythe relates interesting results of the contrary practice:

Modern captains whose charges have consisted onlie of footmen, have (presentlie upon their squadrons formed, and approach or sight of the Enemie) mounted uppon horses or swift Carrires, and either have accompanied their footmen upon the flankes or re-reward, being so well mounted, or els have put themselves into some bands of horsmen...that uppon anie hard accident they might be readie (leaving their soldiers to the slaughter) to save themselves rather with the force of their heeles and spurres, then with any dint of sword, which amongst manie other, hath been one special cause that there have been so great numbers of soldiers at divers times consumed and slaine, and never anie Chieftaines, nor any other of our such men of warre.[13]

So pronounced is Falstaff's distaste for walking, and so un-likely the chance of his escaping from battle on foot, one can only assume that he followed the procedure described by Smythe. This procedure was apparently foolproof, since no chieftain had been lost following it, and it would assuredly have commended itself to a man with Falstaff's studious interest in self-preservation.

Having rescued himself from battle, Falstaff lives to enjoy a hero's due. Dover Wilson has shrewdly observed the signs of Falstaff's new prosperity in 2 *Henry IV,* a change which should be indicated "by a startling change of costume." Now he is "the complete courtier,... fashionably, fantastically, hilariously decked out, according to the very latest and most foppish cut, yards and yards of it, with some absurdity of a cap to crown the sartorial edifice."[14] Wilson ascribes Sir John's prosperity to the reward for his "day's service" at Shrewsbury, when he made the preposterous but inspired claim of having killed Hotspur. But Elizabethans would also have connected the riches with Falstaff's lucrative work as captain. In recruiting his men he had been richly bribed; in losing them, he found solace in collecting their pay. What Dudley Digges has to say about the ridiculous finery of crooked captains amply explains Falstaff's sartorial improvement:

Whereas the right valiant Captaine indeed, that (keeping his Band strong and compleat with armed souldiers, gaining nothing above his bare wages, nor will extort unhonestly upon any Friend or Allie, and his wages ... scarcely sufficient twice in a yeare to buy him a Sute of Buffe) remayneth as a Man contemned and disgraced: Where the other by his Robberies and pickories can florish in Monethly change of sutes of silke, dawbed with Embroderies of golde and silver lace, and Jewels also.... And is it any Mervaile if so brave and gallant a Gentleman ... disdain to haunt the filthy Corps du gardes of ragged, lothsome, lowsie souldiers?[15]

The description should give producers hints for Falstaff's new wardrobe. It is also specially relevant to Falstaff in that only once, and that in *1 Henry IV,* is he shown in the unpleasant company of what Digges calls "ragged, lothsome, lowsie souldiers," and what Sir John himself calls "slaves as ragged as Lazarus in the painted cloth, where the glutton's dogs licked his sores" (*1 Henry IV* IV.ii.27–29).

Like many Elizabethan captains, Falstaff preferred the amenities of London, particularly its taverns, to the inconveniences of the battlefield. Concerning Falstaff's delay in getting from the tavern to battle, Professor Webb has interestingly shown that Shakespeare meant to satirize Elizabethan absentee captains.[16] While Falstaff is wantoning in the Boarshead Tavern with Doll and the Hostess, word comes of a "dozen captains,"

> Bareheaded, sweating, knocking at the taverns,
> And asking every one for Sir John Falstaff.
> (*2 Henry IV* II.iv.388)

These are workaday captains, the kind we shall meet in *Henry V.* They would not be dressed in "sutes of silke, dawbed with Embroideries of golde and silver lace."

Still we have not exhausted the riches available to a dramatist who took the pains to read current descriptions of the captaincy in newsbook and military treatise. One of the major types of peculation practiced by Falstaff remains to be considered. But since this, his recruiting procedure in both parts of *Henry IV,* is interesting mainly in relation to its wretched victims, it may more relevantly be studied in the chapter on common soldiers.

III

By the time he approached the writing of *Henry V,* Shakespeare was as well versed as he was ever to become in knowledge of army affairs and, more specifically, in the aspects of army organization which made for good drama. Indeed, as Miss Campbell has demonstrated, *Henry V* is a sustained dramatization of Elizabethan ideas and procedures of war.[17] Whereas in both *Henry IV* plays Shakespeare confined the mechanics of degree to the comic characters, in *Henry V* an Elizabethan system of rank is imposed upon the entire English army, even though not all offices are well represented. The result makes an effective contrast with the sharp feudal split in the French army between the dainty nobles and the peasants, with no dignities or responsibilities given to the latter. All are lumped together without personality or gradation; and indeed there tends to be no personality anywhere among Shakespeare's humbler military population unless there is gradation.

In the French army there are certainly no equivalents of Henry's four unmistakable captains—Fluellen, Macmorris, Jamy, and Gower. These men, though probably of humble birth, have pride in their station. As successors to Falstaff in an army now under an ideal command, they reveal Shakespeare's ability to portray captains who are competent as officers and yet not without realistically wayward and contentious traits.

Fluellen, the Welshman, and Macmorris, the Irishman, emerge with special vivacity as specimens of argumentative Elizabethan captains. In no other army relationship, with the exception of that between Iago and Cassio, has Shakespeare more successfully translated for the stage a controversy made famous by military journalism. It is true that he has not so firmly as in *Othello* placed the controversy within a context of military rank. The two causes of the unpleasantness between Captain Fluellen and Captain Macmorris might arise between other officers than captains. But it was captains who gave the controversies their greatest publicity.

Whereas corrupt captains were best known for their pecu-
lations, reputable captains appeared in the public eye mainly
as earnest, irascible disputants on military theory. It was these
serious students who, in their plentiful hours of leisure, produced so many of the textbooks on war. Many of these works,
lacking the customary objectivity of instructive manuals, told
readers less about the art of war than about the spleens of the
authors. These animated treatises represented one of the most
amusing battles of the books waged in Shakespeare's day and
gave to the participating captains a public character as comically quarrelsome personalities.

As one of the authors testifies, with rare understatement,
"such bookes have bene written by men of sundrie humours."[18]
Barnaby Rich recalls "upon what splene" one of the most
controversial works was conceived.[19] Heated language was
frequent, with expressions like "very arrogant" and "mere
follie" being applied to rival theorists.[20] One zealous participant complained of his opponents that "in steade of alleadg-
ing reasons and examples, according to the use of other Nations, with quietnes and courteous phrase of speach, they
argue for life and death, with hastie and furious wordes."[21]

It was an unlucky irony for the captains that the subject
which they were so hotly debating was the need for order in
war. The more insistent of them resembled Shakespeare's
Fluellen in pleading, with increasing warmth, for a reasonable recourse to the disciplines of the ancient wars. There was
further irony in the fact that many of the disputants were
meagerly educated captains and had only precarious control
over the classical works which they commended. They were
enchanted by the orderliness of war which they found in the
Greek and Latin treatises; but unluckily, as their modernist

opponents pointed out, they were unable to make practical application of the old system to modern warfare. Procter's grandiloquent description of the "auncient orders" of warfare illustrates the vague, uncomprehending kind of admiration which Shakespeare genially mocked in Fluellen:

Reason will easelye discusse that the knowledge of the auncient orders and government of warre, with the sundrie sortes and attyre of batail, used amonge sundry nations, their maners and practises, the examples of the antiquitie, the experience, pollicies, prudent counsailes, most profitable and pithye preceptes, and admonishmentes, most exellent experimentes, instructyons, behaviour and discipline of the greatest chyeftaines, and most renouned conquerors that ever weare, be requisite and needefull unto a good Captaine.[22]

Similarly, Fluellen rouses himself to his most stately and vacuous eloquence when, in deploring the noisiness of Gower, he tells of the wonders of Pompey's wars (*Henry V* IV.i.72): "I warrant you, you shall find the ceremonies of the wars, and the cares of it, and the forms of it, and the sobriety of it, and the modesty of it, to be otherwise." When Fluellen attempts to be more specific, he is less successful. He objects to the mining operations outside Harfleur "because the mines is not according to the disciplines of the wars," but is unable to explain just what "disciplines" (his favorite word) are being violated. What Fluellen really means, and finally manages to blurt out, is simply that the enemy has countermined and "will plow up all" (III.ii.67). Although, as G. G. Langsam has argued,[23] Fluellen is no contemptible soldier, his erudition in "the Roman disciplines" is of small practical value.

Modern readers may be in little danger of overrating Flu-

ellen's knowledge of the ancient wars, but they are very likely
to mistake the good captain's earnestness for belligerency.
Fluellen was not spoiling for a fight; all he wanted, or
thought he wanted, was a reasonable discussion. He admires
worthy captains who, after a "few disputations," can agree
with him about Roman disciplines. Gower has apparently
proved reasonable, for he is "a good captain, and is good
knowledged and literatured in the wars" (IV.vii.156–157).
Captain Jamy is likewise of "great expedition and knowledge
in th' aunchiant wars.... By Cheshu, he will maintain his
argument as well as any military man in the world in the
disciplines of the pristine wars of the Romans" (III.ii.82–88).
But Macmorris—"he has no more directions in the true disciplines of the wars, look you, of the Roman disciplines, than
is a puppy-dog" (III.ii.75–78).

What makes Macmorris especially trying as a fellow captain is that he refuses a perfectly courteous invitation, during
the heat of battle, to enjoy a discussion on this all-important
subject. It is to be merely "in the way of argument, look you,
and friendly communication" (III.ii.101–105). The relationship between the two captains would then be that ideal kind
which forms the basis for one of Barnaby Rich's entire books.
A Souldiers Wishe to Britons Welfare is presented as the
"second incounter betweene Captaine Skill and Captaine
Pill."[24] Captain Pill, an unlearned soldier, appears "in his
humorous fit" and Captain Skill "in his temperate judge-
ment."[25] Apparently the first "incounter" between the two
captains had achieved print, though no record of it exists, and
apparently on this occasion Captain Pill had, like Macmorris,
proved resistant to instruction. Formerly, he confesses, he had
"presumed of as much skill as might have beseemed the great

Captaine of Cartege, yet now experience hath taught me to know, that indeed I know nothing." Captain Skill commends this humility: "I see it hath inlightened your understanding to know your owne imperfections, and there cannot be a more learned ignorance, then for a man to confese his own ignorance."[26] Thus the "dispute" takes the amicable and leisurely form desired by Fluellen. Throughout the book the pattern of the discourse scarcely varies. Pill offers his respectful opinion on a military subject; Skill counters it with his more learned judgment. But Macmorris, "an ass, as in the world," will not play the patient Captain Pill to Fluellen's maddeningly slow and helpful Captain Skill. He protests:

> It is no time to discourse, so Chrish save me! The day is hot, and the weather, and the wars, and the King, and the Dukes. It is no time to discourse. The town is beseech'd, and the trompet call us to the breach, and we talk, and be Chrish, do nothing. 'Tis shame for us all. So God sa' me, 'tis shame to stand still, it is shame, by my hand! and there is throats to be cut, and works to be done, and there ish nothing done, so Chrish sa' me, la! (III.ii.112–121).

Macmorris' impatience with his disputatious and erudite fellow captain probably paralleled the feeling of the Elizabethan public toward the book-writing captains, who spent their valuable time reading and disputing. As the populace awaited the constantly threatened attack from Spain, they too would have muttered, "It is no time to discourse. The town is beseech'd, and the trompet call us to the breach, and we talk, and be Chrish, do nothing."

But so far, despite the Irishman's animated manner and a few unpleasant terms like "ass," the conversation between the two captains has been relatively pacific. Real violence is threatened only upon Fluellen's ominously quiet remark, after his invitation to dispute has been rejected (III.ii.129–131): "Captain Macmorris, I think, look you, under your correction there is not many of your nation—" Macmorris, suddenly taut with rage, can hear no more. "Of my nation?" he asks. "What ish my nation? Ish a villain, and a bastard, and a knave, and a rascal." "So Chrish save me," he promises, "I will cut off your head!"

A second and more stimulating source of friction has obviously come between the two officers. They are no longer simply British captains, but one is Irish and the other Welsh. And so far as this is a problem of different nationalities serving in one army, it relates to Henry V's responsibilities as general and not merely to their own office of captain. Certainly Shakespeare seems to have had some purpose in enlarging both the challenge and the significance of Henry's command; and interesting attempts have been made to identify this purpose. Richard Simpson, who interpreted the play at large as a case for the militant ideals of Essex, saw the Earl's hope for British unity in Welsh, Scotch, Irish, and English captains serving side by side.[27] On the other hand, it has been suggested that not commendation of an ideal but satire of an actuality was intended. In support of this theory it is contended that these captains were introduced only for Jacobean performances, when the Scotch were common subjects of ridicule and the Irish, now doomed as a nation by the successes of Lord Mountjoy, were keenly sensitive to allusions to their country.[28] This explanation is more satisfactory than Simpson's in that it recognizes the incident as controversy rather than harmony, for Shakespeare is elsewhere in this play at pains to show the discords rather than the harmonious elements with which the general must contend. Moreover, there can be little question that the reference to Macmorris' nation does not seem to be in the interest of British unity.

But may not, one wonders, a more specific cause of this discord be found in an active military situation in Elizabeth's army? Miss Campbell has shown beyond question that it is to this source, rather than Jacobean politics, that the rest of the military affairs in *Henry V* may be traced. This approach proves enlightening if we try to ascertain what Fluellen was about to say in his ponderous, cautious, but unluckily fore-shortened sentence: "Captain Macmorris, I think, look you, under your correction, there is not many of your nation—." No critic has, I believe, accorded the Welshman the courtesy of returning to his interrupted thought.[29] I suggest that he intended to go on (with allowance for his unpredictable manner of speech) somewhat as follows: "who is one of his Majesty's captains." And he would have added, or implied, that an Irish captain was not only a rare species, but one unqualified to talk of the "disciplines" of war. This conclusion, I believe, was what Macmorris might certainly have expected from the scornful talk about Irish soldiers, and particularly about Irish captains, going on in 1599.

The use of Irish soldiers in the Queen's army was one of the most hotly questioned military policies in the 1590's. According to Camden, it was during this time that the "meere Irish ... were first taken for leaders and souldiers, but not very providently, as the wiser sort then judged, and the English found afterward by experience."[30] The difficulty did not lie in any deficiency of the Irish as fighters, for they were terrifying opponents. Moryson wrote that "they rather know not then despise the rules of honor, observed by other nations"; that they advance "with rude barbarous Cryes ... and barbarous lookes..., being terrible Executioners by their swiftnes of Foote upon flying Enemyes never sparing any that yeild to mercy," and never "beleeving them to be fully dead till they have cutt of their heads."[31] Serving with English forces in the Netherlands, they made an awesome impression; for, records Stow, "none were so ready to burne, nor so readie to kill all that came in their daunger." After the English horsemen had vainly tried approaches to a strongly fortified position, the "wilde Irish kernes, neither fearing shot nor threat, ranne up the sides of the sconce, tooke it presently, and put to the sword all in it."[32] Their reputation here and elsewhere justifies the ferociousness of Macmorris, who "would have blowed up the town, so Chrish save me la! in an hour"; who hates to stand idle when "there is throats to be cut"; and who assures his fellow captain, "I will cut off your head!"

But because they were so unlearned in war, and because they were undependable after they had been instructed, the Irish had been used only with reluctance. Late in 1598, possibly while Shakespeare was at work on *Henry V*, Elizabeth wrote to the council in Ireland "that you do use all convenient meanes to clear our army of the Irish."[33] There was special reluctance to endow them with the same dignities as their English fellow soldiers. "Heretofore," Elizabeth wrote in 1601, "when they have beene used, it hath not beene seene, that either they were entertained at the same rate of pay with our owne Nation, or so mixed in common with them in regiments, but ever kept apart, both in companies severall, and used in places and in services proper for them."[34]

Above all, the Queen was reluctant to honor any of the Irish fighting men by making them captains, but the necessity had arisen, and a few Irish captains are found in muster lists of the time. By 1599, she was determined to stop the practice. In that year she wrote Mountjoy that although "we have beene content to grace some such as are of noble houses, and such others as have drawne blood on the Rebels, with charge of Companies, ... we command you, not onely to raise no more, when these shall be decaied, but to keepe them unsupplied that are already, and as they waste to Casse their bands."[35] By 1599, then, the year of *Henry V,* there were not only to be no more Irish captains commissioned, but those already appointed were to be steadily deprived of their companies.

The plight of Irish captains in 1599 has been recorded in a letter written in that year by one Rowland Whyte. This describes the conduct of St. Laurence, an Irish captain, in answering the charges that he had used "undecent Speaches" of Robert Cecil. St. Laurence, with a spirit and vocabulary worthy of Macmorris, denied the charge and affirmed "that who soever told hym of yt, was a Villain, and that if he wold Name hym, he wold make hym deny yt; I by God, that he wold." As a special irritant, he was told "he was an Irish Man." He replied, "I am sory that when I am in England, I shuld be esteemed an Irish Man, and in Ireland, an English Man; I have spent my Blood, engaged and endangered my Liffe, often to doe her Majestie Service, and doe beseach to have yt soe regarded."[36]

There was a fine aptness in Shakespeare's having made his Irishman a captain rather than one of the common soldiers, like Bates and Williams. In 1599, Elizabethans might well have found his rank to be the most noteworthy thing about Macmorris; and he too was possibly most sensitive on this score. An Irish captain in 1599 would have been in a painfully hopeless situation. As one of the first and last of his nation to hold this rank, Macmorris would find intolerable the condescending manner of Fluellen, with his display of erudition and, as a final and well-aimed thrust, his reminder that "there is not many of your nation—."

Compared with the genuineness and ability of his captains, Henry V's other company officers strike one as ridiculously counterfeit figures, incredibly serving in the same carefully governed army. Lieutenant Bardolph, Ancient Pistol, and Corporal Nym are the only officers between the private soldier and the captain, and, except for Bardolph, none has any legitimate connection with his rank. Bardolph's preoccupation seems to be pillage, but he does labor as a lieutenant in one curious respect. Early in the play he is busy pacifying his brawling subordinates, notably Pistol and Nym, and this is the job most frequently assigned the lieutenant in military handbooks. Garrard is typical in writing: "The Lieutenant ought to carie with him a diligent care of concord, for that particularly the pacification of discords and differences amongst the souldiers of his company, appertains to him."[37] Pistol, likewise, may as ensign have had not a pointless but an outrageously reversed relationship to his office. The ensignship, as will become clearer when we turn to Iago, was a rank which above all others called for courage and honor; and there was doubtless intentional irony in the fact that it is here applied to the most wretched of Shakespeare's cowards. Although, therefore, both Bardolph and Pistol were apparently alone responsible for their appointments in *Henry V*, each may well have known enough military theory to choose a congenial rank.

Certainly the captains in *Henry V* cannot be held accountable for either appointment. Both the lieutenant and the ensign seem to be blissfully detached from any company, a situation which doubtless gives them freedom for more profitable
enterprises. Significantly, none of them is well known to the
captains, although Pistol temporarily impresses Fluellen as
an "aunchient lieutenant" who is "as valiant a man as Mark
Anthony" (III.vi.13–15), and later impresses the King himself by the caliber of his voice. Shakespeare did, as we shall
later see, find full and serious use for the common soldiers in
this play, but he was apparently willing to neglect the sources
of friction among the authentic lower commissioned officers
in favor of this roguish threesome.

He did so, partly, as he had done in *Henry IV,* in order to
provide a comic substratum for the serious level of the play.
And with Ancient Pistol in particular, as Leslie Hotson has
demonstrated, the gross humor paid off superbly in box-office
appeal.[38] But there was usually, as we have seen, realistic intent
in whatever military business Shakespeare placed on a comic
level. Pistol and his friends are no exception. Though regular
rank was not provided for them, men of their type played
an important and inevitable role in even the best-governed of
Elizabethan expeditions. Henry V's army, the fullest and
most complex military organization in Shakespeare, would
have seemed both incomplete and ill-proportioned without
these rogues to carry on their own private warfare with their
self-designed ranks and duties. In including them, Shakespeare demonstrated as competent a knowledge of army organization as he did in creating authentic officers like Fluellen
and Macmorris.

Barnaby Rich has circumstantially recorded how the Pistols

in Elizabethan army life made their way. After these men "have bene a moneth or two in the lowe Countries ... and can speake a little of the newe Discipline, they will discourse of greater exploytes than ever was performed before Troy." "With these toyes," Rich adds, "they have deceived men of reasonable wit, though of little understanding."[39] In *Henry V* it is, of all persons, the erudite Captain Fluellen who is deceived. Captain Gower disillusions the Welshman concerning the real nature of this Mark Anthony by describing the type to which Pistol belongs; and Gower's description is very similar to Rich's (III.vi.70–75):

Why, 'tis a gull, a fool, a rogue, that now and then goes to the wars to grace himself, at his return into London, under the form of a soldier. And such fellows are perfect in the great commanders' names, and they will learn you by rote where services were done: — at such and such a sconce, at such a breach, at such a convoy; who came off bravely, who was shot, who disgrac'd, what terms the enemy stood on; and this they con perfectly in the phrase of war, which they trick up with new-tuned oaths. ... But you must learn to know such slanders of the age, or else you will be marvellously mistook.

Pistol had, however, a more tangible plan in mind for profiting from Henry's great enterprise (II.i.116):

> For I shall sutler be
> Unto the camp, and profits will accrue.

The office Pistol plans to fill was purely a self-appointive one. With the exception of the captaincy, none had a less savory reputation, and probably no lines in the play would have evoked more resonant raspberries from ex-soldiers in the audience. Sutlers, or victualers, to the army were usually not even accepted as regular soldiers. James Digges sent to the

Privy Council as one of the "doubts to be resolved concerning musters" the following question: "Whether sutlers, victuallers, purveyors, cooks, merchants, etc., dwelling in a garrison, shall be capable of her majesty's pay unless they perform the ordinary duties of a soldier?"[40] It is certain that not many sutlers had any intention of meeting this requirement. In "An Admonition before the Musters," an actual document used to encourage soldiers to report unauthorized persons, special mention is made of victualers as drains upon the honest soldier, for they do not stand watch or help in battle.[41] However, it was more than their independent status that gave sutlers their bad name. A typical "Complaint from Soldiers of Ostend Against the Victuallers," sent to the Queen, protested the extortionate rates demanded for food and told of "what rotten, unsavoury, and unwholesome victuals" resulted.[42] Shakespeare would doubtless also have heard lively and gratifying stories of how soldiers reciprocated. On one occasion, shortly after the above complaint, they caught a victualer's man and threw him off the bridge, and when he regained the shore, pelted him with stones.[43] Shakespeare could scarcely have devised a more suitable office for Pistol; and though we do not see him practicing it, neither do we see Bardolph at work on the church pillage which results in his vital thread being cut.

Between the offices of captain and general in *Henry V* there is a more serious irregularity of rank than between captain and private: all the intervening offices are lacking. This hiatus is found also in all of Shakespeare's other plays, but in *Henry V,* where Elizabethan military matters are so studiously represented, its existence is the most striking. In Elizabeth's army, there were abundant and important offices between the commander in chief and the captain. The most common of these are listed by Blandy as the "high Martiall with his Provostes," "Serjeant generall" (usually called the sergeant major), and "Corownell" or colonel." Of the senior offices the sergeant major was especially important in Renaissance armies, and an entire book about this rank was written by Francisco de Valdes and translated into English in 1590.

Perhaps, as Cooper proposes, Sergeant Shakespeare had little opportunity to learn about the upper echelon. There was, however, one exception to his ignorance: he had an accurate knowledge of what pertained to the general. But since, as I shall presently suggest, this knowledge came from books rather than from direct experience, there is still a chance that Shakespeare as sergeant would have gotten his knowledge of senior officers only from reading. Still one is not satisfied. Why did he consistently fail to read about the colonel, the sergeant major, and—one must add—the sergeant?

Fortunately, in the case of the missing field-grade officers, there is a far more substantial clue, one which demonstrates the futility of too much biographical speculation. These officers are also missing in virtually all English drama until well into the seventeenth century. This clue, to be sure, does not solve the mystery; but in transferring it from Shakespeare to the drama generally, it suggests that there must have been something about the military titles which made them unsuitable for stage use. Probably even more than the offices of corporal and sergeant these upper ranks were not well enough known to permit easy stage allusion. Moreover, the military treatises make clear that their duties on the field pertained to technically strategic affairs and called for large-scale surveillance of men and supplies; in contrast, the localized responsibilities of the lower offices permitted dramatic focus. Then, too, the higher officers were not involved, as representatives of their ranks, in controversies such as gave the captaincy a public reputation.

As a matter of fact, the public was more likely to know these officers not as colonels or sergeants major, but as captains of companies. Julian Corbett has pointed out that in the seventeenth century "no substantive rank higher than captain was known; and no matter how exalted a staff rank a man held, in his soldiership he was no more than a captain at the head of his company. Even till the dawn of the eighteenth century every general officer continued to have, not only his own regiment, but his own company in it. His duties as major-general, or commissary, or quartermaster, were still regarded as something apart and distinct from his soldiership, as in fact non-combatant."[45] That the situation described by Corbett existed during Shakespeare's time is clear from Professor Webb's disclosure that Sir Francis Vere "was not only a sergeant-major-general of Elizabeth's army, he was captain of a company of horse and of foot and is so listed in 'A breef note of the weekly payments to her Majesty's forces.' " Similarly, Webb notes, "Sir Edward Cecil was both general and 'Captain of a Band of 240 Foot.' "[46] This dual system of rank may well be one reason that Elizabethan newsletters and journals mention so many captains and so few colonels. Certainly it would help to explain the dearth of staff officers in the drama.

In his portrait of Henry V as general, Shakespeare demonstrated that whatever deficiencies the play might have in representing army life were not due to lack of pains. In no other military portrait—Falstaff not excepted—can we say with more assurance that here the dramatist made a careful study of military theory, and sketched character with the theory constantly in mind. Not even Holinshed was more closely studied for this purpose. In fact, although from Holinshed (and partially from *The Famous Victories of Henry the Fifth*) came the outline of Henry V as a religious, efficient warrior, Shakespeare derived most of Henry's conduct and speech as a general from the precepts of military books.

The indebtedness which resulted was different not merely in degree from that of his other military portraits; it was different in kind. For the first time, Shakespeare risked the consequences of drawing a handbook-perfect officer. In all of his other portraits he selected types or ranks interesting for wayward traits, either of contentiousness or of fraudulent practices. To attempt making his main dramatic figure not only "the mirror of all Christian kings" (V.Chorus.6) but the mirror of a Christian general, and to deprive him further of the dissensions available in a divided command, was to forfeit in advance most of the playwright's dependable stratagems for good drama. We shall, to be sure, find that Shakespeare discovered opportunities for a few instances of minor tension within this model portrait, but these are insufficient to make Henry one of Shakespeare's most interesting military studies.

Especial difficulty confronted Shakespeare in his plan to create Henry as a Christian conqueror. Marlowe made a luckier choice in his pagan Tamburlaine, for more interesting irregularities were thus possible: keeping captive emperors in cages, using them as horses for the conqueror's chariot, and making spectacular slaughter of virgins delegated to plead for mercy. All this was denied Shakespeare by the handbooks which he conscientiously followed. According to Sutcliffe, for example, the Christian king as general is distinguished from the heathen Turk by his mercy toward opponents.⁴⁷ And Henry V assures his enemy, "We are no tyrant, but a Christian king" (I.ii.241). More specifically, Paul Ive's translation of Fourquevaux's *Instructions for the Warres* (1589) demands of the general: "If so be that he should have to do with a strong and puissant towne, I would never be of opinion he should use any force, if he might have it lovinglie and by honest composition."⁴⁸ Following this precept meant for Shakespeare softening an episode that in Holinshed had spectacular elements—the siege of Harfleur. In the historian's account, the city is sacked after a vigorous battle.⁴⁹ Inducements of decorum might, of course, have deterred Shakespeare from presenting the full realities of such a spectacle, but a more immediate reason is evident in Henry's remark (III.vi.118–120): "for when lenity and cruelty play for a kingdom, the gentler gamester is the soonest winner."

The same influence accounts for his emphasizing, instead of more exciting material rewards, a pious forbearance in victory. Henry's soldiers get no pillage or concubines like Tamburlaine's. Instead, the audience is treated to a rather somber episode involving the sentencing of Bardolph for stealing a pax from a church. The precept behind this austere substitution is typically expressed by Garrard: "Immediately upon the taking of the Towne, the prince or Generall . . . must enter into the Towne, with his sworde naked in his hand, and must goe to the principall Church to give God thanks for this victorie, and also to defend, that the ornaments which appertaine to the Church be not pulled down nor robbed. . . . Incontinently he must make cry through the

Cittie, that none uppon payne of hanging neither take nor spoyle any Churches."⁵⁰

If rejection of pillage was hard for the soldiers, refusal of personal glory in victory was the special austerity which Christian precepts demanded of the general. Henry is so solicitous in ascribing his victory to God, with no boasting or even close attention to the mechanics of triumph,⁵¹ that one wonders how Elizabethans, having tasted the richer meat of Tamburlaine's boasting, reacted to Henry's piety. Possibly, having heard his stern command (IV.viii.118),

> Come, go we in procession to the village;
> And be it death proclaimed through our host
> To boast of this, or take that praise from God
> Which is his only,

many would innocently have asked, like Fluellen, "Is it not lawful, an please your Majesty, to tell how many is kill'd?" (IV.viii.121–122).

Elizabethans had, however, been well instructed in their own victories over Spain not to usurp any credit for themselves; and they would have recognized, though with suppressed regret, that Henry's conduct was praiseworthy. What is more, military literature of the age would have convinced them that his modesty was practical as well as model. In *An Arithmeticall Militare Treatise, named Stratioticos,* the work of Thomas and Leonard Digges, the general is advised to credit the victory first to God and secondly to his army, for by so doing he will "not only make his honourable Actions shine the more gloriouslie, but also wonderfully combine with harty good wyll his Souldiours to love and honor him."⁵² The penalty for violating this code is even more tangible than the rewards for observing it. John Norden warned that if

God finds generals attributing "their successe unto them-selves, either in regard to their power, multitude, valour, policies or military stratagems, hee forthwith becommeth their enemie, and diminisheth their number, weakeneth their power, besotteth their devises, and maketh their policies of none effect."[53]

Although, as we observed in the first chapter, Shakespeare's plays as a whole are almost consistently lacking in detailed enactments of battles, the Christian character given to Henry V as general made this play particularly inattentive to what Norden calls "policies or military stratagems." For Henry to stress these would be to have them work against him. Hence, although Holinshed credits Henry with "good pol-icie" on more than one occasion,[54] Shakespeare's King care-fully disclaims all credit for strategic skill, even that famous device of the stakes (IV.viii.111):

> O God, thy arm was here!
> And not to us, but to thy arm alone,
> Ascribe we all! When, without stratagem,
> But in plain shock and even play of battle,
> Was ever known so great and little loss
> On one part and on th' other? Take it, God,
> For it is only thine!

There were, however, a few classical precepts for success in battle which Shakespeare apparently thought not inhar-monious with his governing ideal of Christian generalship. A minor one, but interesting because it so sharply contradicts the facts of history, is speed. Sutcliffe and Barret, among Elizabethan authors, both stress this classical ideal.[55] In *Henry V* the King's speed gives special distress to the French, who stand and talk and threaten while Henry moves from

an incredibly swift arrival in France (II.iv.143) to an almost
unresisted attack on Harfleur. Historically, the campaigns
of Henry were characterized by delays and false moves. The
capture of Harfleur alone, as Oman notes, "wasted many
weeks of time."[56]

But of the classical ideals for generalship which Henry V
embodies, the most important are not tactical but psychological and moral. One of these is an Aristotelian moderation
between courage and fear. Unlike Shakespeare's later and ill-
fated generals, Macbeth and Antony, Henry never loses a
wise sense of fear, partly for himself but mainly for his army.
Although virtually all Renaissance manuals make this an
important precept, its seriousness is best analyzed by Shakespeare's Enobarbus in *Antony and Cleopatra* when he recognizes that his leader is doomed (III.xiii.195):

> Now he'll outstare the lightning. To be furious
> Is to be frighted out of fear, and in that mood
> The dove will peck the estridge. I see still
> A diminution in our captain's brain
> Restores his heart. When valour preys on reason,
> It eats the sword it fights with. I will seek
> Some way to leave him.

Contrariwise, the advantages of "moderate fear" are well expressed in the classical play *The Misfortunes of Arthur*. The
Nuncius reports of Arthur:

> And fortune pleasde with Arthurs moderate feare,
> Returnes more full, and friendlyer than her woont
> For when he saw the powers of Fates opposde,
> And that the dreadfull hour thus hastened on:
> Perplexed much in minde at length resolves,
> That feare is covered best by daring most.[57]

Arthur's courageous confronting of fear, rather than insensitivity to it, is paralleled at length in *Henry V*, with considerable attention to "perplexed much in minde."

Holinshed does not refer to Henry's misgivings about his army's courage. Shakespeare not only invents the anxiety, but shapes it into one of Henry's few effective internal tensions. Before battle Henry prays (IV.i.306):

> O God of battles, steel my soldiers' hearts,
> Possess them not with fear! Take from them now
> The sense of reck'ning, if th' opposed numbers
> Pluck their hearts from them.

While disguised as a soldier, he confesses to Bates that even the King has fears as the rank and file have (IV.i.113–117): "Yet, in reason, no man should possess him with any appearance of fear, lest he, by showing it, should dishearten his army." This statement provides a much-needed clue to a deeper and richer personality behind much of Henry's jovial good cheer during the play. Interpreting the heartiness literally has led critics to regard the King as a simple man of action. Actually he is, like Arthur, valiantly counterfeiting optimism. If, according to Barnabe Barnes, real dangers are present, the general must "extenuate them by some cheerfull and ingenious excuse, which hath in it a strong taste of fortitude."[58] Such an "ingenious excuse" appears in Henry's encouragement to the nobility on the morning of battle. His cheery words belie the fact that he has spent a sleepless night going from "watch to watch" (IV.i.3):

> Good morrow, brother Bedford. God Almighty!
> There is some soul of goodness in things evil,
> Would men observingly distil it out;

> For our bad neighbour makes us early stirrers,
> Which is both healthful, and good husbandry.
> Besides, they are our outward consciences,
> And preachers to us all, admonishing
> That we should dress us fairly for our end.

But suddenly he realizes that he is misplacing his advice, since he is addressing not his simple soldiers but his fellow noblemen. And so, with a deft change of pace, he mocks his own brave pose—probably with good psychological effect:

> Thus may we gather honey from the weed
> And make a moral of the devil himself.

On an earlier occasion, however, Henry had confronted a more somber mischance; and in covering up its ominous significance, he could not afford to be frank even with his brothers. Just before embarkation the treason of three trusted noblemen was discovered. This untimely and high-level instance of disaffection might disastrously have lowered the morale of the entire army, but Henry quickly interpreted it as good luck, not bad (II.ii.184):

> We doubt not of a fair and lucky war,
> Since God so graciously hath brought to light
> This dangerous treason, lurking in our way
> To hinder our beginnings. We doubt not now
> But every rub is smoothed on our way.

The hint for this speech apparently came from the following passage in Holinshed: "King Henrie after the returne of his ambassadors, determined fullie to make warre in France, conceiving a good and perfect hope to have fortunate successe, sith victorie for the most part followeth where right leadeth, being advanced forward by justice, and set foorth by equitie."[59] Shakespeare's alteration is significant. Where Holinshed places this remark in an auspicious context, Shakespeare intensifies it dramatically by making it serve as a strained response to shocking news. The ingenious interpretation of bad omens is a favorite form of military encouragement recommended by authorities on generalship. Procter writes that since soldiers often "stumble muche at signes or tokens which fall before battail," reading in them the word of God, the wise general "will cheerefully expounde all such chaunces for hys advauntage, as if an auncient happen to fall, uppon the Captaines head, before the battaill, he sayeth, the same is a happie signe of the victory fallinge unto him."[60]

In his two great battle orations (III.i.1; IV.iii.19), Henry employs another model procedure for allaying the fears of his men. Because of the traditional importance of the oration, generals are universally required by the handbooks to be good speakers. Thereby, as Styward explains, "the Generall comforting the souldiers easilie maie perswade everie one of them to despise all perils, and to attend to the glorious enterprise. For the sound of the Trumpet cannot so much inflame the mindes of men to take their weapons, and constraine them more valiantlie to fight, then the convenient and according to the time the sugred talke of the Generall."[61] That Henry's orations follow a traditional pattern may be seen by comparing them not only with the model oration, cited by Miss Campbell, in Richard Crompton's *The Mansion of Magnanimitie* (1599),[62] but with two supposedly actual orations from Elizabethan warfare: one by Sir Philip Sidney (recorded by Stow) and the other by Sir Roger Williams (recorded in Blandy's *The Castle*).[63] These "actual" orations have a manner so stylized, and follow so closely the details of the literary orations, that they may well have been fabricated or reconstructed by their historians—an approved and common practice.

Even more valued than the oration as a source of morale, but not so commonly represented in literature, was the facial expression of the general. "Surely it is better," writes Onosander, "and doth more agree with the wisdom of a Captaine [general], with the semblaunce of the face, to fayne cherefulnesse unto men, and with his merines, to make them glad, then with wordes and orations to comforte them, whylest they be afflicted with malincoly. For as muche unto wordes, often tyme they doe not give credite."[84] This classical precedent had, as Shakespeare recognized, dramatic value more penetrating and subtle than the stock-in-trade oration. Certainly it explains the dramatist's close attention to the King's face during the bleak hours before battle (IV.Chorus.35):

> Upon his royal face there is no note
> How dread an army hath enrounded him;
> Nor doth he dedicate one jot of colour
> Unto the weary and all-watched night,
> But freshly looks, and overbears attaint
> With cheerful semblance and sweet majesty;
> That every wretch, pining and pale before,
> Beholding him, plucks comfort from his looks.
> A largess universal, like the sun,
> His liberal eye doth give to every one,
> Thawing cold fear.

There is a specially close resemblance between the last three lines of this description and the advice given in 1595 by an anonymous work, *A Myrrour for English Souldiers,* which was precisely the sort of book to which the playwright might turn for help in depicting his "mirror" of generals. This reads: "Let everie Generall know himselfe to be the sunne in the heaven of his host, from whose beams every soldier borroweth his shine."[05]

Not merely in countenance and speech, but in actions, Henry is exemplary in sustaining the spirits of his soldiers. These actions, which likewise may be traced to conduct books, concern primarily the general's relations with common soldiers. The model general must show a tireless attention to the "state and necessities of pryvate persones and common souldiers."[06] In encampments this entails, according to Sutcliffe, that "at all times so especially in the nightes, and carelesse times of others, it behoveth the Generall to be carefull for his people."[07] At the beginning of Act IV, Shakespeare translates this dull commonplace into one of his most beautiful scenes, as Henry is pictured visiting his "ruin'd band" at night, "walking from watch to watch, from tent to tent," mingling with rowdies like Pistol and with troubled but loyal commoners like Bates and Williams, learning their point of view and assuring them of the King's willingness to share their danger without ransom.

Though by freely mingling with his soldiers Henry gives a democratic impression, we should not make, with Falstaff, the mistake of assuming that he is ever spontaneously on a lower level than that of king and general. Like his cheerfulness, Henry's vigorous geniality conceals a firm sense of rank (as shown in the much-maligned episode of Williams' glove). Henry never goes too far in fraternizing. In fact, he goes only so far as the handbooks deemed desirable for practical purposes. "I am a soldier," he says in one of his genial moments (III.iii.5), "A name that in my thoughts becomes me best."

The sentiment is handbook perfect. So Whetstone: "And although, for difference of Aucthorities and Offices, requisit in Martiall government: There is Generall, Lieutenant, Coronell, Captaine, Ensigne, Corporal, &. Yet the hyest to the lowest only glorieth in the name of Souldier."[68] Whetstone makes it perfectly clear, as does Henry, that the difference in rank is not to be obscured except figuratively. Similarly when Henry calls his soldiers "brothers, friends, and countrymen" (IV.Chorus.34), he is likening himself less to common soldiers than to Alexander and Caesar, who, according to Whetstone, "usually cal'de the meanest Souldiers, Companions, fellowes and alwayes greeted them by such like familiar salutations."[69] The ideal traditionally sought by such greetings was not the slackening of rank nor the lessening of the dignity and responsibility of the general, but a greater unity of purpose within the army, especially during periods of danger.

With all his geniality, Henry is unparalleled in Shakespeare as a disciplinarian, and if any soldier strays from the strict code—as does Bardolph—punishment is swift and impersonal. Private soldiers like Bates and Williams who grumble, as soldiers will do, are listened to sympathetically, for the general is expected to do as much. It is customary, Purlilia warns, for even valiant soldiers "to speake yll and backbute theyr capytayne [general].... But yet the capitayne must take no displeasure therwyth, but rather showe hymselfe liberall and gentle, that afterwarde they maye the more wyllynglye, followe hym at nede, then any other."[70] *A Myrrour for English Souldiers* likewise enjoins the general, "If a poore souldier take upon him to speake of militarie discipline, repell him not: but bee thou judge of what he speaketh."[71] Henry is especially careful not to neglect the latter part of this advice; for, as we shall see more fully in the next chapter, he is emphatic in setting the soldiers' minds straight on the subject of their complaint.

The episode which best reveals the disciplined intelligence beneath the King's jovial exterior is that in which he apprehends the three conspirators. In this scene he behaves toward the culprits as though he knew nothing of the conspiracy, and he even welcomes their advice on how to punish a commoner who has offended. In so doing, he has been suspected of reverting to his earlier fondness for dramatizing an episode. At best, the scene of exposure has been thought unnecessarily elaborate and inappropriately playful. Henry's strictly utilitarian purpose in the episode becomes clear if it is recognized that he is simply and conscientiously following a recommended procedure for dealing with treason. The illumination is especially revealing when we encounter the precept in the military treatise of the most cunning of Renaissance theorists. In his *Art of War* Machiavelli tells a general how to extinguish sedition. The "headdes of the faultes" must of course be punished, "but it must be doen in such wise, that thou maiest first have oppressed them before they be able to be aware: The way is, if they be distante from thee, not onely to call the offenders, but together with theim all the other, to the entente that not beleevynge, that it is for any cause to punishe theime, they become not contumelius, but geve commoditie to the execution of the punishment."[72] This stratagem works perfectly for Henry. The three disaffected noblemen, condemned by their own sentence on the base criminal, have no chance to become "contumelius" and thus for their own punishment "geve commoditie to the execution."

It is not to be expected that a model general should also

be an engaging human being. There is something too calcu-
lated in even the most relaxed behavior of Henry V to assure
us that he is ever subject to unstudied emotion. To be sure,
we have noticed certain inner tensions beneath the mask of
heartiness and optimism. Henry feels fear, and must steel
himself not to show it. On the other hand, our study also
revealed a less winsome kind of conscious effort in his good
fellowship with his men. This is, of course, not entirely
studied; Hal can enjoy occasional fun where Henry cannot.
But even Hal, early in *1 Henry IV,* indicated that there was
method in his relaxation. There he promises (I.ii.240):

> I'll so offend to make offence a skill,
> Redeeming time when men think least I will.

That there is nothing idle about his fellowship with base-
born persons is evident from his account of what he had
learned from drinking with "three or four loggerheads"
(II.iv.5–22): "I have sounded the very bass-string of humility.
Sirrah, I am sworn brother to a leash of drawers and can call
them all by their christen names.... To conclude, I am so
good a proficient in one quarter of an hour that I can drink
with any tinker in his own language during my life." In
Henry V he is angered by the Dauphin's failure to recognize
how purposefully he had been idling in his youth (I.ii.266):

> And we understand him well,
> How he comes o'er us with our wilder days,
> Not measuring what use we made of them.

If we can justify—and most critics now tell us we must—
Henry's disciplined amiability as a youth, we can surely justify it when he is a general. The dramatic stiffness which
results is, of course, regrettable. Shakespeare might have given

greater play to Henry's struggle in counterfeiting. On the other hand, his beautiful, sensitive soliloquies reveal a greater tension than the scene in which he rejects Falstaff. Most important, of course, is the fact that Henry *is* a great general, and becomes one at a time when a great general is critically needed. The undisciplined generalship found in *Troilus and Cressida* leaves a bad taste in the mouth, and we read with pain and impatience even the poetic account of Antony's slovenly, self-indulgent leadership. Henry is, by contrast, refreshingly right in what he does. He knows his office, and observes its responsibilities scrupulously. It is not by accident that he is best appreciated during times of war, for *Henry V* was written during, or just before, a major Elizabethan expedition.

IV

In turning to *Othello,* the last play to make important use of specific rank, we find Shakespeare wisely reverting to his favorite practice of dramatizing not the model but the imperfect embodiments of rank. The resultant military portraits are some of Shakespeare's best. It is therefore unlucky that in a play depending so considerably upon the concept of military rank, it has been impossible to ascertain just what ranks Shakespeare had in mind.

The fundamental difficulty concerns the status of no less a character than Othello. Both Fortescue and Draper have provocatively questioned whether Shakespeare, in referring to the Moor now as general, now as captain, had a clear idea of the difference.[73] Draper proposes that Othello's real rank must be the "capitano generale" of the Venetian army, but that Shakespeare, confused by the Elizabethan habit of referring to this simply as captain, gives Othello the military duties of a captain. His function in selecting minor officers, for example, relates "almost entirely to the command of a single company."

We have seen that in his portraits of Falstaff and Henry V Shakespeare demonstrated his knowledge of the ranks of both captain and general, and it would be surprising to find him a few years later unable to tell them apart. If he momentarily lost the distinction in 1604, he would seem to have recovered it by 1608 when he put the following dialogue in *Coriolanus* (V.ii.55):

> *Menenius.* Sirrah, if thy captain knew I were here, he would use me with estimation.
> *1. Watch.* Come, my captain knows you not.
> *Menenius.* I mean thy general.

Nevertheless, as Professor Draper might remind us, we have to confront the facts of the play itself; and *Othello* does present at least apparent inconsistencies and blunders.

The ablest defense of Shakespeare's accurate use of rank in this play is that by Professor Webb in "The Military Background of *Othello*." A short digest cannot do justice to the fullness of his research and argumentation, for he utilizes detailed references to comparable elasticities of rank in Elizabeth's army. His conclusion, most generally stated, is that Othello as general, Cassio as his lieutenant general, and Iago as his ensign, are consistently represented as field-grade rather than company officers. Attention has already been called to Webb's valuable disclosure that Elizabethan field-grade officers had also a different company rank. This contemporary practice helps to explain the fact that Othello is sometimes called general, sometimes captain. But Webb does not admit the dual command idea into Othello's military functions in the play. Othello is consistently general, and never captain.

Certainly one cannot disagree with the interpretation that as commander in chief of the Venetian army and as military governor of Cyprus, Othello is serving in his capacity as general. It is, however, less easy to allay Draper's misgivings about Othello's appointment of Iago as ensign and Cassio as lieutenant, not to mention his unceremonious cashiering of his lieutenant general. Webb may quite rightly point out that although generals were not supposed to do so, they sometimes did appoint their second-in-command. And he may, somewhat more ingeniously, explain the unlikelihood of Iago as ensign aspiring to the rank of lieutenant general (and becoming murderously indignant upon not getting it) by pointing out that Iago was an unusual kind of ensign—in fact, ensign to the general. Still, one is not convinced that this business does not belong, where almost all Elizabethan treatises say it belongs, on a company level.

Although, in the treatises, the term lieutenant may occasionally refer to the second-in-command of an army, the ensign never appears in connection with the lieutenant among staff officers, and never appears as a participant in strategic discussions. But he does, almost without exception, appear in close relationship with the lieutenant in specifications for company appointments. Barret—basing his observations upon the practice of the Italian and Spanish, "who have had the chiefe managing of warres in Europe these 50. or 60. yeares"— first tells how the prince appoints the general and other staff officers. Then, in a clearly distinct section, he turns to the company appointments: "Now the Captain, having his company appointed which he is to direct, govern and commaund,

he chuseth his Lieutenant, Ensign, Sergeant" and lower officers.[74] The same division is observed by Rich in describing
the English army hierarchy.[75] The handbooks, moreover, universally make the captain's appointment of his officers a critical matter, as it is in *Othello*. Garrard states that the merit of
a captain is shown in the wisdom of his appointments; and
Styward emphasizes that "captains must be verie circumspect
in choosing of souldiers to their officers of their bands, placing
ancient, travailed and skilful men, to charge according to
their experiences, as lieutenantes, ensign-beres, sergeants of
bands, and other whose duties are herafter mentioned."[76] But
the most important reason for believing that Shakespeare
meant the appointment of Cassio and Iago to be on a company
level is the dramatically interesting relationship of lieutenant
and ensign as company officers, a relationship which does not
exist on a staff level. Shakespeare's intentions in using these
offices becomes especially clear in view of changes he made
in Cinthio's narrative, his probable source for *Othello*.

The important fact overlooked by scholars is that in Cinthio, although Iago is an "alfiero" or ensign, Cassio is not a
lieutenant, and certainly is not a lieutenant general. He is
"un Capo di squadra." This discrepancy between the dramatist and his source has escaped notice probably because (1)
it does not seem important enough to merit attention, and
(2) the correct meaning of "Capo di squadra" has been obscured for many readers by the perverse durability of Wol-
stenholme Parr's mistranslation of it (1795) as "lieutenant."
Collier reprinted Parr's translation of Cinthio in the first
edition (1843) of *Shakespeare's Library,* and W. C. Hazlitt
again used it for the second edition (1875). In this latter
edition the error appears not only in the text of the transla-

tion but is singled out for special prominence in the introduction (p. 283): "It is to be observed that the only name introduced by Cinthio is that of Desdemona: Othello is called by him the Moor, Cassio the Lieutenant, and Iago the ensign or ancient."

Still another translator, J. E. Taylor, had rendered the title "Captain of a troop."[77] This, though not so mistaken as Parr's translation, was only literally accurate and would continue to mislead readers unfamiliar with Renaissance armies. For the *capo di squadra* was not a captain in either the Elizabethan or modern sense. His closest equivalent was the corporal; indeed, the title of corporal was derived from that of the *capo di squadra*. Barret explains this derivation: "The word *Caporall,* which is meere Italian, and also used by the French, we corruptly do both write and pronounce *Corporall:* for Caporall doth signifie the head and chiefe of a squadra or small company of souldiers:...and is in Spanish more aptly called *Cabo de esquadra* which is the head of 20 or 26 souldiers."[78] Cassio's command in Cinthio, then, was that neither of lieutenant nor of captain, but of corporal in charge of a band (*squadra*) of twenty or so soldiers.

Did Shakespeare recognize this fact? We cannot be sure, but there does seem to be a significant survival of Cassio's Italian title in Iago's contemptuous reference to him as a bookish theorist "that never set a squadron in the field" (I.i.22). Certainly the expression takes on a richer tone of scorn if "squadron" is emphasized. Moreover, corporal existed as a rank in England by as early as 1585, when each company was given three of these officers, who were responsible for training "the three squads or platoons into which a company of 100 or 150 men would be divided."[79] Even more important, Shakespeare probably read Cinthio in the Italian. If so, it is unlikely that the title of one of his main characters would have escaped his notice, even though he did not grasp the technical significance of "squadra."

The first thing, therefore, to recognize in Shakespeare's recreation of his source is that he found in it not a lieutenant general and an ensign, nor even a lieutenant and an ensign, but a corporal and an ensign. The vital relationship between the two men was clearly on a company level, and their traits of character which formed the basis for the tragedy were suited not to nobility but to untitled soldiers.

The second, and major, consideration to keep in mind about Shakespeare's use of his source is the motive behind any change that he might make in it to suit his purposes. His primary dramatic need was to produce a relationship of intense friction between Cassio and Iago. In Renaissance armies no such relationship was likely to exist between ensign and corporal. It was extremely likely to exist between ensign and lieutenant. In fact, Shakespeare's reason for making Cassio a lieutenant leaps at the reader from any section devoted to this office in the military books. In *An Arithmeticall Militare Treatise, Named Stratioticos,* under "The Lieutenant of a Bande, his Office," is the following statement: "This officer I find not in the Romane Armies, neither see I any cause why in these Dayes we shoulde neede them, if the Ensigne and other officers sufficiently knewe theyr dutie."[80] This suggests a troublesome overlapping of the two offices, and an occasion for friction. The difficulty of the relationship is made even clearer by Garrard's description of the lieutenant's duties:

He must observe great affabilitie and fraternitie with the Alfierus, and friendly consult with him (specially if the Lieutenant doth not manage both the one and the other office, as the Spaniards and other nations doe use, and might very well be used of us . . . , both for avoyding of emulation and charge of pay,) but if they be two particular officers, and beare distinct sway in a band, then let the Lieutenant be very carefull (as he that is the chiefe) to avoide all stomaking and strife that might arise betwixt him and the Al-fierus, for thereby oftentimes great scandales have falne out, and the division of the company, a thing above all other to be carfull shunned.[81]

Here the main implication is that, because of "great scan-dales" arising from the "stomaking and strife" between en-sign and lieutenant, it is urgent that the lieutenant be considerate of the ensign's jealousy; and it may even be ad-visable to merge the two offices, as other armies have done. It is understandable why Shakespeare took advantage of so highly charged a relationship. And that he did so consciously is suggested by a remark made by Cassio while drunk (II.iii. 113): "The lieutenant is to be saved before the ancient." That is, the lieutenant, even in theology, takes precedence over the ensign. Cassio quickly senses the gravity of what he has said and tries hard to sober up: "Let's have no more of this; let's to our affairs." But it is certain that the slip did not go un-noticed by Iago. It is not, moreover, a remark that would have much meaning if it were made by a lieutenant general to an ensign.

These two company offices proved valuable to Shakespeare individually as well as in their relationship to each other. The lieutenant was expected "many times to review the bodies of the Watch, to see how they execute their duties, keeping them Vigilant and diligent to their charge."[82] And his principal responsibility, as already noticed, was "to carie with him a diligent care of concord, for that particularly the pacification of discords amongst the souldiers of his company, appertains unto him, which must be done without choler or passion."[83] The significance of these two specifications helps to clarify and deepen the drama of Cassio's disgrace, for he was passionately involved in a street brawl when it was his special duty not only to prevent such behavior in others but also to supervise the watch.

A richer tradition attaches to the office of ensign. His inferiority to the lieutenant was more in command than in honor and had not been of long standing. Before the lieutenant came into prominence, the ensign had been not a junior officer in a company but the specially honored bearer of the standard. According to Sir Charles Oman, the change in the ensign's status to one of company command came during the middle of Elizabeth's reign.[84] The older meaning persisted, however, both in the military books[85] and in Shakespeare's general usage. So late a play as *The Tempest* shows the association of ensign with standard-bearer (III.ii.18):

> *Stephano.* Thou shalt be my lieutenant, monster, or my standard.
> *Trinculo.* Your lieutenant, if you list; he's no standard.

And a remark by Cassius in *Julius Caesar* (V.iii.3) reflects the honored responsibility of the ensign:

> This ensign here of mine was turning back;
> I slew the coward and did take it from him.

Since Iago is not shown in military action, we have no opportunity to know him as a soldier upholding unto death the company standard. Nevertheless, his reputed character bears an interesting relationship to that required of his office by the handbooks.

These stress the need for especial courage in the ensign; because he is a symbol of his company's honor, he cannot show the weaknesses of the average soldier.[86] Iago is therefore appropriately described as "the bold Iago" (II.i.75), "brave Iago" (V.i.31), and "a very valiant fellow" (V.i.52). On the other hand, because he is a dedicated personage, the ensign is entitled to a distinction of dress and manner. "He shall," writes one authority, "alwaies go gallant & well armed, with a faire corslet, Burgonet, short sword and meane dagger, which are his proper arming, with a faire Halberd, when he beareth not his Colours, borne after him to his lodging, or elsewhere, thereby to be the better respected and known."[87] Likewise it is desirable, for the "greater glorie to his place," that "hee be comely of person, strong and ameable."[88] An Elizabethan staging of the play might well have taken advantage of these distinctions of dress and person, thereby emphasizing the qualities to be expected of Iago as a representative of his rank.

Besides boldness, these qualities included one other important virtue: the ensign had to be liked and trusted by his fellows, "that in all hazardes and great exployts, he being beloved of the Souldiers, may be verie much ayded and defended by them, where as otherwise they doe either suffer open ignomie, or danger of death, when as they be either abandoned at the point of extremities, or traiterously slaine or wounded by their owne companions and followers."[89] It was therefore vital for a man in Iago's position to have earned, as Garrard puts it, "not onely ... the love of his confederates, and friendes, but of all the entire companie."[90] This Iago has superlatively done.

He has secured not only universal affection but the singular

degree of trust required of his office. When the Duke asks
Othello to name some officer to conduct Desdemona to
Cyprus, Othello answers (I.iii.284):

> So please your Grace, my ancient.
> A man he is of honesty and trust.

The choice is made without hesitation. The ensign should be,
as writers of handbooks almost unanimously state, a man of
signal honesty. Thomas and Leonard Digges prescribe that
"the Ensigne be a man of good accompte, honest and vertuous, that the Captayne maye repose affiance in."[91] Garrard
likewise requires him to be "honest and vertuous."[92] And
Markham demands the "great vertues" of "Valour, Wisedome, Fidelitie, and Honestie."[93] Honesty is the one common
factor.

So significantly and accurately are these two company
offices used in *Othello,* that to insist on a consistently maintained staff level for the principal male characters means
sacrificing Shakespeare's clearest military clues to their personalities. It is more rewarding in this case, as in many others,
to admire Shakespeare's versatility rather than his consistency. If Othello, except for his company appointments, is
obviously a general, and if Cassio rises later from company
rank to become military commander of Cyprus, the instability
is no more troublesome than the double standard of time for
which the play is famous. Considered more positively, both
phenomena are symptoms of the play's subordination of
steady detail to shifting mood. And the military instability is
the more defensible in that it reflects, though not with perfect
accuracy, the dual system of rank prevalent in Elizabethan
armies. Admittedly the explanation which I have here offered

is not a "solution" to the problem raised by other students. Where Shakespeare himself presents conflicting facts, no infallible interpretation is possible. The exact army rank of Othello, Cassio, and Iago is a problem that may profitably trouble critics as long as has the mystery of Hamlet's age.

There still remains another of the specially difficult questions in which the play abounds, and one vitally concerned with the psychology of rank: Was Othello at fault in appointing Cassio rather than Iago as lieutenant? Iago, of course, says he was; and Iago's statement is given a prolonged emphasis where emphasis counts—at the beginning of the play. If Iago is right, it means that Shakespeare intended to repeat in this play substantially the pattern which gave tension to *Troilus and Cressida:* discontent and emulation within the ranks because of an impotent commander. Or the fault may be, as Professor Webb has suggested, that Othello has been made indolent by a nine-month idleness from military duties and an amorous dotage. He consequently falls victim to the smoothly persuasive, courtier-like Cassio, in passing by the deserving Iago.[04]

In Iago's mind rankles especially the thought that Cassio's promotion was an acceleration. "'Tis the curse of service," he observes (I.i.35),

> Preferment goes by letter and affection,
> And not by old gradation, where each second
> Stood heir to th' first.

Accelerated promotion, in an army of any period, is bound to produce jealousy and resentment in anyone victimized by it. But would those not personally affected have considered it a fault in the captain? Then as now the question was complicated by the reasons, in any particular case, for irregular promotion. Those who rose because of distinguished service are never complained of in Elizabethan letters or books. There was, however, a less commendable reason which was almost invariably present whenever irregular promotions became subjects of written commentary. This was the sort deplored by Iago in the statement, "Preferment goes by letter and affection." Few military abuses of the time received more criticism than this. Not only malcontent eccentrics like Sir John Smythe called attention to it.[95] Men of solid worth deplored the intervention by influential civilians—usually courtiers—that had hindered their normal promotion. Sir Edward Cecil, as "the oldest captain of our nation that looks for advancement," wrote to his uncle in 1604 that he had been bypassed as a result of a "second letter" written in favor of Sir Thomas Knowles.[96] After twenty years in Elizabeth's service, Sir Thomas Morgan found himself overtaken by "upstart soldiers ... who cannot govern themselves in martial affairs." "The place I know," he wrote Walsingham, "I can discharge as well as any in these parts, if not better, although I cannot dissemble or flatter, or have experience by reading histories of wars."[97] The custom of granting promotions on the basis of "letter and affection" was widely deplored by objective military critics as well as by individual victims of the practice. Knyvett, who was not personally affected but was writing a treatise on *The Defence of the Realme,* makes a plea for "the ancient custome (which woulde from henceforth be observed unviolable) to rise from place to place even from private soldiers, to everie degree in the field not above a Corronell, as the fortunes of the warres maie afforde their worthie actions, And not to be chopped and chaunged and misplaced for favor, as now a daies to the greate discoragement of froward spirites is to much used."[98] To Edmund Spenser, much of the demoralization of veteran soldiers in Ireland seemed due to this abuse.[99] A remarkably close approximation to Iago's temperament and its predicament, as he describes them, is made by Robert Barret: "For many have bin chosen by favor, friendship, or affection, little respecting their experience, virtues, or vices; whereby most commonly, the fawning flatterer, the audacious prater, the subtill make-shift, is preferred before the silent man, the aprooved person, or the plaine dealing fellow."[100] Iago professes to be, and has gained the reputation for being, "the silent man, the aprooved person, or the plaine dealing fellow." There is little doubt that this type of person would appeal to the audience more than the courtier type, who got advancement through favor. In fact, we shall see in a later chapter that Shakespeare and other dramatists made frequent use of the stock contrast between courtier and plain soldier, and tended to favor the soldier.

If this were Iago's only grievance, and if the facts of the play bore it out, there would be good reason for supposing that the audience thought him genuinely wronged. But it is a symptom of minds irrationally convinced of persecution that they think themselves beset all round. Iago has two military complaints, just as he later develops two sexual grievances, against his associates. His second complaint about Cassio's appointment is that his successful rival is "a great arithmetician,"

> That never set a squadron in the field,
> Nor the division of a battle knows
> More than a spinster; unless the bookish theoric
> Wherein the toged consuls can propose
> As masterly as he. Mere prattle, without practice,
> Is all his soldiership.
>
> (I.i.19)

In placing himself on the side of practical experience in opposition to "the bookish theoric" of Cassio, Iago is evoking in the minds of the audience all the controversial associations of a dispute closely related to that between ancient learning and modern practice which Shakespeare had dramatized in *Henry V*. But the theorist resented by Iago need not have been, like Fluellen, a muddled antiquarian. In the history of military science, the Elizabethan theorist and student of books must be recorded as on the side of the angels. He was in favor of tactics and policy, whether new or old; he was interested in contemporary foreign works on war as well as in Caesar's *Commentaries;* and, like Cassio, he was probably an "arithmetician" in that he was studying gunnery, fortification, and the scientific marshaling of troops as presented in Digges's *An Arithmeticall Militare Treatise, Named Stratioticos* and Thomas Smith's *The Art of Gunnery. Wherein is set foorth a number of serviceable secrets, and practical conclusions, belonging to the Art of Gunnerie, by Arithmeticke skill to be accomplished.* It was by the good offices of the bookish theorist that the importance of mathematics to national defense was officially recognized in 1588. Then, as Professor Francis R. Johnson has demonstrated, it was argued and finally acknowledged that "the effective defense of the capital required providing instruction in mathematics for the untrained leaders of the volunteer forces."[101] Such a theorist would then, at his best, be attempting to conduct England from a static contemplation of Agincourt into the cosmopolitan stream of military science. And if Cassio is such a man, there is little question, favoritism or no favoritism, of Othello's wisdom in appointing him. Nowhere, in fact, would the executive intelligence of Othello be more evident than in his rejecting for any office higher than ensign a soldier of limited imagination and no professional promise—however trustworthy and valiant—in favor of a student of military science.

But Cassio, Iago argues, is especially contemptible as a theorist because he has had no experience in the field. As might be expected, this unlucky type got itself into some awkward situations. Barret has this to say of "your reading Captaines":

Many of them that reade, do neither understand the Methode nor meaning of the writer; many do understand the Methode, and not the meaning: yet by want of experience and practise, they are farre from a perfect souldier; and more from a worthie Captaine. The proofe of this is soone seene, for of your first sort, bring one of them into the field with a hundred men, he will never ranke them aright without helpe; and (God knoweth) neither with what puzzeling and toyle.... Now let one of your second sort come into the field with the like number, he will ranke theme three and three, but at every third ranke he must call to his boy, *hola sirra,* where is my Booke?[102]

In its comical exaggeration, very close to Iago's, Barret's description suggests that resentment against this type of officer had found a stock satirical expression. Probably it was a standard joke among the rank and file in Elizabethan armies, who resented not only what they considered to be the low practical intelligence of bookish officers but also the fact that these theorists constantly overtook them in promotion.

On the other hand, some able and farseeing minds of the age pleaded for the learned soldier, even if he was inexperienced. Thomas Smith, one of those to stress warfare as a science, urged the nation to accept as a trained soldier one that knoweth by the sound of Drum, and Trumpet, without any voice, when to march, retire, &., that is able in marching, embattelling, encamping, and fighting, and such like, to performe, execute, and obey the lawes and orders of the field, that hath some sight in the Mathematical, and in Geometricall instruments, for the conveying of Mines under the ground, to plant and mannage great Ordinance, to batter or beat down the wals of any Town or Castle, that can measure Altitudes, Latitudes, and Longitudes, &. such a one may be tearmed in my opinion an expert souldier, though he never buckled with an enemie in the field.[103]

And Du Bellay, "a famous General of our age," is quoted to much the same effect by Digges.[104] A controversy over an important appointment, occurring just a few years before *Othello,* dramatically demonstrated for the nation the fact that a bookish man accused of inadequate experience might still be a superb officer. When, according to Camden, a fit man was sought to quench the Irish rebellion in 1599, the Queen and most of the council were in favor of Lord Mountjoy. But Essex advised them "that hee was a man of no experience in the warres" and that he was "too much drowned in booke learning."[105] As a result, Essex found himself nominated for the job, with what sad success the nation was soon to learn. But the full irony of the situation was not unfolded until two or three years later, when Mountjoy, having been appointed to succeed Essex, proceeded with methodical intelligence to reduce the Irish to submission. There was no question, at least in a historical perspective, that the crying need of English armies was not for old soldiers, but for "arithmeticians," even if these were, like many Italian students of war, tending to become scientists rather than active soldiers.[106]

But there was every reason why Iago should fail to recognize this fact. As a die-hard, self-centered adherent of the old school of war, he would see in Cassio his natural enemy. For many veteran soldiers who lived by warfare, the struggle against the newcomers, the aliens, was one of life and death. Both honor and livelihood were at stake. Iago, passionately involved in this struggle, would be unable to talk of Cassio without distortion. Every theorist to him would be an exclusively bookish theorist (just as any man who talked with Iago's wife would be a lecher), and any captain who appointed him to responsible rank must have done so from ulterior motives.

It is also, of course, possible to defend Othello's appointment of Cassio by pointing out, as Professor Moore has incisively done, that Iago is the villain of the piece, that the facts of the play do not bear out his assertion, and that an audience is in no danger of mistaking him for a righteous man victimized by a courtier's arts.[107] But our condemnation of Iago should perhaps be complicated by an awareness that he has what to him seem real grievances. Shakespeare took special pains to make these grievances appropriate to a man of Iago's army status and limited perspective. There may even be elements of objective truth in them, however slight.

What is important is that Shakespeare gave Iago, in terms of that villain's intelligence and ideals, compelling motives for revenge. The practice is one that the dramatist follows for all his villains. There is, as Kittredge points out, no such thing as a "motiveless malignity" in Shakespeare.[108] Richard III is deformed and Edmund is a bastard. In neither of these should there be too much doubt of the sincerity of the grievance. Shakespeare allows each of them, as he allows Iago, to express his predicament as emphatically as possible, and very early in the play. But to say that Shakespeare makes the motive compelling is not to say that he means the audience to consider it murderously compelling in any other context than the limited, tortured mind of the villain himself. To audiences, whatever may have been their individual feeling about the military issues involved, it would have been clear that Iago felt he had been wronged, and equally clear that Iago's views were not to be accepted as a valid criticism of either Othello or Cassio.

Cassio proves, as Professor Moore notes, that he is a man capable of a more courageously direct action than is Iago. And Othello emerges as one of the most respected and capable military executives in Shakespeare, as a general in governing Cyprus and as a captain in appointing officers for his company. There is never any likelihood that the "bloodless emulation" within the ranks which we found in *Troilus and Cressida* would continue for long under Othello's command. His prompt suppression of brawls and his competent, impersonal discipline of Cassio are unusually strong evidence, for a play which has no active warfare, of his executive strength. What is more, Shakespeare is at pains to find verbal testimony to Othello's ability. Montano prays that the Moor may have survived the storm,

> For I have serv'd him, and the man commands
> Like a full soldier.
>
> (II.i.35)

Even Iago is compelled to testify for the man he hates. The state, he acknowledges, "cannot with safety cast him," for

> Another of his fathom they have none
> To lead their business.
>
> (I.i.150–154)

When Othello errs, it is in a context of peace rather than war, and we shall later have occasion to consider this error at length.

v

After *Othello,* Shakespeare makes almost no use of the Renaissance military hierarchy. Besides the obvious reason that his subsequent battles tend to be ancient rather than Renaissance, a perhaps more practical reason may be proposed for Shakespeare's dropping the subject. The great era of Elizabethan military triumphs ended with the Queen's death. Thereafter warfare dropped into the background of popular interest. English officers were no longer returning to London in great numbers, and the public was no longer curious as to who was an ensign and who was a lieutenant.

A period of about eight years comprises the impressive series of plays in which Shakespeare recognized popular interest by staging the duties, honors, and conflicts associated with army rank. During this time it is certain that he not only observed soldiers in London and talked with them, but read about them. It is almost equally certain that his reading in the treatises was not that of a professional. It was, in part, that of a patriotically alert citizen who wanted to know something about a subject which might determine whether England survived as a free nation. But it was also that of a playwright who wanted to find in the popular military books dramatically usable facts about an army's structure. It was with the irresponsible eye of a busy playwright—rather than a soldier seeking promotion—that he quickly sought only the details of military rank which could be used in character study or plot and which would have a meaning to civilians as well as soldiers. The reading tended to be penetrating rather than exhaustive; and his learning in this respect parallels what Professor Whitaker has found in his learning generally.[109] A glance at one of the more comprehensive military manuals—Barret's, for example—shows how small a proportion of the available material he covered. But what he did read, he comprehended with a psychological insight that spelled the difference between military manual and dramatic character.

It is this superiority to military manual which should be finally emphasized, since so much of this chapter has sought similarities rather than differences between the playwright and the books he may have read. Had Shakespeare's first interest been authentic and full representation of army structure, we should have had more stiff portraits like that of Henry V. His primary interest was, of course, character, rather than the military rank in which it was placed. Only of Henry V can it be said that the military treatise profoundly influenced the character. In other instances he seems to have had the character first in mind and then sought a rank or the details of rank which could best represent the personality he had conceived. With his best portraits this merging of rank and personality was perfectly accomplished. Falstaff best illustrates the ideal process. He seems from the first to have been conceived as a shrewd, unscrupulous, tricky, and impoverished character. When Shakespeare wished to translate this already very much alive creature from peace to war, he did not have to manufacture a new Falstaff. He merely changed his garb from that of a decayed knight to that of a disreputable (and later a prosperous) captain. With other characters the transformation is less natural. But when it fails, it fails always in allegiance to the military treatise rather than toward the character himself.

CHAPTER IV

The Common Soldier: Food for Powder

"Discuss unto me"—it is the commanding voice of Ancient Pistol addressing King Henry—"art thou officer; or art thou base, common, and popular?" (*Henry V* IV.i.37). The distinction to which Pistol gives such awful emphasis is still with us. Even so, a democratic theory of government and a literature which now gives privates full-length portraits make us liable to misinterpret or undervalue Shakespeare's treatment of common soldiers. Cannon fodder may still be cannon fodder, but its ingredients are more highly regarded by the self-conscious citizenry which supplies them. Shakespeare, in contrast, gives us the tattered, nondescript wretches of *1 Henry IV;* the grotesque recruits of *2 Henry IV;* the cowardly, insubordinate plebs of *Coriolanus;* and the parade of common soldiers in *Troilus and Cressida* described as follows by Pandarus (I.ii.262–266): "Asses, fools, dolts! chaff and

120

bran, chaff and bran! porridge after meat! ... Ne'er look, ne'er look! The eagles are gone. Crows and daws, crows and daws!" Even good King Hal, who of all Shakespeare's generals has the highest opinion of his soldiers, makes a careful distinction in his battle oration between the "noble English, / Whose blood is fet from fathers of war-proof," and the "men of grosser blood," who must have inspiring models to make them fight (*Henry V* III.i.17–25). It was a grim misfortune for a nobleman to be slain by these creatures, but Shakespeare permits this humiliation to occur only once (*3 Henry VI* I.i.4). Normally the outcome of battle depends entirely upon the nobility fighting one another.

Most offensive of all to modern taste is the anonymity, verging on contempt, with which private soldiers are treated in death. In the French army of *Henry V* Shakespeare intended, of course, to ridicule the fastidiousness of the gentry who ask leave

> To sort our nobles from our commen men;
> For many of our princes (woe the while!)
> Lie drown'd and soak'd in mercenary blood.
>
> (IV.vii.77)

The English are less dainty, but there is still what may seem a lack of that blood-shedding fellowship which Henry promised even the "most vile" of his soldiers, in his report of English casualties (IV.viii.108):

> Edward the Duke of York, the Earl of Suffolk,
> Sir Richard Ketly, Davy Gam, Esquire;
> None else of name; and of all other men
> But five-and-twenty.

This aristocratic point of view is equally pronounced in *Much Ado*. Leonato asks (I.i.5): "How many gentlemen have you lost in this action?" Upon being told "But few of any sort, and none of name," he happily observes: "A victory is twice itself when the achiever brings home full numbers."

We shall not, of course, find that contempt for the common soldier always obscures sensitive awareness of his mental world—however limited it may be. We have already noticed Shakespeare's able, if somewhat typed and humorous, study of the captains in *Henry V,* men who presumably rose from the ranks. Even for men not yet dignified by offices, there will be observed an occasional compassionate touch. In *3 Henry VI* Shakespeare suddenly introduces into the war of the nobles an interlude showing the effect of that war on conscripts. A youth tells how the ironic circumstances of civil war compelled him to kill his father (II.v.64):

> From London by the King was I press'd forth;
> My father, being the Earl of Warwick's man,
> Came on the part of York, press'd by his master;
> And I, who at his hands receiv'd my life,
> Have by my hands of life bereaved him.
> Pardon me, God! I knew not what I did.

The situation is traditional, but emotionally perceived. It gains added poignancy, and extends its meaning throughout the play, by King Henry's observation (II.v.73):

> O piteous spectacle! O bloody times!
> Whiles lions war and battle for their dens,
> Poor harmless lambs abide their enmity.

On the whole, however, whatever insights Shakespeare achieves into the mentalities of his common soldiers are focused upon their less admirable traits: their reluctance to be drafted, their ridiculous poverty, their fear in battle, their pursuit of booty rather than honor, and their grumbling and insubordination.

II

If we recognize, as probably we must, that of all Shakespeare's military population the commoners benefit from the least penetrating of his insights, we may nevertheless come to a better understanding of both his limitations and his successes if we examine them in the light of sixteenth-century attitudes. In that light we immediately recognize, to choose one of the clearest examples, the inevitability of caste distinction among the victims of war. Although the distinction is easily inferred from the structure of civilian society, one might still expect some wartime leveling in favor of commoners who die in a patriotic cause (as intimated by Henry V). No such leveling can be found in practice. The casualty list of a newsletter sent home to England from Brest records the names of officers down through the rank of corporal (an unusually generous limit), concluding with "and some 16 or 18 sodiors."[1] Aristocratic distinctions are of course even more pronounced in chivalric literature of the time. Although Sir Philip Sidney was capable of the beautiful gesture of refusing water in favor of a wounded soldier, he maintains a less gracious attitude in his *Arcadia*. There he asks, in pity of a knight whose life has been spared by a noble enemy: "But what good did that to poor Phebilus, if escaping a valiant hand, he was slaine by a base souldiour, who seeing him so disarmed, thrust him through?"[2]

Nevertheless, sixteenth-century attempts to catch the point of view of the common soldier succeed better in arousing pity

---

[1] For notes to chapter iv, see pages 324–326.

for him than in inviting respect or the sort of understanding
that informs a solid dramatic portrait. At best he is one of
Henry VI's "poor harmless lambs." One of the earliest and
most remarkable expressions of concern for the untitled soldier was made by Thomas More, whose Utopians "doo no
lesse pytye the basse and commen sorte of theyr enemyes
people, then they doo theyre owne; knowynge that they be
dryven to warre agaynste theyre wylles by the furyous madnes
of theyre prynces and heades."[3] Here, as in *Henry VI,* the
emphatic word is *pytye.* Queen Elizabeth also felt mainly
pity "that the poor soldier that hourly ventures life should
want their due reward,"[4] though we shall later see that the
pity alternated with annoyance.

Occasionally, social critics made a strikingly common-sense
appraisal of the potential military worth of commoners and
pointed out that if the wretches were allowed to famish they
would be unable "forcibly to use their weapons" in national
defense.[5] And Francis Bacon, in his essay "Of the True Greatness of Kingdoms and Estates," perceived that English military strength owed much to its infantrymen, men who in
feudal armies like the French would be merely peasants.
Shakespeare seems likewise to have recognized this fact in
his contrast between the French and English armies in
Henry V.

Soldier authors, as might be expected, have left us the least
condescending records of the humble members of their profession. Even when these records are harshly critical, they
dignify the soldier by recognizing his importance and poten-
tials. Above all, they benefit from fresh, direct observation
rather than traditional feudal prejudices. When these authors
speak favorably of their meaner fellows, they make us see

what only Shakespeare—and he rarely—among literary men perceives. The conscripted soldiers are not, they admit, noted for valor or intelligence; but they do have admirable traits and are more than just pitiable. So Blandy describes them:

For as their leaders, and commanders excell in witt, prowes and value: so have they them in more love, reverence, and admiration. For this may be truely sayd of our Countrymen: that even the rude multitude, doe love their rulers, and superiors, according to their vertues, and magnanimity, that they see in them. No people in the world more faythfull, more affectionate, then are the English Nation, if they be retayned accordingly; neither are they overcome a whitt with the hellish furies, and brutish crueltyes, that doe generally possesse all other Nations in the world.[6]

But tributes of this kind are usually paid only to professional soldiers. Soldier authors, as we shall see, have little respect for the ordinary conscript.

A better guide to the orthodox English view of the common soldier is the copious body of conduct books intended to instruct him in his duties. John Norden designed his *Mirror of Honor* to include this large and important group of customers. Its second treatise tells "how inferiour officers in armies, the common and private souldiers should behave themselves, as touching their obedience to God, their Prince and Commanders."[7] Norden recognizes that his book is not unique. "Many divine labors also of men learned and heavenly disposed, are offered to all, to the ende that all excuses both of idlenes and ignorance might be taken away." But, he regrets, "vaine and lascivious treatises of worldlinges and wicked ones, offensive to God and every good mind, are imbraced of soldiers for the most part."[8] Undoubtedly these vile progenitors of the comic book shouldered out the "divine labors" as claims upon the soldier's leisure. But the exemplary works nevertheless tell us what was expected of him. The marginal headings of sections in Norden's book are typical of the model indoctrination which the soldier received from all sides: "Cowardice voyd of the spirituall life"; "Men cannot perish in the warres before God decreeth it"; "Obedience the mother of all vertues"; "Counterfeit devises to be dispensed from warre, is perjurie"; "The Bible a necessary companion for a soldier"; "Vagabond and begging souldiers a great enormitie"; "It is no dishonor for a souldier to labour."

Obedience has of course been "the mother of all vertues" in armies from time immemorial. In Shakespeare's day, both the religious significance of degree and the dreadful lot of the commoner in war made crucially important keeping the soldier content within his orbit. It is no accident that not only Norden's book but almost all others give generously of space to this purpose. Stephen Gosson, pointing out that "the fourth and last in concurrence with the war is the common souldier," quotes John the Baptist to the effect that the duty of these soldiers "is to do violence to no man, but to be contented with their pay." When they are summoned to fight, "they must remember that in this case they are inferior instruments unto God to punish the offences of the wicked, and setting him before their eies in these actions, they may not consecrate the first fruites of their fingers with robberies and outrage upon their friends."[9] The order in which Smythe places his three precepts for soldiers is illuminating. Their "duetie and sufficiencie," he declares, "dothe first and principallie consist, to be obedient to their Captaines, and all other their superiour Officers. The second, that they doo knowe how to apparell and arme themselves fitlie, and to handle and use their weapons in everie time and place, and to know and observe al orders Militarie. The third is, to be sober, patient, and able to endure labours and travells."[10]

Equally important with these ideals in limiting the dramatic role of the soldier was the literary habit of employing commoners only in comic segments of the plot—often mere interludes of entertainment. Shakespeare's predecessors in the drama had already firmly established this limitation for him. Indeed, the standardization had gone so far that the clown often took the role representing the populace in battle. There had, of course, been occasional serious uses of soldiers in groups. Certain dramatists, notably those with didactic purpose, took special pains to make soldier episodes instructive. In *Horestes,* Idumeus exhorts his men, much in the manner of the conduct books, to be courageous, obedient, and convinced of their just cause.[11] And a few dramatists, mindful of a real social menace, interpose totally irrelevant scenes in which kings or generals look after the comfort and compensation of their enlisted men. Edmond Ironside asks of his general:

> But are ye sure my Lo: that all is fitt
> are all my souldiers furnished for this warr
> what have they meate and drincke to their Contente
> doe not the Capitaines pince them of theire paye.[12]

The incredible hero of *The Wars of Cyrus* refuses any of the booty for himself, ordering that it be divided; for "it pleaseth me to see my souldiers rich."[13] But this noble attitude does not usually become real drama unless a comic bent is given it. This bent is rudely applied in *Tamburlaine* when the victorious conqueror, asking, "Where are my common souldiers now," orders that they be given "Queens apeece (I meane such Queens as were kings Concubines)," equally to "serve all your turnes." Then a final warning, before the soldiers make off with their indignant booty: "Brawle not (I warne you) for your lechery."[14] The episode has intentions clearly beyond instructiveness. And so have, generally, the most vigorous scenes involving common soldiers in the pre-Shakespearean drama. When these soldiers are at all delineated as individuals—when they are given the rare dignity of names—they appear as clownish characters.

In *Horestes,* the best soldier scenes are not the exemplary type in which Idumeus lectures his men, but those featuring two low-life individuals. In these scenes, Haltersycke sings a lusty soldiers' song; then he and his friend Hempstring obscenely contemplate their service under Horestes; and finally they engage in a prewar brawl.[15] Later one of these lads, now called only "Sodyer," distinguishes himself in Horestes' warfare by capturing a beggarwoman. At first she cries "pitifully," but then turns upon her captor "and al to be beaten him."[16] A similar pattern of episodes enlivens the soldierly parts of *Cambises.* Here the soldiers also have doubtfully individual names—Huf, Ruf, and Snuf. They express themselves in tremendous oaths preparatory to war, and then fall victim to a Mistress Meretrix, who puts them shamefully to flight. Low-life warriors of this sort, combining the *miles gloriosus* with the Elizabethan clown, could not have given Shakespeare much inspiration beyond suggesting use for blustering rogues like Pistol. Yet these were the most conspicuous military roles given to commoners in the early drama.[17]

A partial exception to this generalization is to be found in conscription scenes. Episodes involving a forcible levy of men for service became popular as early as *Locrine,* and held the stage throughout the next century. In them there was every chance for a dramatist to penetrate beneath the bumpkin or rogue to the husband or the father who must leave his family, or the artisan who must leave his trade. And dramatists occasionally did so. In both *Locrine* and *The Famous Victories of Henry the Fifth* (the play which suggested the conscription scene for *2 Henry IV*), a cobbler is lamentably torn away from trade and wife; both cobblers, moreover, are given names, even though merely that of John Cobbler in *The Famous Victories.* But the prevailing tone in these two cases, and even more so that in *Histriomastix,* is one of grim and ironic comedy. The dramatists' primary intention was to give the audience amusement, not to present the point of view of the victim.

Shakespeare's recruiting scenes in *Henry IV* cannot be said to be much more humane than those of his predecessors. Superficially, at least, he was interested mainly in getting laughs from his audience. Nevertheless, the scenes will repay detailed study. For one thing, they testify to a knowledge of current practice which, though not professional, is sufficient to exploit the subject for all the humor and indignation it might give a civilian audience. More important, however, is the bearing of these scenes upon the portraits of common soldiers throughout the Shakespearean drama. More than his fellow dramatists, Shakespeare seems to have recognized the relationship between the scandals of conscription and the quality of men in Elizabeth's armies. And it is these men whom he puts on the stage in preference to the clowns and the Hufs of his predecessors.

III

As we noticed when studying Falstaff as captain, it was in *Henry IV* that Shakespeare first became closely attentive to the lower military ranks and first began to give comic and realistic representation of current military scandals. Why, one wonders, did he do so at this particular time? An underlying explanation would, of course, be his growth as a dramatist away from stereotypes and toward the full-dimensional portraits of criminal, roguish, and low-life individuals. But, more specifically, the change marked by *Henry IV*—and particularly by its realistic attention to conscripts—was inspired by the grave impact made on the national economy by an almost total mobilization for defense between the years 1596 and 1599. Intimations of trouble appeared as early as 1595, when the Queen wrote to her generals that Spanish preparations were greater than in 1588 and that "it is not to be doubted but that they intend to invade England and Ireland next summer."[18] "Nothing," recorded her council, "appears to her more necessary than to have her people trained in the discipline of war."[19] Not only were the gentry of the land kept in constant readiness for an attack, but commoners were drafted for service in unprecedented numbers. Whereas 2,800 men had been levied from the counties in 1594, and 1,806 in 1595, 8,840 were taken in 1596, 4,835 in 1597, 9,164 in 1598, and 7,300 in 1599.[20] The years 1596 to 1599 were clearly the years of greatest wartime pressure, and these significantly are the years when Shakespeare, in *Henry IV* and *Henry V,* was writing and staging the plight of the commoner called to war.

Conscription, especially, was in the air, and scenes depicting

it and its consequences could be depended upon to hold the
commoner's grim attention and also get condescending
laughs from the gentles in the audience, who saw themselves
in the "cull'd and choice-drawn cavaliers" of Henry V's army
(*Henry V* III.Chorus.24). For the populace at large, mobilization took the form described by Rumour in 2 *Henry IV*
(Induction, line 11):

> And who but Rumour, who but only I,
> Makes fearful musters and prepar'd defence,
> Whiles the big year, swol'n with some other grief,
> Is thought with child by the stern tyrant War,
> And no such matter?

The type of "fearful musters" to which the commonalty were
subjected, and the futile result of all the effort, are both
illustrated by an episode which took place in 1596. During
Good Friday service at Paul's Cross, the Lord Mayor and
aldermen of London were ordered to press 1,000 men. This
was accomplished by eight the same night, and before morning the conscripts were clothed and armed to be sent to
Dover—only to be demobilized that afternoon. But the terror
was not yet over. The following day, Easter Sunday, came a
new order for 1,000 men, "so that," as Stow records it, "all
men being in their parish Churches readie to have received
the Communion, the aldermen, their deputies, constables, and
other officers, were faine to close up the Church doores, till
they had pressed so manie men." But these likewise, after
having got as far as Dover, were demobilized.[21]

In exploiting the nation's interest in mobilization, Shakespeare might very well have represented a model levy in
Henry IV, since this would have corresponded with the exemplary warfare waged by the King and his sons. A pattern

for such a levy is briefly given—but atrociously misplaced in context—by Falstaff in his tribute to sherris sack (2 *Henry IV* IV.iii.115): "It illumineth the face, which, as a beacon, gives warning to all the rest of this little kingdom, man, to arm; and then the vital commoners and inland petty spirits muster me all to their captain, the heart; who, great and puff'd up with this retinue, doth any deed of courage." Shakespeare found, however, material more tonic and authentic—and better suited to the comic stratum of his play—in scandalous malpractices of recruiting captains and in the decidedly unmilitary material which they pressed.

Elizabethan captains were originally given the task of recruiting because they were supposed to have the most professional knowledge of men and because they could give expert advice on suitable weapons for each recruit.[22] The confidence proved, during the latter part of Elizabeth's reign, to be ill-advised. What formerly had made the captains ideal recruiters, according to Digges, was that they were leaders in their community, and their men were townspeople for whom they felt responsibility. But under the current practice, "the Captaine neither knowes his Souldiers, nor the Souldiers their Captaine before the Service, nor ever meane to meete again when the warres are ended."[23] Hence the terrible anonymity of Falstaff's "food for powder"—representing the 150 citizens whom the captain recruits in *1 Henry IV*. Hence, too, the callous impersonality of the conscription scene in *2 Henry IV*. This latter episode merits more investigation than it has received, if only because it dramatizes in detail what the more famous passage in *1 Henry IV* merely describes. And it has the added merit of presenting the victims not en masse but as separate persons, even though their names have no more individual dignity than the typed names of the conscripts in *Locrine* and *The Coblers Prophesie*. Here are Mouldy, Wart, Bullcalf, Feeble, and Shadow—names chosen simply as labels for physical peculiarities and as words which will permit Falstaff to make puns.

The men, moreover, although distinct from one another in trade, physique, and spirit, have a good deal in common. They are drawn from the rural districts rather than from London, and thus share the clownish marks which Shakespeare usually gives country people. They share, likewise, the more humiliating distinction of having been selected as candidates by Justice Shallow. Writing in 1598, Robert Barret complained that "the Companies that are commonlie levied, are drawn forth by the Justices of peace, who to disburden their towns or shire of corrupt weeds, as they tearme it, do pick out the scumme of their countrie."[24] The talents of both Captain Falstaff and Justice Shallow are therefore combined in making the miserable selection of men in 2 *Henry IV*. Shallow has brought a wretched little lot for inspection, and Falstaff chooses the worst of these.

The first person called forth for the captain's inspection is a surly individual, Ralph Mouldy. Shallow enthusiastically proffers him as "a good-limb'd fellow, young, strong, and of good friends" (III.ii.113); but Falstaff, interested in his name, reflects that it is time Mouldy was used. Mouldy does not join Shallow in applauding the pun. He has, he protests, an "old dame" who needs his help with household drudgery. There were better men to choose. In fact, Mouldy's name and manner suggest that he is not so young as Shallow, his sense of time distorted by age, takes him to be. The next candidate, Simon Shadow, pleases Falstaff, "for we must have a number of shadows to fill up the muster book." Thomas Wart follows, ragged, lowsy, and apparently "little, lean, old, chopt, bald," but he promptly becomes the first of the rejectees. Francis Feeble, woman's tailor, is accepted, however; Falstaff is pleased with the thought that he will be "as valiant as the wrathful dove or most magnanimous mouse."

"Peter Bullcalf o' th' green!" is announced. Falstaff is enthusiastic: "Yea, marry, let's see Bullcalf"; and again, "Fore God, a likely fellow! Come, prick me Bullcalf till he roar again." But Bullcalf is a reluctant selectee. "O Lord! good my Lord Captain," he roars—"O Lord, sir! I am a diseased man." Bullcalf suffers, he confesses, from a "whoreson cold," caught in celebrating "the King's affairs upon his coronation day." Captain Falstaff, however, assures him that he may go to war in a nightgown and that all his friends will accord him the rites of a hero.

In the interval before the final selection, Bullcalf and Mouldy offer Corporal Bardolph a convincing sum of money. Consequently, Falstaff liberates the two whom Shallow calls his "likeliest men" and chooses Wart, Shadow, and Feeble. With wounded professional pride, Falstaff rebukes the justice for questioning his choice (III.ii.275):

Will you tell me, Master Shallow, how to choose a man? Care I for the limb, the thews, the stature, bulk, and big assemblance of a man? Give me the spirit, Master Shallow. Here's Wart. You see what a ragged appearance it is. 'A shall charge you and discharge you with the motion of a pewterer's hammer, come off and on swifter than he that gibbets on the brewer's bucket. And this same half-fac'd fellow, Shadow—give me this man. He presents no mark to the enemy; the foeman may with as great aim level at the edge of a penknife. And for a retreat—how swiftly will this Feeble, the woman's tailor, run off! O, give me the spare men and spare me the great ones.

A caliver is then put into Wart's hand to illustrate Falstaff's conviction that "a little, lean, old, chopt, bald shot" is ideal. One gathers from Shallow's melancholy reaction that the results of the experiment are not persuasive. At any rate, Falstaff's brilliant rationalization scarcely disguises the fact that he has chosen a ragged old man without spirit, an absurdly emaciated fellow, and a feeble, though willing, man of delicate occupation.

Shakespeare depended for appeal in this scene upon a controversial subject understandably interesting in 1597–1598: What men are best suited for military service? The subject was almost comically technical and was the special province of military experts. Generally these were veteran officers like Sir John Smythe, Sir Roger Williams, and Humphrey Barwick, whose treatises, based on either classical authority or modern practice and theory, dealt in part with the problem of recruiting. Since the government made few specific demands upon the recruiting experts other than to request that the conscripts be of good behavior and moderate physical ability,[25] the military career of the average citizen often depended upon the integrity of the recruiting officers and upon their peculiar theories.

Captains relying upon ancient authorities might follow the precepts of Vegetius: "Let the young man therefore that shalbe a souldiour, not looke drowsely, let hym be straighte neckd, broad brested, let his shoulders be well fleshte, let him have strong fingers, long armes, a gaunte belly, slender legges, the calfe and feete not to full of fleshe, but knitte faste with harde and strong synowes."[26] Modern authorities, however, placed less stress on physique. Thomas Procter asserted that in choosing a soldier "to sett downe a precyse order, for the same by his shoulders, brest, armes, thyghes, feete, or composition of anie parte of the bodye: I houlde it most vayne." The "courage and minde is as much to bee respected as the bodye."[27] Matthew Sutcliffe took issue with Pyrrhus' instructions that "bigge and corpulent men" should be chosen. Such physiques are unequal to hard work. Slighter men, Sutcliffe advises, are not to be rejected "if they have strong and active bodies," since these men "are for the most part more vigorous and courageous; they do more easily endure labors, and commonly excell great bodied men in swiftnesse and running, which is a matter in a souldier verie requisite and commendable."[28] Falstaff, as we have seen, thoroughly endorses this view: "how swiftly will this Feeble, the woman's tailor, run off! O, give me the spare men and spare me the great ones." But the greatest commendation in a soldier, Sutcliffe adds, "is the vigor of the mind," and here too Falstaff is in complete agreement ("Give me the spirit, Master Shallow").

When Falstaff recommends Wart as a "little, lean" shot, he is alluding to an especially well-known branch of the subject of scientific recruiting: the relationship of physique and weapon. The council in 1597 ordered captains who were to pick up their men in the various counties to take care that the recruits be "fytt for service and to use those weapons appointed unto them."[29] A more specific order to the muster masters in 1598 explains what the council had in mind: "the strongest to carry pikes; strong and spare men to have muskets, and the nimblest harquebuses."[30] The harquebus, like the caliver entrusted to Wart, was one of the lighter firearms, and agility rather than strength was required in its use. Justice Shallow, sadly watching Wart manage his weapon, recalls "a little quiver fellow" who "would about and about, and come you in and come you in. 'Rah, tah tah!' would 'a say; 'Bounce' would 'a say; and away would 'a go, and again would 'a come" (III.ii.300–306). According to Smythe, the harquebusiers "must be lythe in all their joints and sinewe, that they may stoupe to their pieces, and traverse their grounds, now retiring having discharged, giving place to their fellowes, and then advancing againe, giving their fellowes retiring tyme againe to charge."[31] Moreover, he would have these nimble lads chosen of "the smallest sorte and size of men, because they should be the lesser markes in the sights of their enemies."[32] In this respect, of course, Shadow is an even better choice than Wart, since "he presents no mark to the enemy."

Age was another criterion in the selection of soldiers. Smythe went so far as to place "conveniencie of age and yeares" as the first consideration.[33] Falstaff seems to have been offered, out of five men, one somewhat callow and two approaching the thither limits of warlike vigor. Soldiers of all ages were to be found in Elizabeth's army. In 1577 she had authorized, though probably only for emergency availability, the conscription of all able men between sixteen and sixty.[34] But advantage had obviously been taken of these generous limits by unscrupulous recruiters, for some years later the council complained that the ages chosen were far from satisfactory.[35] And one official protested that he had received mainly old men and boys.[36] In the light of such complaints, Falstaff seems to have had, besides three pounds, a show of virtue when he instructed the two liberated conscripts (III.ii.268): "for you, Mouldy, stay at home till you are past service; and for your part, Bullcalf, grow till you come into it."

In preferring Feeble to Bullcalf, Falstaff also has occasion to make an ingenious interpretation of still another criterion in selecting soldiers: trade. Not only is Feeble of very modest physique; he is of an occupation which, since classical times, was among those least favored for conversion to warlike employments. "Wilt thou," Falstaff sarcastically asks him (III.-ii.164), "make as many holes in an enemy's battle as thou hast done in a woman's petticoat?" Feeble promises to do his best. "Well said, good woman's tailor!" roars Captain Falstaff. Bullcalf, on the other hand, represents the strength and temperament associated with farming. Classical writers generally disapproved of delicate occupations as backgrounds for military service. Vegetius recommended that "linnen weavers, and whosoever that dealeth with any thing that tokeneth a womanishe nicenes, should be utterly banished the campe."[37] Once more Falstaff cannot afford to be a classicist, and so he turns again to modern authority to support his surprising choice of a woman's tailor. Sutcliffe, who had supported him with "the vigor of the mind," is also gratifyingly enlightened on occupation. He would not rule out men of unpromising trades, "for many to win themselves a living, are oftentimes driven to follow base occupations, that otherwise are couragious."[38] And Captain Barnaby Rich rejected the classical notion that the husbandman or laborer necessarily makes the best soldier. The laborer, argued Rich, cannot endure the irregular diet incident to warfare. The ability to maintain courage with slight nourishment "proceedeth onely of the valewer of the mynde,"[39] which is precisely the quality that Falstaff esteems in Feeble.

The recruiting scene is notable, however, not only for Falstaff's droll use of theory in the choice of men, but for the attitudes toward a military future revealed by the men themselves. Of five candidates for conscription, only Feeble has the proper spirit for serving his country. Feeble's attitude is one which the government and unofficial propagandists sought to arouse in the citizens by scores of hortatory tracts.[40] Feeble is willing (III.ii.251): "I'll ne'er bear a base mind. An't be my destiny, so; an't be not, so. No man's too good to serve's prince." It is from his kind—more sturdily built, to be sure—that there will arise the remarkably human, troubled, but loyal soldiers of Henry V.

Imperfectly indoctrinated, however, are Mouldy and Bullcalf, both of whom plead grievous disabilities, offering three pounds as additional evidence. "And yet"—Bullcalf would have the record straight—"for mine own part, sir, I do not care; but rather because I am unwilling and, for mine own part, have a desire to stay with my friends. Else, sir, I did not care, for mine own part, so much" (III.ii.239). The portrait of robust and roaring Bullcalf pleading a bad cold is a comical mirroring of the Elizabethan malingerer. One medical authority has left us a vigorous description of the type; he hopes that there are not

a great nomber of our people, that can roiste, crake, braule, sweare, and bragge, in the tyme of peace.... And when the Quenes majestie shal have nede, to withstand thenemie, or suppresse the rebel: that then thei become not like unto Aristogiton, with sore legges, Agues, broken armes, tremblyng, lamentable lokes, as bolde as Geese, or Lions of Coteswolde Heath. Sendyng their water to the Phisicion, to cloke their knaverie, for lacke of manhode, or els with *Unguentum aurum,* can anointe their Capitaines hande, to blotte theim out of their muster booke, which is a good medicene.[41]

Family ties such as those claimed by Mouldy were naturally of some importance in Elizabethan recruiting. Strictly military reasons favored single men. Leicester complained on one occasion that he had been sent "householders, and maryed men," and asked specifically for single men in the next levy.[42] And as subjects for conscription, family men were, as Falstaff well knew, the most likely to buy their way out. Mouldy is not Sir John's first profitable experiment with husbands. In *1 Henry IV* he had pressed "none but good householders...., contracted bachelors, such as had been ask'd twice on the banes," and these had "bought out their services" (IV.ii.16–25).

Undoubtedly in almost all Elizabethan malingering the major blame rested upon the captain, who, like Falstaff, would choose men least eager for service and then accept their bribes. Council instructions to captains in 1597 stated: "We need not to admonish you after you have your whole companie to take heede that none be dyschardged for anie monie."[43] The council's confidence was, however, misplaced, for exactly two months later it called the counties' attention to the "great offence and greevaunce of her Majesty's good subjectes" caused by recruiters and conductors "in exacting or takinge summes of money or other composicions of diverse persons to keepe them from being imprested and in chaunging or dismissing others for bribes that were leavyed."[44] It was, assuredly, vain to warn Englishmen of the perjury to God involved in malingering,[45] if the chief motivating criminal was the captain.

As a mirroring of contemporary recruiting practice, the episode from *2 Henry IV* is obviously distorted for purposes of satire and mere entertainment. Falstaff, although not necessarily more criminal than occasional real-life captains, is certainly more talented as a manipulator of recruiting theories and a purveyor of puns. But despite their pleasure in the sheer beauty of his performance, citizens would have noticed an ugly stratum of reality beneath the artistry. Reduced to its lowest terms, Falstaff's performance consists in sacrificing the king's service and the welfare of individual citizens for the sake of three pounds and the delight in his own cleverness.

And beneath Justice Shallow's quaint choice of men, citizens would have recognized the serious reality of officials withholding their best townspeople because they had convinced themselves that the low character of warfare made a better selection inhuman. Barnaby Rich's Captain Pill tells how he once met a constable and his men "pulling of a fellow by the head and shoulders (I had thought to some place of execution)." Asking what offense the culprit had committed, Pill "was answered that it was an idle Rogue that had beene a runagate about the countrey, and they had pressed him for a Souldier." Further inquiry of the constable whether he was authorized to take rogues brought an angry answer: "Sir, I perceive by the sound of your words, you are a favourite to Captaines, and I thinke you could be contented, that to serve the expedition of these times, we should take up honest house-holders, men that are of wealth and abilitie to live at home, such as your Captaines might chop and chaunge.... Let me tell you therefore in secret, that we have learned of Scoggin long agoe, to seeke out sleevelesse men, to send of sleevelesse arrands."[46] Though the constable's argument might be the rationalization of a corrupt official, it was substantially based on fact. It leaves not only Captain Pill, but Captain Skill (that is, Rich himself) without a good rejoinder. "Unhappy may those warres be called," he reflects, "where men are but sent as it were to the slaughter, too weak in number, unfurnisht, unprovided, unpaid, and in every way wronged and discouraged; for this usage, and these services, rogues, runnagats and pesants are the fitst men to be sent."[47] There would thus have been a disconcerting element of truth even in Falstaff's justification of his choice of "scarecrows" and ex-prisoners in *1 Henry IV*. When Prince Hal remarks that he has never before seen "such pitiful rascals," Falstaff accepts the fact philosophically (IV.ii.71): "Tut, tut! good enough to toss; food for powder, food for powder. They'll fill a pit as well as better."

If, allowing for comic exaggeration, the procedures and philosophy behind Falstaff's recruiting are surprisingly true to Elizabethan conditions, an even greater authenticity must be acknowledged in the quality of men chosen. Feeble and Wart may at first seem to be incredible representatives of Elizabethan conscripts. And Falstaff's description in *1 Henry IV* of his unlucky 150 may seem yet more preposterous. Here are "slaves as ragged as Lazarus in the painted cloth, where the glutton's dogs licked his sores ... ten times more dishonourable ragged than an old fac'd ancient." In this macabre procession are creatures that "march wide betwixt the legs, as if they had gyves on; for indeed I had the most of them out of prison." In the whole company there is only a shirt and a half, the half shirt being "two napkins tack'd together and thrown over the shoulders like a herald's coat without sleeves," and the full shirt having been stolen. The shortage of shirts does not worry Sir John, for "they'll find linen enough on every hedge"; but meanwhile he is ashamed to march through Coventry with so grotesque a following. "No eye hath seen such scarecrows" (IV.ii.22–52).

One must of course acknowledge Shakespeare's, and particularly Falstaff's, command of language. But the situation was one to inspire vigorous and effective language even in the unliterary. Officials who found themselves the recipients of Elizabethan recruits rose to unwonted eloquence. "There was never man beheld such creatures brought to any muster," complained the Mayor of Bristol; "few of them have any clothes, small, weak, starved bodies, taken up in fair, market, and highway, to supply the place of better men kept at home."[48] The Privy Council had several occasions to comment upon the quality of men drafted. In 1597 it wrote to the justice of Middlesex concerning the recruits that "yt ys not meete that they shalbe sent over in naked and ragged sorte."[49] Failure of officials to observe this order evoked in 1598 a warm protest. The conscripts, reported the council, "were taken out of the gaoles and of rogues and vagrant persons, evyll armed and set forth so naked and bare, without hose or shooes, as they are not any way fytte for servyce nor to appeare amongst men, besydes of that lewd behavyour as they had lyke to have mutyned and made an uprore in the towne."[50] It is such recruits as these, unfit "to appeare amongst men," that Shakespeare saw passing through towns in the late 1590's, or skirting towns if they were being conducted by a Captain Falstaff. And testimony to the ability of such men to pick up clothing as they went has been found by Miss Campbell in Barnaby Rich's *A Right Exelent and Pleasaunt Dialogue, Betwene Mercury and an English Souldier* (1574): "Fyrst by the way as they travayle through the Countrey, where they chaunce to lye all nyght, the godwyfe hath spedde well if she fynde hyr sheets in the morning, or if this happe to fayle yet a coverlet, or Curtins from the bed, or a Carpet from the table, some table clothes, or table Napkins, or some other thing must needes pack away with them."[51]

It was, then, by turning directly to the recruiting going on about him that Shakespeare gained not only the grim comedy but the animated detail and much of the language of the conscription scenes in *Henry IV*. But the scenes are, in a way that has not been recognized, important for reasons well beyond their immediate context. They determine and give credibility to portraits of common soldiers throughout the entirety of Shakespeare's military world. His common soldiers—whether English, Greek, or Roman—are substantially the Elizabethan wretches conscripted in *Henry IV*. Unless we recognize this fact, we cannot accept the truth behind their preposterousness, nor appreciate those vigorous traits—however unflattering—which make them distinct from their feudal predecessors in literature.

IV

Elizabethan military critics could have helped the dramatist forecast the kind of service to be expected of Wart, Feeble, and the nameless 150, particularly since army officers did little to improve life for their men. According to one authority, soldiers may well "perish for could and hide themselves, or Mutenye when they should undertake accions of most moment."[52] How, asked Barnaby Rich, would you persuade such poor rascals to fight for the honor of their country? They have no idea what honor means. Exhort them to defend their lands and livings? But "they have nothing to loose, and less to care for; will you presse them with shame for being reputed Cowards? but they will never blush, that are not onely past shame, but also past grace; why then what lawe to enjoyne, what love to induce them, or what gods to conjure them?"[53] And no less an authority than Queen Elizabeth acknowledged to the emissary De Maisse her opinion of English soldiers in France: "She said ... that they were but thieves and ought to hang, and other words between her teeth which I did not well understand. Also it seemed as if she had put herself in choler about it, for which cause I forebore to discuss the matter further."[54] In the light of these estimates, Coriolanus' statement of the plebs' military value may not seem unduly pessimistic (III.i.122):

> Being press'd to th' war
> Even when the navel of the state was touch'd,
> They would not thread the gates. This kind of service
> Did not deserve corn gratis. Being i' th' war,
> Their mutinies and revolts, wherein they show'd
> Most valour, spoke not for them.

Coriolanus, it will be noticed, credits his soldiers with but one kind of valorous action in battle: "mutinies and revolts." Of this kind of misconduct, however, there is in Shakespeare only one clear instance, and this is not a full-dress mutiny but merely the refusal of Coriolanus' soldiers to follow him into Antium. It is curious that Shakespeare did not make more prominent use of a type of military disorder so prevalent in Renaissance warfare and so clearly indicated by the type of men he shows being conscripted for service.

The explanation is obviously not Shakespeare's reluctance to show common soldiers in a bad light—he seldom shows them in a light of any other kind. More likely the explanation is just the reverse: a full representation of mutinies, with their causes, would have given the soldiers a more favorable case than he cared or dared to make.

A tendency in this direction is evident in his occasional, but unstaged, allusions to mutinies. In *1 Henry VI* a messenger reports (I.i.158):

> The English army is grown weak and faint;
> The Earl of Salisbury craveth supply
> And hardly keeps his men from mutiny,
> Since they, so few, watch such a multitude.

These soldiers, however poor in quality they may be, are not without understandable grievances: lack of supply and inadequate support. Usually the sharpest incentive was monetary. The poor wretches simply were not paid. This explains the revolt reported in *2 Henry VI* when Somerset is accused of having levied vast sums for the soldiers without dispersing the money (III.i.60). In *Timon of Athens,* likewise, Alcibiades complains (IV.iii.90):

> I have but little gold of late, brave Timon,
> The want whereof doth daily make revolt
> In my penurious band.

In reporting these revolts, Shakespeare was surely aware of their counterparts in contemporary wars. The *Henry VI* type of grievance was notoriously common, especially in the years just preceding the composition of this trilogy. The meager funds intended for English soldiers in the Netherlands did not find their way into the pockets of the humbler members of the army. A prolonged and understandable mutiny resulted when their "hard and miserable estate" compelled them, as they said in a supplication to the Queen, to take "under hand" their governor, captains, and other officers. Their hard estate was in part having to lie upon straw, or worse, with "not so much as a candle to answer the allarums" in winter; in part it was being victimized by sutlers; and in part it was having served "without any penny pay." The soldiers' petition is a quaintly pathetic one, assuring their sovereign of their willingness to die in her service, but praying that they might be allowed six months' pay wherewith to "cherish" themselves.[55] The situation in Ireland was, if possible, more steadily worse. On one occasion Sir John Norris wrote to Cecil that "the soldier groweth into desperate terms, and spare not to say to their officers, that they will run away and steal rather than famish."[56]

The Roman citizens in *Coriolanus* who mutiny during peacetime—and who are presumably the same that balk during battle—have a complaint strikingly similar to that of Elizabethan soldiers. "You are all resolv'd rather to die than to famish?" asks their first spokesman (I.i.4). Yet this valid grievance is not kept closely enough before the audience's mind when the citizens prove insubordinate during battle. We see then only mean-spirited rogues. It is clear, therefore, that in his only strong hint of mutiny on the stage Shakespeare resists giving sympathy to the commonalty. And he does so despite Plutarch's careful explanation of why the oppressed and poverty-stricken plebs refuse to risk their lives for their country.

In other instances where he mentions mutiny, Shakespeare carefully refrains, as I have suggested, from dramatizing it. It was safe enough, as most military writers found, to make a not too specific plea for correction of the abuses that resulted in unpaid soldiers. The Queen herself had set a royal precedent when she wrote to Leicester in the Netherlands, "If there be fault in using of soldiers or of making of profit by them, let them hear of it without open shame and doubt not but I will chasten them therefor."[57] But the Queen's expression "without open shame" is a significant caution. No serious disgraces occurred. Indeed, if criticism were to be allowed to seek its proper level, not even Leicester or the Queen herself would have escaped blame. Military critics—with the exception of the unlucky Sir John Smythe, whose book was called in—accordingly concentrated their abuse on the captains, a deserving but not adequate target.

To stage a mutiny with dramatic adequacy would therefore have been for Shakespeare a highly delicate problem. Obviously he could not sympathize with rebellion, the most heinous of Elizabethan political sins. Nor could he, if he wished to motivate his drama, seem oblivious to the intolerable conditions behind the mutiny. Vividly in his mind must have been his painful experience in *Richard II,* when all his immense tact had been needed in the attempt to motivate as well as condemn a rebellion. Even the resultant ambiguity was, as he knew, distasteful to the Queen. The closest Shakespeare ever came to seriously investigating soldierly discontent before rebuking it was, as we shall see, in *Henry V;* but even there one finds no hint of mutiny. For Shakespeare's refusal to present the grievances of the "worshipful mutineers" in *Coriolanus,* there may have been an unusually specific reason. As Brents Stirling has reminded us, the play was "contemporaneous with widely felt enclosure riots," when the government was specially sensitive to any kind of uprising.[58] At any rate, rebellion in this play is far more than a military phenomenon, and to investigate it thoroughly would be beyond the purpose of this study.

V

In dealing with pillage, a related soldierly vice, the dramatist is almost consistently harsh or scornful. There is no ambiguity of feeling, no suggestion of a fuller case that could be made. Mutiny, however opprobrious, was popularly associated with real grievances. But soldiers on irregular pillage were thought of as the rowdies and thieves that they often were and had long been. These were men who would turn to loot in war as they had done in peace. They were the unhappy few in Henry V's army whom the King describes as "making the wars their bulwark, that have before gored the gentle bosom of peace with pillage and robbery" (IV.i.169).

It was not that the soldiers' need for some irregular means of subsistence was unacknowledged by contemporary military critics. Smythe, in a book which brought him painful recognition, accused English commanders of setting down "cunningly and artificiallie" a few laws to terrify soldiers from demanding their pay or "complaining of the misusages of their Captaines and higher Officers"; but "to terrifie them from spoyling, robbing, and taking by force from the common countrie people their friends . . . , there was no prohibition . . . they often terming those to be best soldiers that could live without pay, by stealing and spoyling most."[59] With a less partisan cynicism, Barwick recognized that loot for the average soldier far outweighed honor and patriotism as incentives for heroism, "for no doubt a poore souldiers manner is to venter ten lives if might be, for gold and jewels before all other things whatsoever."[60]

The trouble with this incentive, especially among the rascally element, was that it constituted one of the gravest menaces to concerted warfare by the English. Important expeditions degenerated during critical moments into chaotic scrambles for personal gain. A Spanish monk who made the 1597 voyage with Essex asserted that his nation's fleet might have been captured if it had not been for this failing. As soon, he reported, as the English "have taken some booty they speak of nothing else but going to their homes, and they do nought but plunder."[61] With good reason, therefore, conduct books repeatedly attacked selfish pursuit of plunder. When victory is near, Barret warns the common soldier, "let him set all his care and diligence in execution of the victory with his weapon, and not in the spoile of apparell, robes, and trash: least he be accounted an unruly scraper, as to many now a dayes be: for many disorders doe happen by the disorder of covetous spoilers, many times to the dishonour of the action, and losse of their lives."[62] Blandy even overlooks the sacred virtue of obedience in affirming that "the onely and chiefe grace, that beautifieth the minde of a Souldier, is the contempt of Spoyle, and refusall of riches."[63]

Royal interests gave added emphasis to the denunciation of this abuse. English amphibious expeditions depended financially upon plunder, but the pillaging was to be concerted, not casual or individual, and its principal returns were to be reserved for royal coffers. Few military malpractices were so noisome to the Queen as the soldiers' habit of "embezzling" royal plunder. According to Camden, this habit, which was prompted by "inbred ravenous greedinesse," was officially rebuked in 1592 when "there came forth a Proclamation, (as there had done now and then before) that they should bring forth the goods privily conveighed away, unlesse they would suffer punishment for their faults, as Thieves and pirats." Yet,

Camden notes, "their dishonesty deluded both the industry of the Commissioners, and the strictness of the Edict, even by perjuries. For they said, They had rather hazard their soules in the hands of a mercifull God, by perjury, then their fortunes gotten with perill of their lives, in the hands of unmercifull men."[64] A rebuke to such private profiteers and a plea for the type of pillage desired by Elizabeth are implicit in one of Shakespeare's most famous passages defining the role of the soldier in "the state of man." Using analogy with the bees, the Archbishop of Canterbury pictures the ideal of soldierly enterprise as follows (*Henry V* I.ii.193):

> Others like soldiers armed in their stings
> Make boot upon the summer's velvet buds,
> Which pillage they with merry march bring home
> To the tent-royal of their emperor.

Normally, however, Shakespeare does not dramatically endorse even this orderly type of pillage. Canterbury's idealistic picture is not permitted to govern the ethics of plunder within the play of *Henry V* itself. The King's code of Christian warfare is more stringent than Elizabeth's, for he commands "that in our marches through the country there be nothing compell'd from the villages, nothing taken but paid for" (III.vi.114). One suspects, however, that more than Christian ideals prompted this decree. Henry is uneasily aware that his authority can remain firm only if all temptation to plunder is removed. To permit any kind of pillage is to open the way to a slack, vulnerable army in which disciplined soldiers turn into beasts. Such anarchy is figuratively described in *Lucrece,* when Tarquin's veins are tempted by his eyes to an uproar (line 428):

And they, like straggling slaves for pillage fighting,
Obdurate vassals fell exploits effecting,
In bloody death and ravishment delighting,
Nor children's tears nor mothers' groans respecting,
Swell in their pride, the onset still expecting.

No Shakespearean army seems less subject to mad lust of this kind than that of Henry V. But the King's forces, regardless of their fine discipline and "choice-cull'd cavaliers," are like all other armies in Shakespeare in being made up also of men such as those Falstaff has levied in *Henry IV*. There is consequently more than rhetoric in Henry's warning to the rulers of Harfleur that they submit while his men are still under his control (*Henry V* III.iii.22):

What rein can hold licentious wickedness
When down the hill he holds his fierce career?
We may as bootless spend our vain command
Upon th' enraged soldiers in their spoil
As send precepts to the Leviathan
To come ashore. Therefore, you men of Harflew,
Take pity of your town and of your people
Whiles yet my soldiers are in my command,
Whiles yet the cool and temperate wind of grace
O'erblows the filthy and contagious clouds
Of heady murther, spoil, and villany.

Even the best of Elizabethan commanders would have endorsed Henry's dark picture of "enraged soldiers in their spoil" and of the futility of controlling such a rabble. Ralegh, in his report of the victory at Cadiz, tells how he dared stay no more than an hour in the town, weak as he was from injuries, "for the fear I had to be shouldered in the press, and among the tumultuous, disordered soldiers, that, being then given to spoil and rapine, had no respect ... all running headlong to the Sack."[65] Even if a town capitulated, it was all the generals could do to hold their soldiers from the spoil. When Dowsborough yielded to Leicester, Stow records, "it was a grievous thing to see how [the women] were ransacked, till the earle of Essex and divers other gentlemen came downe the breach, and by smiting and beating the soldiers, made them leave off rifling them.... The captaines and soldiers that were sent to save the towne from spoile, did to the contrarie, for they made havocke and most horrible spoile."[66]

Shakespeare never neglects an opportunity supplied by his sources to point out common soldiers engaged in shameful pillage. In *Julius Caesar* he may do no more than record the fact, given him by Plutarch, that Brutus' "soldiers fell to spoil" at a critical moment (V.iii.7). But since in the play this represents almost the only notice taken of the ordinary soldiers' performance at Philippi, the damaging effect is equal to that obtainable in a larger scene. In *Coriolanus* Shakespeare emphatically goes beyond the hint supplied by Plutarch, in order to ridicule the short-sighted greed of the plebeian soldiers. The historian gives two sentences to the premature pillage.[67] Shakespeare not only dramatizes the episode, but introduces creatures sufficiently clownish and stupid to have come from Falstaff's band of conscripts. They are pictured in the town of Antium, which they had refused to enter during active hostility, hard at work gathering loot for themselves (I.v.1):

> *1. Rom.* This will I carry to Rome.
> *2. Rom.* And I this.
> *3. Rom.* A murrain on't! I took this for silver.

Meanwhile the stage direction "Alarum continues still afar off" underlines their limited view of the battle. But Shake-

speare is not content with this clownish performance. Coriolanus now enters and moralizes about the spectacle with persuasive scorn (I.v.5):

> See here these movers that do prize their honours
> At a crack'd drachma! Cushions, leaden spoons,
> Irons of a doit, doublets that hangmen would
> Bury with those that wore them, these base slaves,
> Ere yet the fight be done, pack up. Down with them!

The coins may be Roman, but the loot and the culprits are
unmistakably English.

VI

Although insurrection and pillage are the most serious vices
of Shakespeare's common soldier, they are far from being his
most shameful or most frequently ridiculed. The characteristic that most clearly distinguishes the dramatist's commoner
from his nobleman in battle is cowardice. There is no doubt
that Shakespeare's enlisted men are poltroons—not patheti-
cally or understandably, but ridiculously. Their cowardice,
moreover, is not the stylized type of the *miles gloriosus* as
exemplified in Parolles, or the reasoned, complex type of Falstaff; nor is it the wise and controlled fearfulness of Henry V.
It is the cowardice of wretched men without spirit or ideals.
It accurately mirrors the abject cowardice, ungraced by intelligence, of Elizabethan conscripts.

These men, except for the rare Feebles, resisted the lure of
battle from the time of conscription to the end of their military careers. Having been pressed for service and given equipment, they had to be closely guarded to prevent their escaping—with equipment—before they even got out of England.
On at least one occasion it was necessary to drive them aboard

ship with cudgels.[68] Since, as Professor Farnham has demonstrated, the average Elizabethan was uncommonly fearless in the presence of death,[69] the fault must have been mainly in the selection of men. "But heare is the maine mischiefe," as Barnaby Rich said of the men chosen for service, "if necessitie should inforce to fight, what hope to confirme those fellowes with a settled resolution, to incounter a warlike enemie, when they are so readie to runne away, before ever they durst to looke foe in the face?"[70]

Running away, as reports from the field and contemporary historians attest, was the most noteworthy activity of the conscripts. "One thing I must complain to your honour of," wrote Sir Edward Norreys to Walsingham, "—of the baseness of our countrymen's minds, that now they hear the enemy is said to come hither do run away daily five and six together."[71] Those who did not successfully disperse themselves before battle could still take to their heels during combat. A notorious and tragic instance occurred in Ireland, when fifteen hundred "common Souldiers, . . . being scattered by a shamefull flight all the fields over, were slaine and vanquished. They that remained alive, reproachfully laid the blame not upon their owne cowardize but the unskilfulnesse of their Leaders, which was now growne to a custome."[72]

Shakespeare is studiously faithful in reproducing this trait of the common soldiers. Disordered retreats, as we have seen, occur in several plays, but the most sustained account is that of the panicky Britons in *Cymbeline* (V.iii.5):

> the army broken,
> And but the backs of Britons seen, all flying
> Through a strait lane—the enemy, full-hearted,
> Lolling the tongue with slaught'ring, having work

> More plentiful than tools to do't, struck down
> Some mortally, some slightly touch'd, some falling
> Merely through fear, that the strait pass was damm'd
> With dead men hurt behind, and cowards living
> To die with length'ned shame.

The shame of the Britons' flight is somewhat assuaged by the fact that within a few minutes the Romans are leading the rout in the opposite direction. A patriotic conclusion of this sort was necessary in any Elizabethan play which matched English forces against aliens; but Shakespeare still makes it quite clear that the concerted valor of a handful of noble Britons, rather than the army at large, effected the change.

In *Coriolanus,* where no comparison of foreigners with Englishmen is implied, Shakespeare presents the cowardice of English soldiers under the thinnest of Roman disguises. After a prodigious curse thrown at his retreating commoners, Coriolanus lambastes their cowardice (I.iv.34):

> You souls of geese
> That bear the shapes of men, how have you run
> From slaves that apes would beat! Pluto and hell!
> All hurt behind! backs red, and faces pale
> With flight and agued fear!

For this damning portrait of Coriolanus' soldiers, Shakespeare was historically justified only by Plutarch's mention of the General's "crying out to the Romans that had turned their backs, and calling them again to fight with a loud voice."[73] That the dramatist's invective had an English rather than Roman inspiration is especially clear in the light of a similar passage in Thomas Heywood's 2 *Edward IV,* some eight years earlier in date than *Coriolanus.* Falconbridge curses his retreating English soldiers:

Why this is to trust to these base rogues,
This dirty scum of rascal peasantry,
This heartless rout of base rascality.
A plague upon you all, you cowardly rogues,
You craven curs, you slimy muddy clowns,
Whose courage but consists in multitude,
Like sheep and neat that follow one another,
Which if one run away, all follow after.[74]

Heywood makes it even clearer than does Shakespeare that he is denouncing not normal Englishmen but the riffraff that made up so large a proportion of Elizabethan armies.

The private soldiers were as slow in advancing to battle as they were fast in retreat. Nonprofessional soldiers have never, of course, been battle-eager. Elizabethan conscripts, however, seem to have had an extraordinary reputation as laggards. This reputation was in part due to the inevitable comparison between them and their officers, particularly the young nobility, who were as famous for a dashing manner of attack as the conscripts were for caution. Whereas the officers often drew lots for the honor of the first onslaught, the commoners would advance "coldly" to the breach.[75] In an Irish action of 1599, the English horse "gave a desperate charge upon the hill, rocks and bogs, where never horse was seen to charge before," with heavy casualties and honor, but in their charge they were seconded by what Sir John Harington called "not Roman citizens, but rascal soldiers, who, so their commanders had been saved, had been worthy to have been half hanged for their rascal cowardliness."[76] Shakespeare has effectively recognized this distinction between nobility and commoner in approach to battle. In Lucrece's "skilful painting, made for

Priam's Troy," the contrast is sharply drawn, and the figures are not Trojans but English (*Lucrece,* line 1387):

> In great commanders grace and majesty
> You might behold triumphing in their faces;
> In youth, quick bearing and dexterity;
> And here and there the painter interlaces
> Pale cowards marching on with trembling paces,
>> Which heartless peasants did so well resemble
>> That one would swear he saw them quake and tremble.

The artistic technique which Shakespeare here applauds is his own, used on more than one occasion. We recall the "interlacing" of noble youths and rabble in *Troilus and Cressida.* In *Henry V,* however, the contrast is brought to life with unusual clarity in two brilliantly juxtaposed scenes. In the first of these scenes, the King is shown directing his noble warriors "once more unto the breach." The second scene shifts the focus to the "grosser blood" element. Bardolph, as lieutenant, is urging his men "On, on, on, on, on! to the breach, to the breach!" But it is doubtful whether either the Lieutenant or his band makes any progress. Nym advises his leader that "the knocks are too hot; and, for mine own part, I have not a case of lives," an opinion judiciously endorsed by Ancient Pistol. But this unofficial council of war is vigorously adjourned by the arrival of Captain Fluellen. "Up to the breach, you dogs!" he roars at the strategists. "Avaunt, you cullions!" Under protest and cudgeling, the band advances, but since Fluellen fails to escort them, they obviously get no farther than is necessary for Bardolph to rob a church. It may be objected that Bardolph's crew are rogues rather than soldiers. Admittedly they are singled out as rascals from the rank and file, and they still carry some of the stage tradition of

Huf, Ruf, and Snuf. But one should not forget Harington's wholesale indictment of his commoners as "rascal soldiers, who ... had been worthy to have been half hanged for their rascal cowardliness."

Under ideal conditions, of course, the superior valor of the nobility would be, instead of a discredit to the common soldiers, an incentive for greater courage themselves. In writing to Cecil for replacements, Mountjoy made a special plea for "as many good spirits, as may be spared, for they must be the soul of the country's body, who ... will not fight but by example."[77] Shakespeare recognizes this quality of common soldiers when he reports their reaction to Hotspur's death (*2 Henry IV* I.i.112):

> In few, his death (whose spirit lent a fire
> Even to the dullest peasant in his camp)
> Being bruited once, took fire and heat away
> From the best-temper'd courage in his troops.

It was the need for exemplary daring that doubtless prompted so many Elizabethan generals—not only Essex, but men with the reasonableness of Mountjoy[78]—to lead an attack in person. There may, accordingly, have been more than impetuosity in Coriolanus' singlehanded assault on Antium. Although at the scene of battle the Romans seem only skeptically impressed by their leader's daring, it is later reported as having been an inspiration to them (II.ii.107):

> He topp'd the fliers
> And by his rare example made the coward
> Turn terror into sport. As waves before
> A vessel under sail, so men obey'd
> And fell below his stem.

Considering the quality of Elizabethan conscripts, however, it was likely that threats would prove more invigorating than would heroic examples. Cudgels got the recruits aboard ship, and both blows and words drove them into battle. On one occasion, Birch reports, Essex's soldiers "went so coldly on, that his lordship was oblig'd, by reproaching their baseness, to drive them into the wood." This "eagerness" of his, according to Birch, "exceedingly improv'd the dulness of the common soldiers, so that, to make amends for their faults, they made a fierce attack on the rebels."⁷⁹ Sir Philip Sidney illustrated, through the person of Philanax, how both invective and example might prevail upon fearful soldiers. "For, crying to them (and asking them whether their backes or their armes were better fighter) he himselfe thrust into the presse."⁸⁰ In the light of these examples, one may well wonder whether Coriolanus' harsh treatment of his army is wholly unwise, particularly since he reënforces it with his own heroism. "Mend and charge home," he growls at his men,

> Or, by the fires of heaven, I'll leave the foe
> And make my wars on you!
>
> (I.iv.39)

And the judicious Captain Fluellen, we recall, beat and cursed the laggards in the direction of the breach.

VII

Although he generally attributes the "coldness" of the common soldiers to plain cowardice, Shakespeare may sometimes lay the blame on the weakness of the cause. This interpretation of soldierly morale was one strongly endorsed by divines, since it suggested, as human incompetence did not, God's hand in battle. The orthodox religious view is summarily put by Sutcliffe: "The cause, as it is good or evill, so either abateth and breaketh, or whetteth the souldiors courage."[81] *The French Academie* goes one logical step further and makes divine favor the sole determiner of fear in battle: "Onely God is able to arm us against this, because it is he that giveth or taketh away the heart of man, that sendeth feare or boldnesse, as pleaseth him." Granted that God has endowed certain men with aptitudes for either fear or courage and the means of using these traits, "yet he hath not subjected himselfe to all those meanes . . . , but hath alwaies reserved in his power both Feare and faintnesse of heart, and boldnes and assurance, which are their contraries." When, therefore, God "is minded to punish men, he taketh away their hearts whom hee will destroy, causing them to tremble and to flie for feare."[82]

Obviously there is none of this Christian doctrine in *Coriolanus,* and it is only faintly outlined in most of the other plays. The fear deriving from a doubtful cause is briefly sketched in *Richard III* when Ratcliff admits that Richard's supporters are "Unarm'd, and unresolv'd" to beat the enemy back (IV.-iv.436). In Macbeth's comparable army, "none serve with him but constrained things, / Whose hearts are absent too" (*Macbeth* V.iv.13). The predicament is more fully expressed in *The Two Noble Kinsmen* (I.ii.95):

> Yet what man
> Thirds his own worth (the case is each of ours)
> When that his action's dregg'd with mind assur'd
> 'Tis bad he goes about.

In none of these plays, however, is the predicament really translated into the thoughts of the ordinary soldier. That it does become so translated in *Henry V,* and almost nowhere else in the Elizabethan drama, is a remarkable distinction—possibly the major distinction of the entire play. There are other studies of ideal generalship and splendid patriotism in the Elizabethan drama; there are none other in which the ideological misgivings of the common soldier are so thoughtfully and sympathetically presented.

Shortly before battle, it will be recalled, Henry makes the rounds of his camp in the guise of an ordinary soldier. Coming upon three enlisted men, he listens to their unenthusiastic forecast of the day before them, their cynicism concerning the King's willingness to share dangers with them, and their uneasiness about the spiritual welfare of soldiers who die in an unjust war. He reassures them on the last two misgivings, but not before he has drawn angry words and a promise of settlement from one of the men.

The unusual role of the three soldiers in this episode is suggested at once by their names. These are not Wart, Bullcalf, or Feeble, but genuine English names of individual dignity: John Bates, Alexander Court, and Michael Williams. Their speech, also, immediately distinguishes them from their predecessors in the drama. They do not talk like clowns, rustics, or simpletons. It would have been easy and natural for Shakespeare to make derisive comedy out of their pessimism. Instead, we find dialogue like the following (IV.i.87):

Court. Brother John Bates, is not that the morning which breaks yonder?

Bates. I think it be; but we have no great cause to desire the approach of day.

Will. We see yonder the beginning of the day, but I think we shall never see the end of it.

These men, like their general, are fearful, but they are not cowards. Bates swears that however brave a pose Henry may make, the King would rather be in the Thames up to the neck; "and so I would he were, and I by him, at all adventures, so we were quit here" (IV.i.118). The attitude is not exemplary, and Henry has to rebuke it; but even the cynicism has a stubborn strength that bodes well. Bates will argue, but he will not mutiny or run away. He is resolved, as he says later, to "fight lustily" for the King (IV.i.201). What troubles him, Williams, and presumably any other intelligent, questioning, but loyal commoner, is the fact that they are fighting a war which has never been explained to them, and in which they may, through no fault of their own, come to a bad end. It is, in part, the desire to reassure soldiers like these that has led Henry to mingle with his men.

"Methinks," he declares as a loyal commoner should, "I could not die anywhere so contented as in the King's company, his cause being just and his quarrel honourable" (IV.i.-131). But this easy attitude only brings to the surface the major source of his soldiers' resentment. "That's more than we know," Williams replies. Bates, however, refuses to get into the controversy about the justness of the cause: "Ay, or more than we should seek after; for we know enough if we know we are the King's subjects. If his cause be wrong, our obedience to the King wipes the crime of it out of us." Bates's attitude was discreet. The subject was a dangerous one in Shakespeare's day since, as Richard Simpson has pointed out, Cardinal Allen had attempted to alienate English soldiers by sowing in their minds scruples "about fighting against Catholic enemies in an unjust war."[58] With Christians fighting Christians, religious justification of warfare was apt to involve extremely nice distinctions—certainly beyond the trustworthy intellectual range of the common soldier, who, as Gosson had declared, was "the fourth and last in concurrence with the war." On the Essex expedition of 1596, a severe decree had prohibited soldiers from conversations like the one Bates and Williams are engaged in: "No man is to dispute of matters of religion, unless to be resolved of some doubts, when he is to confer with the minister of the army, as it is not fit that unlearned men should openly argue of so high and mystical matters. If any person shall forget himself and his duty herein, he shall receive open punishment, and be banished the army."[84] Intelligent caution, therefore, may very well have dictated Bates's refusal to carry on the argument with a strange soldier, possibly someone sent to try their loyalty.

But there was more than discretion in Bates's disinclination to know more. In rejecting responsibility, he had a valid reason for moderate peace of mind. "What the meanest souldier doth," as one writer put it typically, "hee must doe it by authority, which doth warrant him to doe many things, which otherwise were unlawfull."[85] John Norden advised soldiers in 1597 not to be concerned over whether the authority is right or wrong: "As touching the justice and lawfulnes of the cause present, it sufficeth us to know it is to preserve our state, the superiour Magistrate commandeth it, and we are to obey it in a treble dutie, to God, our Soveraigne and commonweale."[86]

Not all writers, however, offered the comfort of a blanket dispensation. In Barret's dialogue between a gentleman and a captain, the former asks whether if one's prince makes war against other Christians, it is "no grudge to the souldiers conscience to fight against them." The captain's reply is cautious:

"I suppose none, for the souldier is bound to serve his Prince, and to defend his desseines; and it toucheth him not, much to examine whether the warre be just or unjust, not being against Gods true religion: but in such a case, I would wish men to be well advised."[87] Fourquevaux is also uncertain about the spiritual future of a commoner killed in a doubtful cause. In order to remove all responsibility from the soldier, he recommends a compulsory levy, which gives men no opportunity to volunteer or refuse.[88] Sutcliffe, one of the most learned of English authorities on the subject, advises soldiers that "if the warres be notoriously unjust, let every man take heed howe hee embrewe his handes in innocent blood." If, however, "the unjustice of the warres be not notorious, the subject is bound to pay and serve, and the guilt shall be laide to his charge that commandeth him to serve," an opinion supported by reference to St. Augustine.[89]

The commoner in Henry's army had been given no opportunity of knowing whether the King's aggressive warfare against fellow Christians was "notoriously unjust." Presumably he had learned nothing of the King's questioning of the prelates, "May I with right and conscience make this claim?" (I.ii.96), or of the Archbishop's reply, "The sin upon my head, dread sovereign!" It is therefore with some semblance of reason that Williams, as the most stubbornly thoughtful of Henry's soldiers, refuses to be content with Bates's comfortable attitude. Williams pursues the inquiry (IV.i.140):

But if the cause be not good, the King himself hath a heavy reckoning to make when all those legs and arms and heads, chopp'd off in a battle, shall join together at the latter day and cry 'We died at such a place!' some swearing, some crying for a surgeon, some upon their wives left poor behind them, some upon the debts they owe, some upon their children rawly left. I am afeard there are few die well that die in battle; for how can they charitably dispose of anything when blood is their argument? Now, if these men do not die well, it will be a black matter for the King that led them to it; who to disobey were against all proportion of subjection.

Williams' argument, perhaps the most beautifully literate and logical statement made by any of Shakespeare's commoners, is answered patiently and sympathetically by the disguised King. The gist of Henry's answer is to be found in the parable with which he begins his explanation: "So, if a son that is by his father sent about merchandise do sinfully miscarry upon the sea, the imputation of his wickedness, by your rule, should be imposed upon the father that sent him." Obviously, as the King says, "this is not so." Nor, by analogy, is the sovereign "bound to answer the particular endings of his soldiers." Even a king whose cause is spotless is unable to muster an army consisting entirely of unspotted soldiers. Men who were scoundrels in peacetime are now, regardless of the cause for which they fight, liable to God's punishment which they escaped in peace. "Then if they die unprovided, no more is the King guilty of their damnation than he was before guilty of those impieties for the which they are now visited. Every subject's duty is the King's, but every subject's soul is his own." Therefore, let every soldier purge his own offenses in preparation for death in battle.

Williams appears satisfied by this explanation: "'Tis certain, every man that dies ill, the ill upon his own head—the King is not to answer it." And probably Shakespeare himself was satisfied by it—at least by its eloquence and sincerity. As a *logical* answer to Williams' perplexity, it leaves something to be desired; and one may even suspect a baffled, tentative quality in Williams' acquiescence. The truth of the matter—whether Shakespeare intended it or not—is that the King has explained away only a fraction of what is troubling Williams.

The soldier, in his simple, dogged way, has a real point. "But if the cause be *not* good," is his premise. The King in his argument makes no mention of a bad cause; the entire premise of his argument is a *good* cause. The parable of the father depends for its meaning upon a blameless venture and a blameworthy son. Williams, on the contrary, was talking about a blameworthy venture and a blameless soldier. At least he was so talking during the first part of his speech—the longest and most effective part. There he expresses the plight of mutilated bodies at the "latter day," the destitute wives and children, the debts unpaid. What if these victims of war were virtuous men damned because they fought in a bad cause? The King does not answer this question. Instead he concentrates upon the last part of Williams' speech—the segment beginning "I am afeard there are few die well that die in battle; for how can they charitably dispose of anything when blood is their argument?" This segment was an unlucky addition as far as Williams was concerned. What he wanted to say, judging from his earlier words, is that it is difficult to die well in an unjust battle. The idea he actually conveys before he is done is manifestly imperfect, and invites an eloquent rather than a nicely logical rejoinder: it is that soldiers, because of their own sinfulness and the sinfulness of war in general, cannot die piously in battle. It is easy for Henry to interpret this as an attempted defense of wicked soldiers in war—scoundrels who would place upon the king responsibility for their own transgressions. Williams of course had no intention of pleading on behalf of wicked soldiers—men who, in Henry's words, "have on them the guilt of premeditated and contrived murther;...of beguiling virgins with the broken seals of perjury;...making the wars their bulwark, that have before gored the gentle bosom of peace with pillage and robbery." Henry is understandably able to wax eloquent and persuasive on this theme, and probably that is what Shakespeare wanted. Williams had to be put down; and Shakespeare probably recognized that mere logic can never allay the most fundamental misgivings of common soldiers.

What is important in the episode is that in it Shakespeare gave such a rare credibility and authority to the perplexed mind of a soldier, recognizing that not all soldiers were clowns or rogues. As Brents Stirling has said of Williams' speech, "If humanity is the capacity to entertain, not only intellectually but also emotionally, the views of less fortunate men, we have it here in generous measure."[90] Here, certainly, for the first and last time in Shakespeare, is a recognition of the views of the "less fortunate" soldiers expressed by the soldiers themselves. In Falstaff, of course, there is an equally telling expression of soldierly cynicism; but Falstaff's cynicism is a hard, intellectual sort. It is not the spontaneous, humble expression of a lesser intelligence actually undergoing and trying to master personal inadequacies in the face of battle. Williams may not be so brilliant a character study as the far more famous Falstaff; but, if only because there is not (except for his impoverished relative Feeble) a close parallel to him in the Elizabethan drama, he is as an artistic achievement equally astonishing.

CHAPTER V

War and Peace

One would expect Shakespeare, as a competent student of society, to distinguish between war and peace as basic settings for human activity; and it does not seem especially noteworthy to say that he usually does so. One is therefore surprised to find that this distinction has been almost ignored in the main body of Shakespearean criticism. Whereas the finest shadings of imagery and of diction have been studied in an attempt to wrest the full meaning from the plays, few critics have presumed to ask so broad a question as whether the background for the play was war or peace, or what difference either of these made in the drama. The major exception to this critical indifference has been Lily B. Campbell's study of Renaissance attitudes toward war and peace in *Henry V.*[1] That this study resulted in possibly the first basic interpretation of this deceptively simple play, emphasizes what should be done for Shakespeare's plays generally.

---

[1] For notes to chapter v, see pages 326–329.

The subject is admittedly a large one. Within the bounds of this chapter I can hope merely to describe a few of Shakespeare's habitual uses of Renaissance concepts of war and peace, and to suggest that these concepts not only are of considerable sociological interest but tend often to be of central importance in setting the scene for the drama.

II

It will be advisable to begin—as Shakespeare usually does—with peace, and to question at once the common assumption that the term connoted nothing more positive than an absence of war. It tended, rather, to describe a political condition, a social atmosphere, more troubling and more provocative of human drama than its usual associations of concord and tranquility. The pleasant meanings are, of course, occasionally to be found.[2] But when Shakespeare wishes to indicate an ideal peace—as he does in Burgundy's great speech in *Henry V* or in Cranmer's prophecy in *Henry VIII*—he takes pains to emphasize it as an ideal, to distinguish it from its usual associations in his plays. In thus giving peace a frequently ominous or unwholesome connotation, Shakespeare was but sharing with his countrymen a pessimism encouraged by current political writings and events.

Although most Elizabethans did not like war, they had small encouragement to develop a corresponding delight in peace. Publications did appear in praise of peace, but these could scarcely have been heard in the larger and louder company of books which spoke of the dangers of unwarlike states. Most of these were the writings of military alarmists, who made themselves audible in one of the largest volleys of tracts ever discharged in Elizabethan England.[3] If they accomplished nothing else, these stern soldiers must have deprived the public of any possible contentment during peacetime. Thomas Churchyard, to cite only one of the most vociferous, dourly compared peace to calm weather "that smoethly loeks tyll doskye clowds, have clean oercast the ayre."[4] Not only soldiers but men in high public position helped arouse anxiety concerning peace. Dudley Digges considered "warre sometimes lesse hurtfull, and more to be wisht in a well governed State than peace," and tried to "disswade bewitched men from ease and pleasure, two seducing Syrens in whose beastly servitude too too many are inthralled past recoverie."[5] The Earl of Essex again and again pleaded, with all his immense popular appeal, against a treaty with Spain, and not simply because of its precariousness. More positively, he foresaw Englishmen "growen generally unwarlike; in love with the name, and bewitched with the delights of peace."[6] On the stage the public could see spectacular dramatizations of the militarists' admonitory tracts. *A Larum for London* (1602), which belonged to Shakespeare's company, presented a frightening picture of the sack of Antwerp, a prosperous city with peace-loving citizens,

> Their bodies us'd to soft effeminate silkes,
> And their nice mindes set all on dalliance,
> Which makes them fat for slaughter, fit for spoile.[7]

The Coblers Prophesie (1594), another stage enactment of an "alarm" tract, demonstrated how a proud, content, sinful land—contemptuous of the soldier's trade—suffers from "heavens ire" in the form of war.[8]

Religious spokesmen took an almost equally troubled view of terrestrial peace. In their war against Anti-Christ, Protestant ministers offered spiritual encouragement to soldiers and sailors.[9] Those who did not serve as military chaplains could still exhort warriors and harass civilians from the pulpit. But a more fundamental reason than Anti-Christ inclined churchmen against an advocacy of peace. From St. Augustine and the older Church still survived a distrust of perfect concord on earth, where life itself was warfare. The Spaniard was regarded as "a pricke and thorne to Englishmen, insomuch as we shall never bee so assured of peace, but wee may alwaies live in suspition of warre."[10] And in times of peace sin was especially rife. Many Elizabethan sermons consequently had an alarmist purpose comparable to that of the soldier authors.[11] Congregations were reminded of the deceptive comforts of peacetime by the fates of luxurious cities like Nineveh and Jerusalem.

It is significant that military writers should have found religious authority to be so suitable to their own purposes: that Barnaby Rich, for example, should quote from Osorio da Fonseca in his *Allarme to England:* "Christe hath especially commended us into peace: no doubt, that peace hee hath commended, which hee him selfe gave us, which doth not consist in pleasant reste and quietnes . . . but that peace, by the which we were reconciled into the grace and favour of God."[12] Geoffrey Gates, another alarmist, likewise uses religious authority to warn his nation against the enjoyment of peace: "When the Lord meaneth to plague a wicked nation for sinne and to translate them to the power and scepter of another nation: then he filleth them with the fatnesse of the earth, and geeveth them peace that they may wax rotten in idleness, and become of dulle wittes, and slowe of courage, weak handed, and feeble kneede."[13]

Of the pernicious qualities of peace which Shakespeare might exploit for his plays, there was one which lay most ready to the hand of any dramatist: its deceptiveness. It was this quality, conveyed always with the broadest of irony, that formed the sole dramatic value of the alarmist plays. The formula for dramatic episodes was to depict first the complacency, then the disillusionment. Both parts of this formula lent themselves to a lively staging. In *A Larum for London,* the Dutch, "merry at theyr Feast ... sit swilling in the pride of their excesse," just as Danila orders a cannon to be discharged on them. Their grim enlightenment is indicated by the stage direction: "A great screeke heard within."[14]

Shakespeare did not write alarmist plays, but neither was he indifferent to their popular appeal. An apt discipleship is shown in *Coriolanus,* when he depicts the complacency of the plebs and their tribunes after they have apparently banished, with their disturbing warrior, all civil dissension. At the very time when the exiled General is burning his path toward Rome, Sicinius is commenting on Rome's newly won peace (IV.vi.2):

> We hear not of him, neither need we fear him:
> His remedies are tame. The present peace
> And quietness of the people, which before
> Were in wild hurry here, do make his friends
> Blush that the world goes well.

Apart from this ironic stereotype, the passage as a whole leaves one impressed with the recurrent menace of war, a menace of which the tribunes and populace are oblivious. Early in the play the Volscians are preparing for war; and even before Coriolanus offers the enemy his services, they are planning another invasion.

Indeed, Shakespeare's interest in the deceptiveness of peace is not limited to its value in building scenes of dramatic irony. Persistent commentaries throughout his works betray a deeper concern with its menace. Hector, though opposed to the futile Trojan war, agrees that "the wound of peace is surety, / Surety secure" (*Troilus and Cressida* II.ii.14). The Dauphin in *Henry V,* foolishly contemptuous of the English threat, is yet well enough versed in Elizabethan military philosophy to mouth what is wrong with his country (II.iv.15):

> It is most meet we arm us 'gainst the foe;
> For peace itself should not so dull a kingdom
> (Though war nor no known quarrel were in question)
> But that defences, musters, preparations
> Should be maintain'd, assembled, and collected,
> As were a war in expectation.

Treaties of peace have a curiously unpleasant role in Shakespeare's plays, being almost always viewed as deceptive or humiliating. In *King John,* France withdraws

> From a resolv'd and honourable war,
> To a most base and vile-concluded peace.
>   (II.i.585)

And John's reconciliation with Cardinal Pandulph is with some reason called an "inglorious league" and "base truce" (V.i.65–68), while an earlier concord is termed a "painted peace" (III.i.105). "I speak of peace," Rumour acknowledges at the beginning of *2 Henry IV,* "while covert enmity, / Under the smile of safety, wounds the world." The mockery of professed concord is dramatized not only in the notorious treaty in this play but in the cynicism of the French truce in *1 Henry VI*. In this latter instance, Alençon advises the Dauphin to "take this compact of a truce, / Although you break it when your pleasure serves" (V.iv.163); yet this truce is referred to by the English as a "solemn peace."

So consistently pessimistic is Shakespeare's picture of truces, that one may wonder whether it does not betray a personal bias. But his bias need have been merely that of any loyal citizen. As an Englishman, he could have had only the most vexing memories of trust placed in the good faith of the enemy. An authorized "Psalm and Collect of Thanksgiving" for 1588 complained of the Spaniards, "They communed of peace, and prepared for most cruel war; for they think that no faith nor truth is to be kept with us, but that they may feign, dissemble, break promise, swear, and forswear, so they may deceive us and take us unawares, and oppress us suddenly."[15] Later Spanish tenders of amity provoked even keener distrust. In 1596, one writer warned against rumors of peace: "I pray GOD there be not some false-harted subjects amongst us, that give out reports of peace for some ill purpose, when they are perswaded the Spanyard is approaching."[16] Rumour's speech in 2 *Henry IV* may be topical in mirroring English reaction to a proffered treaty of 1598.

But defeat and humiliation resulting from a deceptive peace have limitations as subjects for thoughtful drama; and if the subject of peace had connoted nothing more than this for Elizabethans, Shakespeare would not have used it in his more sophisticated plays. In actuality, the subject had less spectacular aspects which conduced to serious, probing studies of society. Although in these aspects the enemy was of minor interest, the function of war was all-important. When, therefore, we study the aspects of peace that were available to Shakespeare for his subtler portraits of society, we must study

them as they were conventionally studied in Elizabethan
treatises and plays: from the point of view of their corrective
counterpart in war. It is war rather than peace that is the
clearer, dominant force.

III

What is essentially Shakespeare's complete dramatic program
for the concept of war is conveniently stated in Arcite's great
prayer to Mars in *The Two Noble Kinsmen.*[17] There are two
parts to this prayer: the supplication and the acknowledgment. In the former, Mars is praised purely in awe of his
splendid, amoral power:

> Thou mighty one that with thy power hast turn'd
> Green Neptune into purple; [whose approach]
> Comets prewarn; whose havoc in vast field
> Unearthed skulls proclaim; whose breath blows down
> The teeming Ceres' foison; who dost pluck
> With hand armipotent from forth blue clouds
> The mason'd turrets; that both mak'st and break'st
> The stony girths of cities.

This is the war of the sonnets: a pagan, destructive, but
wonderful power, described always in lines of appropriate
strength. So, in Sonnet 55:

> When wasteful war shall statues overturn,
> And broils root out the work of masonry,
> Nor Mars his sword nor war's quick fire shall burn
> The living record of your memory.

In its lack of Christian purpose, usually one of correction,
this aspect of war is well suited to the pagan world of the
sonnets.[18] But its very lack of motive makes it ill suited to
the needs of thoughtful drama. Only spectacle or language

could make it impressive on the stage, and Shakespeare employs it only where he cannot suitably employ a more philosophical—usually Christian—concept. It is almost invariably associated with Mars or Bellona. The prelude to Bertram's rather pointless warring in *All's Well That Ends Well* is the young gallant's speech dedicating himself to Mars (III.iii.8). Hotspur's notion of war does not extend beyond Bellona and Mars as slaughterers. To the "fire-ey'd maid of smoky war" he will offer up the enemy "all hot and bleeding," while "the mailed Mars shall on his altar sit / Up to the ears in blood." (*1 Henry IV* IV.i.114–117). *Henry V* is a more complex mixture of pagan spectacle and Christian purpose, of which only the former need be noted here. Shakespeare's Prologue complains of the inadequacy of the stage for dramatizing so grand a martial spectacle when he describes Henry in terms of Mars:

> Then should the warlike Harry, like himself,
> Assume the port of Mars, and at his heels
> (Leash'd in, like hounds) should famine, sword, and fire
> Crouch for employment.

The same figure is used by Holinshed, except that Bellona appears there instead of Mars.[19] We shall presently see that more than stage limitations deterred Shakespeare from fully employing this hint.

The second part of Arcite's prayer complements the first by describing war's more purposeful aspects:

> O great corrector of enormous times,
> Shaker of o'er-rank states, thou grand decider
> Of dusty and old titles, that heal'st with blood
> The earth when it is sick, and cur'st the world
> O' th' plurisy of people!

With one omission, these lines account for every sociological use made of warfare in Shakespeare; and the one omitted function—healing or diverting civil dissension—is easily related to the others. All have a corrective purpose.

Of the functions of war employed by Shakespeare, we may most conveniently take up the less complex first. "Grand decider of dusty and old titles" is not usually a clearly defined purpose for warfare in Shakespeare, though the endless fighting described in the English histories is superficially directed toward this end. Only in *Henry V* is the question of "dusty and old" titles talked about, and even in this play that question cannot be said to give the war its principal meaning. Like the idea expressed by the Prologue, the question of titles is obscured as soon as Shakespeare settles upon a worthier basis for his hero's military crusade.

Curing the world of its "plurisy of people" is likewise rarely mentioned as a motive. Only one clear reference is made to it, and this is not the real purpose of the war referred to. Coriolanus, hearing that the Volscians are again in arms, expresses his pleasure (I.i.229): "I am glad on't. Then we shall ha' means to vent / Our musty superfluity." The social need that Plutarch treats at length and with understanding—that of sending superfluous Romans to populate a devastated town—is by Shakespeare reduced to this one reference. No facts in the play, except the populace's ridiculously expressed need for grain, suggest a plethora of people. If Shakespeare deliberately minimized this subject, it was not because it was no longer a live one in his day. The use of war to control population was soberly contemplated by Elizabethan thinkers and statesmen. Ralegh foresaw how arithmetical progression in population might lead princes to make wars for reasons of which they were unaware.[20] And Ralegh's theory was discreetly abstract compared with others. Certain commanders, according to Sir John Smythe, expressed their pleasure in the heavy mortality among the English, contending (much in the perverse manner of Coriolanus) that these "were the very scomme, theeves, and roges of England . . . and that the Realme (being too full of people) is very well ridde of them."[21] That Shakespeare did not expect his audience to endorse this severe attitude may appear from his placing it in the irresponsible mouth of Captain Falstaff. Sir John complacently accepts the grim fate awaiting his conscripts by regarding them as "the cankers of a calm world and a long peace" (*1 Henry IV* IV.ii.33).

With another controversial function of war, however, Shakespeare is more troublesomely noncommittal. His wars deliberately undertaken as a cure for domestic discord are seldom placed in a definitive context. They leave one uncertain how to view the characters who initiate them.

The earliest appearance of this ambiguity in Shakespeare is the easiest to analyze. Clifford, pleading with the "rabblement" to forsake Cade and his revolutionary claims, appeals to their common grievance against the French. While the English "live at jar," Clifford warns, the French may take advantage of "this civil broil"; better far that ten thousand Cades miscarry than that an Englishman should stoop to a Frenchman's mercy. Therefore,

> To France, to France, and get what you have lost!
> Spare England, for it is your native coast.
> (*2 Henry VI* IV.viii.43–52)

Modern readers, schooled in the economic interpretation of history, may censure this plea for diverting, as it triumphantly does, the people from their intended reform. But there is little likelihood that the Elizabethan audience, having been moved to tears by Talbot's stand against the French, would now hear anything more subtle in this appeal than a trumpeting to their manhood.

The philosophy of war in the foregoing episode is never explicitly identified as a political device. It is so identified, and therefore more conspicuously invites criticism, in 2 *Henry IV*, where it appears as the King's advice to his son (IV.v.213):

> Therefore, my Harry,
> Be it thy course to busy giddy minds
> With foreign quarrels, that action, hence borne out,
> May waste the memory of the former days.

This counsel is not one likely to endear Henry to present-day readers. But that Shakespeare intended it to stigmatize the King is questionable. In the first place, he had earlier announced—publicly and candidly—his intention to end English civil war by launching a crusade. Secondly, at the end of 2 *Henry IV*, when only patriotic sentiments are appropriate, Prince John prophesies that the English will bear their "civil swords and native fire / As far as France" (V.v.112). It is true that in *Henry V*, a play which can use only exemplary motives, Henry's advice is never allowed to become overt. But this could well be because Shakespeare found somewhat more stirring grounds for an ideal English war.

Admittedly, the evidence is still ambiguous. The most that can be said is that Shakespeare does not betray any decisive distaste for foreign war as a cure for civil dissension. Those who would seek in his plays a clearer partisanship might first try their hand on the utterances of nondramatic writers from whom a forthright statement could reasonably be expected.

La Noue, wisest of contemporary military philosophers, is as noncommittal as Shakespeare in discussing this function of war as a "polytik rule ... which many verie excellent persons both have and still doe allowe." He describes the "rule" with objective accuracy: "A great estate replenished with warlike people, ought still to have some foreine warre wherewith to keepe it occupied, least beeing at quiet they convert their weapons each against the other."[22] But aside from reporting the case for and against the rule, and arguing against drastic remedy, La Noue does not decisively take sides. Among English writers I have found only two, Ralegh and Digges, who betray any partiality. Ralegh is the more cautious of the two, for he merely explains the case for foreign war as an inescapable predicament presented by historical laws: "And it is more plain there is not in nature a point of stability to be found; everything either ascends or declines: when wars are ended abroad, sedition begins at home, and when men are freed from fighting for necessity, they quarrel through ambition."[23] The fact that Ralegh found this view in Machiavelli's *Discorsi* may help to explain English reticence on the subject.[24]

The least reticent by far of Elizabethan authorities was Dudley Digges, whose *Foure Paradoxes, or Politique Discourses* constituted perhaps the most candid description of the prevailing English military policy to reach print. Although Digges later got into trouble through his outspokenness, he was but putting down the logical interpretation of what he had observed. The government did, as Cruickshank has recently pointed out, employ conscription to quiet unrest at home, as well as to increase its military strength.[25] And occasionally it seems to have connived at the drafting of social undesirables for the sake of domestic peace.[26] Digges does not, however, go so far as to cite English policy as evidence. He describes, rather, how Philip II held his nation, "of a rebellious disposition," in harmony, "by keeping his active subjects in continual employment, farre from home, where there Eaglelike piercing eyes might not come to prie into his Actions, nor malitiously observe the distastes his government occasioned." So dramatically disruptive is peace, Digges believes, that if no war happens to be spontaneously available, governments should look about for enemies.[27]

Digge's most interesting historical evidence, for its bearing upon Shakespeare, is what he calls "the wise proceeding of the Senate of Rome in Coriolanus time." For, so he interprets Plutarch,

the populousnesse of that Citie, by reason of their peace occasioning a dearth and famine, and their idlenesse stirring up lewd fellowes to exasperate the desperate need and envious malice of the meaner sort, against the nobility, whose pride and luxurie grown through sloth intolerable, caused them to contemne and injurie the poorer people, ... then the Senate ... were at length enforced to flie to this medicine, which wisely applied before, had well prevented all those causes, and their unhappie effectes. Then they resolved on a warre with the Volsces to ease their City of that dearth, by diminishing their number, and appease those tumultuous broyles, by drawing poore with rich, and the meane sort with the Nobilitie, into one campe, or service, and one selfesame daunger: sure means to procure love and quietnesse in a contentious common wealth.... [Despite the excellence of this plan] there wanted not home tarrying housedoves, two peacebred tribunes Sicimus [sic.] and Brutus, [who] hindered that resolution calling it crueltie, and it may be some now will condemne this course, as changing for the worse.[28]

The passage is valuable as an interpretation of Plutarch that invites comparison with Shakespeare's. Here, more prominent than in the play, is the dearth and the proposed remedy, which Digges ascribes to the Senate, and not to an isolated militarist. Even more striking are divergences in the martial remedy for civil dissension. Shakespeare, differing from both Plutarch and Digges, does not expressly employ this remedy at all. And it is this omission, hitherto unnoticed by critics, that marks one of the dramatist's most puzzling departures from his source. Shakespeare could easily and consistently have retained Plutarch's political motivation for the Roman war, assigning it either to the Senate or, if he wished to limit it to an erratic spokesman, to Coriolanus. Instead, a distorted fragment of it is expended, totally out of place, on the Volscian servingmen near the end of the play. One servingman deplores peace because "it makes men hate one another," and the other adds that it does so "because they then less need one another. The wars for my money!" (IV.v.246–248). Shakespeare surely did not mean to entrust the political moral of his play to the muddled intelligence of clownish menials, even though these might conceivably have learned their philosophy from their masters. The only certain meaning in the episode is a comic one, appropriate to a farcical interlude: Elizabethan servingmen were exempt from conscription (Falstaff is able to "press" only *discarded* unjust servingmen").[29]

But if the theory of foreign war as a cure for dissension is not expressly present as a motivation in *Coriolanus,* its influence survives in the play's action. War *does* heal the rift between plebs and patricians. The tribunes and citizens who are bravely calling for reform as the play opens slink away when war is announced. And upon the General's return, Rome forgets its differences as all classes come out to welcome

him. It is only when the unifying excitement of war has sub-
sided that domestic troubles begin again. And Shakespeare
parallels Digges in showing the "peacebred tribunes" as
stirrers of sedition. In war they fade away; upon the resump-
tion of peace they go again into action. They become almost
symbols of the ferment habitually troubling a peaceful society.

Why did not Shakespeare make explicit use of the military
philosophy which he embodies in the play? As in *Henry V,*
the most likely answer is that other dramatic emphases made
this political message inconvenient. The best clue to Shakespeare's intention is the reason he *does* assign for the war. It
is defensive and necessary, whereas Plutarch's (and Digges's)
was offensive and voluntary. And only one obvious reason is
possible for this change: to make the demurring plebs and
tribunes appear ignoble and at the same time make more
prominent an ideal that rises above the imperfect characters—
the ideal of Rome itself.[30] With Rome presented as a state in
danger, individuals will be judged by how well they respond
to the national challenge. Populace and tribunes would, for
partisan gains, leave their city vulnerable to aggression; Coriolanus, on the other hand, serves Rome magnificently in war,
but is, as we shall see in the next chapter, an encumbrance in
times of peace.

Coriolanus does, then, conspicuously involve war and
peace, and shows, though in subordinate dramatic position,
the domestic hazards of peace and the temporary blessings
of war. It does not, however, betray any more than does
Henry V Shakespeare's partisanship in the question of busy-
ing "giddy minds in foreign quarrels." Though he is now
inescapably aware of this issue in his materials, and though
his contemporary Digges interpreted them vitally in terms of

current problems, Shakespeare still, and finally, refuses to use this issue as a significant motive for war. At best it can be said that he shows the principle effectively at work. And it is probably more than accidental that only Henry IV, Shakespeare's master of *Realpolitik,* actually formulates the principle in words. Others may silently put it into action; he alone seems to understand it as a philosophy.

Related to the above in severe political function is the role of war described by Arcite in the phrase "Shaker of o'er-rank states." The rankness, the decadence, the excessive civilization to be corrected are consistently attributed by Renaissance thinkers to a decline in warlike aptitude. Essex was not alone in fearing an English treaty with Spain because of its damage to the fiber of Englishmen. Sir John Smythe is speaking with an authority larger than that of a military alarmist when he places "long peace" first of two things that have "been the occasion of the great decay, and oftentimes, the utter ruine of many great Empires." This decay comes after "great warres to divers Nations that have had notable Milicias and exercises Militarie in great perfection, [when] they by enjoying long peace, have so much given themselves to covetousness, effeminacies and superfluities." These declining nations yield eminence to hardy peoples beginning to develop their militias.[31] Now a historical commonplace, this principle of war and peace was still a subject of disturbing interest to Elizabethans. The thesis that war ennobles nations is cited by Digges as one of his *Foure Paradoxes.* Fulke Greville also treats it as a troubling paradox. Inquiring,

> What is the cause, why States, that war and win,
> Have honour, and breed men of better fame,
> Than States in peace, since war and conquest sin
> In bloud, wrong liberty, all trades of shame?

he suggests as an answer:

> *Peace is a quiet Nurse*
> *Of Idlenesse,* and Idlenesse the field,
> Where wit and Power change all seedes to the worse.[32]

But a purely sociological explanation was not enough for most Elizabethans, and so Geoffrey Gates adds to this the reassurance of divine purpose when he explains national decline in a passage cited earlier in this chapter. His thesis, it will be remembered, was that when the Lord wishes to plague a wicked people and "translate" them to the power of another nation, he gives them peace and luxury.

It is this Christianized version of Mars as "Shaker of o'er-rank states" that Shakespeare uses for his philosophy of war in *Henry V.* The French, as Miss Campbell points out, are represented as a nation vain, secure, idle, and soft.[33] They would have interested both military alarmists and divines. The English, on the other hand, represent the ascendant type of nation in Gates's thesis: "And likewise when the Lord meaneth to advance a nation and to make any people famous and honourable upon earth: he stirreth them up to high courage, and maketh their mindes and bodyes apt to the warre, and in all points sufficient for the pursuite and accomplishment of militarie travaile."[34] Henry V's Englishmen are not wanting in these virtues. The Dauphin ruefully complains (III.v.28):

> Our madams mock at us and plainly say
> Our mettle is bred out, and they will give
> Their bodies to the lust of English youth
> To new-store France with bastard warriors.

Indeed, so impressive does Shakespeare make the lustiness of the English that one suspects an elementary chauvinism to have been his original interest and the military philosophy an afterthought. Actually, of course, the unphilosophical chauvinism was not Shakespeare's contribution to the story. *The Famous Victories of Henry the Fifth,* representative of what English audiences had long wanted to hear about Henry's warring, has virtually no military philosophy at all, and Holinshed has Henry's piety without the philosophy.

But to say that Shakespeare provided a thoughtful military basis for a story traditionally lacking in one is not to say that the basis proved altogether desirable. To be sure, it makes a better ideal for Henry's warring than the elaborate argumentation about "dusty and old titles," relegated by Shakespeare to a suspiciously motivated sponsorship by the churchmen.[35] Nor is there, as we noted in the third chapter, any question that Henry's pious execution of the war is ideal. Critics have, nevertheless, been persistently troubled by something false about the play, and have even suspected deliberate satire. The fault is more likely to be found in the unsuitability of the subject for thoughtful drama. In attempting to dignify Henry with exemplary purposes and conduct, while refusing to discard the cruder excitements, the arrogance, the personal vindication of *The Famous Victories,* Shakespeare forces his hero into the position of a hypocrite. The fact that popular audiences have proved less resistant than have critics to the play suggests that its military philosophy is now lost in the theater.

By far the most important social function of war in the Shakespearean drama is that described by Arcite as "great corrector of enormous times ... that heal'st with blood the earth when it is sick." This function is more fully expounded by Barnabe Barnes in a political treatise appearing just a few years before *The Two Noble Kinsmen.* War, states Barnes, "is the noble corrector of all prodigal states, a skillful blood-letter against all dangerous obstructions and plurasies of peace, the most soveraigne purgation of all superfluous and spreading humours or leprosies, which can breed in any generall politicke body."[36]

The peace-bred imperfections of a state are described in morbid imagery by so many Elizabethan writers that peace itself becomes almost synonymous with disease. Thus Fulke Greville in "A Treatise of Monarchy":

> So doth the War and her impiety
> Purge the imposthum'd humors of a Peace,
> Which oft else makes good government decrease.[37]

Churchyard visualizes peace as "a swelling soer, that festers sowndest mynd and so bursts owtt in bylls, in botch or ulcerrs greatt."[38] There is an important tendency to select a hidden type of disease to describe the sinister workings of peace. John Norden, asking why England must, in the apparently peaceful year of 1596, fear aggression, answers that "the bodie may be most sicke when it feeleth no griefe at all.... And therefore saith the wise man, A disease knowen is in a manner cured."[39]

The concealed nature of the disease has dramatic significance. Whereas the didactic war plays of minor authors suppress none of the morbid symptoms, Shakespeare's better plays, concerned primarily with personal relationships, must keep sociological considerations in the background. There they need not be uninfluential. The background workings of

peace can be the more realistic in the light of its conventionally hidden activity. *Hamlet,* compared with dramas of a
res publica theme, does not make constant reference to morbid peace. That this social condition is none the less important is manifest from Hamlet's description of its nature
(IV.iv.27):

> th' imposthume of much wealth and peace,
> That inward breaks, and shows no cause without
> Why the man dies.

Consonant with the notion of peace as a disease, the corrective work of war is viewed as therapy. "Warre," writes
Sir William Cornwallis, "is the remedy for a State surfeited
with peace, it is a medicine for Commonwealths sicke of too
much ease and tranquilitie."[40] So Shakespeare's Archbishop
of York appears (2 *Henry IV* IV.i.63)

> awhile like fearful war
> To diet rank minds, sick of happiness,
> And purge th' obstructions which begin to stop
> Our very veins of life.

Is there, then, as Samuel Daniel asks,

> no means but that a sin-sick land
> Must be let blood with such a boist'rous hand?[41]

Shakespeare's answer is usually, though not always, No. Pala-
mon prays that "peace might purge / For her repletion,"[42]
but the purgation of Creon's corrupt city is accomplished only
by Theseus' invading army. Providence may work in *Hamlet*
through its scourge and minister, the Prince, but Fortinbras
enters finally, with "warlike noise" and "warlike volley," as
a not too subtle assurance that a more drastic remedy was

available. Elizabethan sermons on war stress that only if a nation effects its own cure can it escape less discriminate purgation by an alien force. For this purpose, the menace of Spain was always in the offing. Since Hamlet is largely responsible for purging what is rotten in the state of Denmark, there is more reason than has usually been recognized that he should be borne "like a soldier" in death and "the soldiers' music and the rites of war / Speak loudly for him."

In *Macbeth,* more typically, the sick country must be purged by war. Macbeth himself asks of the doctor a question similar to Samuel Daniel's—whether there is any remedy for his sick land that "would scour these English hence" (V.iii.50):

> If thou couldst, doctor, cast
> The water of my land, find her disease,
> And purge it to a sound and pristine health,
> I would applaud thee to the very echo,
> That should applaud again.

But even before the question is put, the Scotch exiles, their entry announced by "drum and colours," are marching to meet Malcolm, "the med'cine of the sickly weal," to pour "in our country's purge / Each drop of us" (V.ii.27–29). Salisbury, in *King John,* regrets that he is summoned to apply the surgery of war to the "sore of time" suffered by his country, and that he must "heal the inveterate canker of one wound / By making many." It grieves his soul that he must be a "widow-maker,"

> But such is the infection of the time
> That, for the health and physic of our right,
> We cannot deal but with the very hand
> Of stern injustice and confused wrong.
> (V.ii.12–23)

Coriolanus sees himself as more than a private individual seeking revenge, when he turns against his "cank'red country" (IV.v.96). And Tullus Aufidius, in the same play, understands his own role as a corrective one: "pouring war / Into the bowels of ungrateful Rome" (IV.v.134).

The therapeutic function of war assumes a still more satisfying and orthodox meaning when it becomes the scourge of God. "War is nothing else," writes one religious spokesman, "but a divine scourge for sinne."⁴³ However, neither the divinely ordered war nor its agent need be exemplary. Otherwise, why should the Spaniards be feared? How might their barbarous tactics be reconciled with a divine purpose? Marlowe's Tamburlaine, as Professor Battenhouse has demonstrated, is not disqualified by his own wickedness from serving the purposes of God.⁴⁴ Shakespeare's Clifford recognizes both the divine sponsorship of war and its diabolical aspects when he exclaims (2 *Henry VI* V.ii.33):

> O war, thou son of hell,
> Whom angry heavens do make their minister.

And Henry V acts as an avowedly blameless part of "impious war, / Array'd in flames like to the prince of fiends," when like Tamburlaine he demands that Harfleur either yield or suffer the ravaging of virgins and spitting of infants on soldiers' pikes (III.iii.15). His war (despite a personal vexation with the Dauphin) is not for himself, but God: "War is his beadle, war is his vengeance" (IV.i.176). Even so selfish a monarch as King John sees himself as "God's wrathful agent" (II.i.87).

Despite the frequency with which war appears in Shakespeare as a corrective, there is only one of his plays in which this function rivals human friction as a center of interest; and this play, *Timon of Athens,* is significantly weak as a study in character, strong as a study in society. Timon himself, as has been increasingly recognized,[45] is not built like other Shakespearean tragic heroes. What happens to him personally is not important in the way that the sufferings of Othello and Lear are important. Timon's excesses and misfortunes have meaning primarily as they relate to his Athens, where he is the most prodigal citizen of a society in the conventional last stages of peace. These stages are part of a larger cycle—commonly accepted by Renaissance thinkers—carrying a nation irresistibly from war to peace, from peace to war. The full cycle is thus described by one writer: "Warre bringeth ruine, ruine bringeth povertie, povertie procureth peace, and peace in time increaseth riches, riches causeth statelinesse, statelinesse increaseth envie, envie in the end procureth deadly mallice, mortall mallice proclaimeth open warre and battaile: and from warre againe as before is rehearsed."[46]

This cycle is not brought full circle in *Timon,* but for the segment shown it is helpfully explanatory. And for the larger context in which the play should be viewed, we must turn to contemporary plays which do present the full cycle. *Histriomastix,* written before 1600, best illustrates how a play must be constructed if it is to stage the complete rotation of war and peace. Each of the six acts is given to one period in the cycle. In Act I Peace is the dominant character, and her ideal status is suggested by learned attendants such as Grammar, Logic, and Rhetoric. In Act II, the decadent aftermath is suggested by the entrance of *"Plenty* in Majesty, upon a Throne, heapes of gold, *Plutus, Ceres;* and *Bachus* doing homage."[47] The deterioration is carried further in Acts III and IV, which are dominated respectively by Pride and Envy, with stiff characterizations of these conditions in terms of vocational types. Envy gives place in Act V to War, who is followed in Act VI by Poverty, and ultimately by Peace again.

Though didactic, *Timon* is not so fully a "moral" play as *Histriomastix,* and its structure—a feature much disliked by critics—is not so symmetrical. Yet if viewed as an imperfect version of such a politically didactic play, at least secondarily concerned with the relationship of war and peace, its structure becomes more meaningful. The first stage of peace is not shown, though there are rotten remnants surviving in the Poet and Painter. What we see at first in *Timon* is a society rank with Plenty, Pride, and Envy. Such a society will lead an individual to disaster unless he is restrained by temperance. So, in *Histriomastix,* the moderate Chrisoganus tells how he moved safely through the entire peace-war cycle (VI.i, p. 296):

> Nor yet did *Plenty* make me Prodigall:
> *Pride* I abhor'd and term'd the Beggers shield:
> Nor ever did base *Envie* touch my heart.
> . . . .
> Nor could the ratling fury of fierce warre
> Astonish me with more than the mid-night clock,
> The Trumpetter to Contemplation;
> For *Poverty,* I shake her by the hand,
> As welcome Lady to this wofull Land.

Timon lacks this temperate attitude: he is made "Prodigall" by "Plenty"; his generosity is motivated partly by pride; and he is passionate in confronting both poverty and war. But if not ideal, he stands on a plane above the rest of decadent Athens, and the political lesson of the play applies mainly, as it does in *Histriomastix,* to the society at large.

When war threatens corrupt Athens, it does so in the person of Alcibiades, a soldier whose sudden motivation for the war is usually thought undramatic. But if we disapprove of Alcibiades' emergence as an important character late in the play, we have not properly felt the ominous quality of his taciturn presence during the early revelry. We are especially likely not to feel his early significance because we read rather than see the play, and his four brief utterances are scarcely noticed. On the stage, in military garb, he would have been strikingly distinct from the gaudy revelers. His later prominence is of course sudden, but dramatically and frighteningly so. He enters at precisely the right time, just as War enters suddenly in his appropriate act in *Histriomastix*. And like War, Alcibiades is less a person than an impersonal force. Whatever personal animus he has becomes subordinate to his larger purpose, much as Coriolanus' private revenge against the plebs gives way to a passionless, corrective crusade against corrupt Rome generally, in which he symbolizes fiery, indiscriminating war.

Alcibiades' larger purpose is so fully expressed in the later scenes as to leave no doubt concerning Shakespeare's intention. Timon, who now speaks with the authority of a tragic chorus, addresses the General as though he were not a person at all (IV.iii.108):

> Be as a planetary plague when Jove
> Will o'er some high-vic'd city hang his poison
> In the sick air. Let not thy sword skip one.
> Pity not honour'd age for his white beard;
> He is an usurer. Strike me the counterfeit matron;
> It is her habit only that is honest,
> Herself's a bawd.

Timon further stresses the representative, rather than the personal, quality of Alcibiades when he prays (IV.iii.103):

> The Gods confound them all in thy conquest,
> And thee after, when thou hast conquered!

And again (IV.iii.127):

> Make large confusion; and, thy fury spent,
> Confounded be thyself!

War's directions to Horror, his servant, in *Histriomastix* are no more impersonal (V.i, p. 284):

> Horror shall greet the bosome of greene youth,
> The melting liver of pied gallantry,
> The wrinckled vizard of Devotion,
> The cheverell conscience of corrupted law,
> And frozen heart of gowty Merchandize,
> Horror wound these, strike palsies in their limmes.

Alcibiades himself exhibits the same attitude toward his function when he announces, with warlike sound, his "terrible approach" to Athens; and he indicates a similar type of victim for correction (V.iv.3):

> Till now you have gone on and fill'd the time
> With all licentious measure, making your wills
> The scope of justice.
> . . . .
>   Now the time is flush,
> When crouching marrow in the bearer strong
> Cries, of itself 'No more!' Now breathless wrong
> Shall sit and pant in your great chairs of ease,
> And pursy insolence shall break his wind
> With fear and horrid flight.

In this climactic period ("the time is flush") may be noted important resemblances to Hamlet's Denmark. Here is "pursy insolence" breaking his wind; in *Hamlet*, "the fatness of these pursy times" and the "insolence of office." In both plays, too, there is moral license and miscarriage of justice. One gets a better appreciation of Hamlet's problem by recognizing that almost alone he must do what Alcibiades can perform with an army: set the time right.

Actual war ultimately proves unnecessary in *Timon*. Its threatening music is finally muffled, as in *Hamlet,* because those responsible are no longer living and the city submits willingly to whatever correction Alcibiades may impose. With reform accomplished, the General offers, to complete the cycle, new and disciplined peace (V.iv.81):

> Bring me into your city,
> And I will use the olive, with my sword,
> Make war breed peace, make peace stint war, make each
> Prescribe to other, as each other's leech.

In accepting the facts of the peace-war cycle, Alcibiades' program for peace is in accord with the counsel of military writers and most political realists of the day. Neither war nor peace should be expected to exist permanently in a healthy commonweal. Peter Whitehorne so contends in dedicating his translation of Machiavelli's *Art of War* to Elizabeth: "For soche truly is the nature and condicion, bothe of peace and warre, that where in governements, there is not had equalle consideration of them bothe, the one in fine, doeth worke and induce, the others oblivion and utter abholicion."[48] Sir Philip Sidney, according to Fulke Greville, felt that this doctrine was most applicable to Englishmen: "His opinion being that

Ilanders have the air and waters so diversly moving about them, as neither peace, nor war, can long be welcome to their humors."⁴⁹

Shakespeare's recognition of the case for this theory is perhaps shown by its acceptance—as a fact rather than a moral principle—by his ideal statesman, Henry V. Among other proposals for the welfare of the state, he plans "noble counsel" so

> That war, or peace, or both at once, may be
> As things acquainted and familiar to us.
>   (*2 Henry IV* V.ii.138)

Indeed, the philosophy of war and peace that we now refer to as pacifism is espoused by not a single admirable character in Shakespeare. And possibly Shakespeare's best commentary upon a state dedicated to such a philosophy is its embodiment in Gonzalo's mock utopia, where there would be no "sword, pike, knife, gun, or need of any engine" (*The Tempest* II.i.161).

IV

The main obstacle in the way of a philosophically grounded lasting peace was the everlasting cycle. And since the most critical stage in this cycle was that inauspicious union of peace and plenty, Shakespeare's occasional references to this stage have more than fragmentary meaning. Richmond's prayer at the end of *Richard III* requests for him and his Tudor descendants "smooth-fac'd peace, / With smiling plenty." Hamlet, on the other hand, considers these qualities unwholesome symptoms in "th' imposthume of much wealth and peace," and Alcibiades offers major surgery to an Athens suffering from such an imposthume. In *Cymbeline,* there are three references to peace and plenty. Imogen is the first to speak on the subject (III.vi.21):

> Plenty and peace breeds cowards; hardness ever
> Of hardiness is mother.

But she is speaking of herself, and it is doubtful whether she implies a criticism of the court she has just left. The next appearances of "peace and plenty" are unquestionably relevant to Cymbeline's Britain, and both have a hopeful connotation. The prophecy made to Posthumus states that after certain conditions are fulfilled, "then shall Posthumus end his miseries, Britain be fortunate and flourish in peace and plenty" (V.iv.143). The Soothsayer's interpretation of this prophecy emphasizes the auspicious future of this happy peace: Cymbeline's "issue," proceeding through his lost sons, "promises Britain peace and plenty." And this durable peace, the Soothsayer finally says (V.v.466), has a divine sponsorship.

In Shakespeare's favorable references to peace and plenty, the presence of at least one of two elements is invariable. The first is divine favor. None of the peaceful, wealthy nations which Shakespeare brings under a military scourge are God-fearing. And in both instances where he expressly invokes hope for lasting peace and plenty, there is a strong religious context. In thus opposing religious optimism to the cold logic of the cycle, Shakespeare was in accord with most contemporary religious writers. For although Elizabethan divines took a dim view of comfortable peace, they could not endorse the cyclical theory of war, which was a classical and not a Christian doctrine and which in its mechanical rotation left little room for Providence. War as they saw it had only one function: it was a scourge of God. As such it could be avoided by a repentant nation, even in prosperity. While the people of Israel dedicated themselves to the Scriptures, it was recalled, "they injoyed peace throughout their borders, and great plentie within their Pallaces. And such feare God strocke into the harts of their enemies round about, that none durst stirre against them."[50]

A second reason for a durably prosperous peace in Shakespeare is the character of the sovereign, including the promise of his issue. The conclusion to *Richard III* is a paean to the house of Tudor and, by implication, Elizabeth. The Queen did, indeed, deserve praise for a government both thriving and moderately peaceful. But she had no apparent philosophy of war and peace. Her comments on war concern almost exclusively its costs in men and money, her dissatisfaction with her allies and generals, and her personal interest in the quality and welfare of English soldiers.

With King James it was entirely otherwise. Possessing none of his predecessor's interest in the execution of war or her ability to inspire heroic effort, he had instead a lively theoretical interest in war and peace; and whereas Elizabeth could be called neither pacifist nor militarist, James was extraordinarily dedicated to the idea of peace. In a key speech to Parliament, delivered in 1603, he cited "peace abroad with all forrein neighbours" as the first of the blessings "which God hath joyntly with my Person sent unto you." This new peace, he declared, had brought prosperity at home and abroad.[51] James's idea of peace, in fact, was entirely favorable: it was divinely sent through his person, and it consisted with and encouraged prosperity. To be sure, he acknowledged that although the blessings of peace are great, they are worth little if they do not "have perpetuity or long continuance." But in this respect, his new-brought peace was not wanting: "so hath it pleased Almighty God to accompany my person also with that favour, having healthful and hopefull Issue of my body." He did not doubt that it would please God to continue for many years all the "blessings of Inward and outward Peace, which I have brought with me."[52] Although James was not frightened by peace, or the combination of peace and plenty, he did in one unofficial discussion, the preface to his *Counterblaste to Tobacco* (1604), ponder academically the conventional threat to his happy government: "Our Peace hath bred wealth: And Peace and wealth hath brought foorth a generall sluggishnesse, which makes us wallow in all sorts of idle delights, and soft delicacies, the first seeds of the subversion of all great Monarchies." But "for remedie whereof," he foresaw not war but "the Kings part (as the proper Phisician of his Politicke-body) to purge it of all those diseases, by Medicines meete for the same." It is evident that James was troubled not by peace and plenty, but by a few corruptions—notably smoking—distasteful to him personally.[53]

The full influence of the King's assertive political creed upon Shakespeare's Jacobean plays has yet to be determined; but the findings made by recent students of *Macbeth* suggest an influence considerably greater than has so far been recognized.[54] And although the year 1603 marks no radical change in Shakespeare's attitude toward war and peace, it is only natural that he should have paid tactful heed to one of his sovereign's most deeply felt convictions. That other authors found it impossible to overpraise James's pacifism is shown by Markham's effusive statement: "He enters not with an Olive Branch in his hand, but with a whole Forrest of Olives round about him; for he brought not Peace to his Kingdome alone, but almost to all the Christian Kingdomes in Europe."⁵⁵ Barnabe Barnes wrote of his new sovereign that "hee raigneth and governeth upon earth in comfort, peace, and plentie."⁵⁶ And still another Jacobean opportunist, apparently Middleton, wrote an unctuous tract called *The Peacemaker* (1618) which speaks even more complacently than James himself of the blessings of "the Land of Peace under the King of Peace."⁵⁷

The evidence of Jacobean pacifism in Shakespeare's later works is, of course, not so gross as that in the writings of opportunists. If we except the possible allusion in the famous line from Sonnet 107—"peace proclaims olives of endless age"—there is only one direct compliment to James as peacemaker. In Cranmer's prophecy on the blessed government of Henry VIII's successors, it is predicted of James that "peace, plenty, love, truth, terror" shall "be his and like a vine grow to him" (*Henry VIII* V.v.48). Besides its accord with James's major interest generally, the prophecy has a verbal similarity to a claim made by the King in a speech of 1607, wherein he specifies among the "Commodities" brought by the union of England and Scotland: "Peace, Plentie, Love."⁵⁸

Cymbeline provides a more sustained mirroring of Jacobean policy. As Warren D. Smith has observed, "About the same time Shakespeare was preparing *Cymbeline* for performance at Blackfriars, James appears to have been bending every effort to effect peace between Spain and the Dutch republic."⁵⁹ Professor Smith's interesting contention is that the political role of Cloten, as advocate of war to the death against Rome, is consonant with this lout's ridiculous part in the rest of the play. James did not approve of alienating foreign emissaries by rude conduct. Nor did he favor militaristic counselors, like Ralegh. Therefore, Cloten's defiance of Caius Lucius, emissary from Rome, and his haughty counsel for war, would not have drawn Jacobean applause. One might go further than Professor Smith (who is concerned only with Cloten's role) and find in the remarkably pacific ending of the play other royal interests. There is, for example, an unusual hope for lasting peace and plenty, and in this ideal condition the role of Cymbeline's issue is stressed. Equally striking is the possible reflection of James's policy of appeasement. *Cymbeline* is the only Shakespearean play in which the English finally submit to a foreign power after winning the war. James was much criticized for his truce with Spain, a nation which the English had more than once defeated. Greville regretted the abandoning of the late Queen's "wisedomes too suddenly, by exchanging that active, victorious, enriching, and ballancing course of her defensive wars, for an idle—I feare—deceiving shadow of peace."[60] From the garrison at Flushing, Sir William Browne complained to Cecil on behalf of his soldiers "that the very name of our peace with their enemies is so unpleasing as that it seems in short time all pleasures past that we have done with them will be more than half forgotten." And he reflects nostalgically upon "the old pathway of our late Queen."[61]

Indeed, a clear distinction soon became felt between James and Elizabeth in their attitudes toward war. This distinction is visible in Shakespeare's remarkably different treatments of two militaristic counselors: the Bastard Faulconbridge and Cloten. The former, created when England could breathe defiance to her enemy, persuasively advocates war, fulminates against appeasement, and denounces John's submission to the Pope. But in *Cymbeline,* when comparable defiance is to be addressed to Rome, Shakespeare puts it in the mouth of the one totally contemptible person in the play.

Advocacy of war became highly unpopular in James's reign. Only a few anonymous tracts carried on furtively the militarism of Essex,[62] and the drama reflects this caution. Philosophical arguments for war, or against peace, that might formerly have been assigned to a Hamlet are now given to Cloten, Timon, Coriolanus, or the Volscian servingmen.

The practice of Chapman interestingly parallels Shakespeare's. Chapman, too, had developed his political ideas during the Elizabethan era, and these are reflected in the heroic manners of his dramatic protagonists. But the martial doctrines that might once have befitted model heroes are now subordinated. The following opinion appears in a play written at about the time of *Coriolanus:*

> Peace must not make men cowards, nor keep calm
> Her pursy regiment with men's smother'd breaths.[63]

Ten years earlier the utterance would have been exemplary. Now it must be assigned to the scheming malcontent La Fin, who is properly banished by the model (Jacobean) sovereign Henry IV, with the reprimand: "Thou art at peace with nothing but with war."[64] At about the same time that Shakespeare was creating Cloten, Chapman was penning the following lines:

> Now all is peace, no danger: now what follows?
> Idleness rusts us, since no virtuous labour
> Ends ought rewarded.[65]

Yet this persuasive indictment of the new ideals is given to a "politican" who is craftily sounding out the discontent of another character. Nor was this curious practice limited to

Chapman and Shakespeare. Cyril Tourneur, apostrophizing "noble warre" as the "first originall Of all man's honour," regrets how his age has fallen from this ideal.[66] But his dramatic spokesman is a villain, trying to get his nephew off to war.

All these speeches are stirring echoes of a former age; and for theatergoers they may still have carried a message beyond their dramatic context. Would not, for example, Chapman's audience have felt a measure of social truth in Byron's outcry,

> The King hath now no more use of my valour.
>
> . . . .
>
> The world is quite inverted, Virtue thrown
> At Vice's feet, and sensual Peace confounds
> Valour and cowardice, fame and infamy,[67]

even though Byron proves to be only a villain hero? Shakespeare does not always give a similar poetic endorsement to the militarism of his later characters; certainly he does not do so for Cloten or the Volscian servingmen. But the intensity of utterance that he gives to Coriolanus, for example, makes one wonder whether he, like many of his countrymen, did not have misgivings about James's "whole Forrest of Olives."

v

The evidence reviewed in this chapter does not warrant our assigning a definite—certainly not a consistent—meaning to every reference to war or peace in Shakespeare. But it does justify attributing to both war and peace a more important function in the play than Shakespearean criticism usually accords them. This function, moreover, is not limited to background ideas, but often affects the dramatic qualities of the play. Peace, for example, especially in its decadent form, provides an ominous atmosphere rich in dramatic tension. As potently as the villain's soliloquy, it may announce impending trouble and ultimate war. *Richard III,* for example, begins inauspiciously in a society relaxing from war and dedicated, as Edward proclaims at the end of *3 Henry VI,* to "stately triumphs, mirthful comic shows, / Such as befits the pleasure of the court." It is in "this weak piping time of peace," with its "idle pleasures," that Richard III begins the civil ferment that produces outrage and war. Similarly at the beginning of *Richard II* there is indicated an antecedent period of unwholesome peace. The King has not warred, but "basely yielded upon compromise / That which his noble ancestors achiev'd with blows." "More hath he spent in peace than they in wars" (II.i.251–255). Richard's court, while avoiding war, has turned to idle flattery, "lascivious meters," and the "report of fashions in proud Italy" (II.i.17–21). In *Hamlet* there has apparently been a prior period of peace dating back to the Prince's birth, when the elder Hamlet overthrew Fortinbras. In Hamlet's description of the rank social atmosphere of Denmark, Elizabethans would have caught the ominous note which Shakespeare more obviously communicates through the sentries and the omens of war. The evils of Claudius' peace-rotten Denmark are strikingly similar to those which John Norden listed in 1597 as symptoms of an abscess to be lanced by war: falsehood, deceit, "dissimulate" love, flattery, adultery, drunkenness, cruelties, and injustice.[68] And Norden makes it clear that such a state of peace is perilous indeed.

In all three of these plays, the structural pattern is peace giving way to war, actual or threatened. In them, Shakespeare takes advantage of the dramatic value of peace as an unrestful beginning for his play, and of war (or a symbolic army) as an agent of resolution. And we have already noted the same sequence in *Timon of Athens*. In addition to its sociological significance, this procedure had also a certain justification from literary theory. In Renaissance Italy, as Professor Swedenberg points out, there was considerable controversy as to whether a nonmilitary theme was proper for serious literature, particularly the epic, and a playwright might very well have felt an equal obligation to emphasize war as his drama progressed—at any rate to use warriors as major characters in the central action.[69]

But Shakespeare does not, of course, always follow the dramatic formula of peace turning to war. War yielding to peace was an almost equally formidable segment of the cycle and had comparable dramatic value, particularly in terms of human readjustment. For many of Shakespeare's heroes, as we shall see in the next chapter, peace proves to be a battlefield far more harrowing than war.

In any event, it is helpful to the reader not to miss cues that for Elizabethans were implicit in the social scene. Cues announcing the advent of warfare one is not likely to overlook, though some of the traditional omens were less obvious than the appearance of soldiers or the distant rumble of drums. But the foreboding presence of peace, particularly as announced in the opening scenes, may often be indicated by symptoms that today are mistakable for general malaise. And when one of Shakespeare's characters complains of these rank conditions eloquently and at length—as does Hamlet—we today may notice only the virtuosity of the performance, or what it tells us about the character of the speaker.

The plight of modern audiences is aggravated by producers' changes in a play's structure made with regard only to present-day acting expediency. Thus in *Hamlet* we may have totally deleted for us the role of Fortinbras, who was vital to Shakespeare's design of war and peace in the play. It should be remembered that the Folio *Hamlet,* which was probably the acting version, omits the great speech "How all occasions do inform against me," but does not omit what we today are most likely to cut—the episode provoking the speech, in which Fortinbras and his soldiers pass across the stage.

Further dangers of modern indolence in interpreting war and peace in Shakespeare's plays are suggested by the conclusions reached by a recent writer. Miss Zabelle Boyajian, studying "War and Peace in Shakespeare" against a present-day rather than Renaissance background (she commends *Henry V* for its "satire on warfare"), concludes that Shakespeare "thoroughly understood the philosophy of pacifism." "His warfare," she finds, "is conventional—that of epics and fairy stories; his peace, reasoned, calm and internal."[70] Miss Boyajian is surely wrong; but she is merely expressing an attitude that many of us had less consciously accepted.

Failure to recognize that warfare in Shakespeare tends to have a function more than decorative will blind us to the significance of rare occasions when it has no worthy function at all. Such is the case in *Troilus and Cressida,* where the lack of a good cause ("All the argument is a whore and a cuckold")[71] helps explain the most disagreeable picture of war to be found in Shakespeare. Failure on the other hand to recognize that peace is not a neutral or normal condition, that it is almost never "reasoned, calm, and internal," is to deprive Shakespeare's wars of virtually all their meaning and to take from the plays, generally, a major source of tension and social criticism.

CHAPTER VI

The Soldier in Society:
From Casque to Cushion

Although the abstract forces of war and peace penetrate to the imagery and design of Shakespearean drama, in only one play—*Timon of Athens*—do they become almost characters in the plot. There was, however, a more tangible way in which Shakespeare might dramatize the impact of war upon society. This way—already foreshadowed in remarks upon Richard III, Alcibiades, and Coriolanus—was to embody certain of the rude forces of war in the personalities of human characters and then bring those characters from the battlefield into a milieu of peace. The present chapter is devoted to major instances of this practice. Guided perhaps by literary theory and precedents, Shakespeare frequently chose for his major roles noblemen, such as Othello and Coriolanus, who make war almost their only occupation. Upon returning from the wars, these men clash with society in ways that significantly reveal their own limitations of character and also the flaws of the social group to which they return. And in addition to these noblemen, conscripts and common soldiers must also be considered, though briefly. Their pathetic rather than noble distress as veterans, and their economic plight rather than their corrective friction with society, place these unfortunates in a class by themselves, and they may conveniently be studied first.

II

The returning conscript troubled society for reasons similar to those for which he was drafted. He had no employment and threatened to be a social nuisance. In view of the serious problem presented by the Elizabethan veteran, it is curious that Shakespeare has not a single episode dramatizing a private's return. We must fall back upon occasional commentary for whatever Shakespeare seems to know about the postwar plight of the common soldier.

A particularly revealing commentary occurs in Shakespeare's most authentic soldierly conversation: the talk of Bates and Williams with the disguised King in *Henry V*. One significant aspect of this conversation is that the two common soldiers, neither of them cowardly, think of the future in terms of death rather than survival. Their view of the future is not troubled by thoughts of regaining an old job or finding a new one. Instead they worry about the mutilation of battle, their unpaid debts, their wives and children left "rawly" provided for, and the state of their souls. Shakespeare's perception in this scene had more than a psychological accuracy. The shocking truth was that Elizabethan warfare, with its dysentery, famine, and crude surgery, allowed conscripts relatively little reason for anxiety about a postwar future on earth.[1] The proportion of casualties in Falstaff's company (147 out of 150) may be abnormally high because of the Captain's exceptional problems of finance, but it was less incredible for Shakespeare's time than for our own.

Henry V, we recall, is uninterested in the economic anxieties of Bates and Williams. He promises no pensions for their widows or children. Instead, after clearing himself of any responsibility in the matter, he advises both men to look after their own souls so that they may have the comfort of dying well. Probably neither Henry nor Shakespeare thought of this advice as an irrelevancy. Dying well meant providing for a future which was more certain, more important, and considerably more attractive than a return to human society. And Henry is merely reflecting the practice of conduct manuals for the soldier in stressing how death may be "to him advantage."[2] These manuals not only prescribe the correct attitude for meeting death, but occasionally indicate the ideal future awaiting a soldier who dies virtuously in battle. Thomas Styward typically describes the Christian "camp of everlasting life" which, he says, the chaplain should hold before the minds of common soldiers. In this Christian Valhalla are "souldiers on white horses, clothed in white and pure silkes."[3] And like Henry V, most of these manuals are relatively uninterested in the economic plight of the returned soldier. At most, they advise him to go back to work in an orderly manner. Nor is Henry's indifference to postwar economics at all untypical of Shakespeare's habitual practice.

In fact there is only one important statement about the veteran's plight that seems at all subversively realistic. This

---

[1] For notes to chapter vi, see pages 329–333.

is Falstaff's brief, but startling, prediction of the career awaiting the two or three survivors of his company (*1 Henry IV*
V.iii.39): "They are for the town's end, to beg during life."
This line reads today like unmistakable criticism of cruel
governmental neglect; and possibly it produced in audiences
uneasy recognition of a royal failing. It was not, however, an
obvious attack on the crown. Elizabeth was frugal in dispensing funds to wounded or indigent soldiers, but not un-
reasonably so. There were occasional, though inadequate, hos-
pitals for the maimed, and pensions for a few deserving
veterans. The Queen could not afford much more. Besides,
she was apparently quite at ease with her own conscience
in the matter. She insisted that the individual counties which
had levied the men were responsible for the maimed veterans.
The sincerity of this conviction is evident in the injured tone
of frequent letters from her council to county officials complaining that their responsibilities had been neglected. In
1595, for example, the council wrote to the justice of Mon-
mouth:

One William James, a poore maymed souldier in whose behalfe
wee have heretofore written unto you by som yearly pencion or
allowance to be given him according to the statute, hath again by
peticion made known unto us that notwithstanding according to
the said letters he was enrolled amongst the rest of the maymed
souldiers of that county to be provided for as abovesaid and received allowance for one whole yeare, yet is the same wrongfully
and without cause with the certificate of his mayms and hurtes
(his maims being apparent) deteyned from him.[4]

Even Falstaff later recognizes that pensions were available
for wounded veterans. Suffering from either the gout or the
pox, or both, he is in a crippled condition—"his maims being

apparent," in the words of the council. "'Tis no matter if I do halt," he reasons. "I have the wars for my colour, and my pension shall seem the more reasonable" (2 *Henry IV* I.ii.272).

Moreover, his earlier reference to veterans' begging during life would not necessarily—even without the transfer of blame to county officials—have seemed indiscreet. Wounded soldiers were officially and unapologetically granted licenses to beg, just as royal favorites were accorded monopolies. These licenses were special favors, and were granted for a limited period. Thus in 1592 the council issued

an open warrant to all Maiours, Sherifs, Justices of Peace, Bailifs, etc. for Thomas Smith, a poore wounded soldier in her Majesty's services, to collect the devocion and benevolence of the inhabitants within the county of Suffolk in all places, onely chappels, churches and such like places of publick assemblie empted, without any your unlawfull lets or interruptions, behaving him self orderly as becometh a good and dutifull subject, which license shalbe continued for six monthes onely.[5]

Of course, the fact that the government had no qualms about licensed begging as a reward for wounded veterans did not necessarily mean that Shakespeare's audience was equally complacent. Falstaff's words, as always, may have meant quite different things to different people. The Queen liked Falstaff, but so also did commoners in the pit.

Shakespeare is least reticent about the postwar economic problems of disreputable soldiers like Parolles and Pistol. In their resourcefulness and adaptability, these men are miniatures of Falstaff; and however scornfully Shakespeare may have viewed their military disgrace, he took an obvious pleasure in acknowledging their ability to digest the shame and face life with a brave pose once more. Parolles, finished as a soldier by one of the best-staged humiliations in dramatic literature, does not contemplate suicide or obscurity. Like Falstaff, he has splendid rebound, and instantly decides that there is a place for him as a civilian (*All's Well* IV.iii.373):

> Rust, sword! cool, blushes! and, Parolles, live
> Safest in shame! Being fool'd, by fool'ry thrive!
> There's place and means for every man alive.

And Pistol, who in war had a job planned for himself as sutler to the camp, approaches his postwar career with equal resourcefulness (*Henry V* V.i.89):

> Old I do wax, and from my weary limbs
> Honour is cudgell'd. Well, bawd will I turn,
> And something lean to cutpurse of quick hand.
> To England will I steal, and there I'll steal;
> And patches will I get unto these cudgell'd scars,
> And swear I got them in the Gallia wars.

Besides his pleasure in portraying men with the vitality of these two rascals, Shakespeare had the satisfaction of knowing that the government—not to mention the victimized public—would applaud his comedy about these nuisances to society. So industriously did Elizabethan rogues exploit their dubious army service that the council wrote to county officials complaining of "divers mysdemeanors, insolence and enormyties that were dailie commytted in sondry places of the Realme ... by soche as had been emploied in the warres in forraine parts and others that did pretend and beare a shewe to have served in the warre as souldiers, being the most parte of them indeed ydle and vagrant persons and soche as lived by pillfring, stealinge and wandred from place to place."[8]

By highlighting the postwar difficulties of rogues and paying relatively little attention to the tribulations of ordinary citizen soldiers, Shakespeare was reflecting a governmental practice. Because a large percentage of Elizabethan conscripts were either rogues or misfits in society, it was easy for the government to take the righteous attitude that all discharged soldiers who caused trouble were scoundrels. Upon the demobilization of Essex's troops from the Ireland expedition, when it was murmured among the soldiers that peace would leave them destitute, Secretary Cecil firmly denounced this "libel": "No; whatsoever is concluded, we shall think of them; they will always be regarded, and her Majesty has a special care of such as be soldiers in deed; but those that live in drunkenness and looseness I hold are no more worthy of the name than a hedge priest that can scarce read a homily to be made a bishop."[7] It would, therefore, be not only pleasant but politic for a dramatist to show in civil distress only obvious rogues like Pistol. A more convincing representation of the economic plight of the considerable number of honest soldiers—however small a minority they represented—would have amounted to criticism of the government.

III

As we turn from commoners to noble warriors and professional soldiers of rank, we find a situation almost exactly the opposite. It was not merely that Shakespeare was willing to examine seriously the problems faced by superior officers in peace; he seems to have specially chosen military men as tragic heroes, and the dramatic friction for which they are noteworthy results from the fact that they are shown primarily in peace rather than in war. Coriolanus is the clearest example of the general who succeeds in war, his occupation, and comes to ruin when he is forced into a nonmilitary situation. It was his nature

> Not to be other than one thing, not moving
> From th' casque to th' cushion, but commanding peace
> Even with the same austerity and garb
> As he controll'd the war.
>   (IV.vii.42)

In other Shakespearean generals the tragic disability is less clearly marked. The dramatist does not always point to this as a reason for disaster, any more than he feels it always necessary to comment upon Renaissance attitudes toward peace as a troubling background for his plays. Moreover, he did not constantly wish to highlight the theme of the misplaced warrior. Occasionally, as in *Macbeth,* he had other frictions so much more pertinent to the individual's nature that a study of soldierly disabilities would lie mainly outside the play. No two of Shakespeare's generals fail as citizens for exactly the same reason. Nevertheless, almost to a man they do fail. And several of them fail for reasons closely enough related to justify a common study of these men as warriors moving inexpertly from the casque to the cushion.

For Elizabethans, "cushion" connoted mainly the court, with all its elegance, niceties, intrigue, and flattery. It was not, however, merely the setting of the fashionable courtier, for it included government and politics—with all the behind-the-scene machinations which the soldier had to contend with on distant battlefields and which he viewed with rightful suspicion. For Essex, courtiers would connote not vapid gallants but shrewd politicians like the Cecils. It was natural that one of the most conventional and important cleavages in Elizabethan society was that between the court and wars.

Soldiers sensed that the world of the court was not their world. "The Campe," wrote Barnaby Rich cautiously, "is better befitting a Souldier than the Court."[8] And Overbury, describing "A Worthy Commander in the Warres," states that "hee is so honourably mercifull to women in surprisall, that onely that makes him an excellent Courtier. He knowes, the hazards of battels, not the pompe of Ceremonies are Souldiers best theaters."[9] The soldier-poet Thomas Churchyard wrote a work called *A Pleasant Discourse of Court and Wars* (1596), contrasting the two theaters of activity. And a more significant book, since it deals with actual Elizabethan examples of the two occupations, is Sir Robert Naunton's *Fragmenta Regalia*. Naunton uses as almost his single theme of characterization the contrast between courtier and soldier. Sir Francis Vere, for example, is characterized as belonging to the soldier type: "I finde not that he came much to the court, for he lived almost perpetually in the campe." Yet Vere was remarkable in that when he did come to court, "no man had more of the queene's favour."[10] Less fortunate, according to Naunton, was Lord Willoughby. A "great master of the art military," he failed to prosper with the Queen because he scorned adapting himself to the court; "and it was his saying, though it did him no good, that he was none of the *reptilia,* intimating, that he could neither creep nor crouch, neither was the court his element, for indeed he was a great souldier; so was he of a suitable magnanimity, and could not brooke the obsequiousnesse and assiduitie of the court."[11] Sussex, too, suffered because he "played not his game with that cunning and dexteritie, as the Earl of Leicester did, who was much the more facete courtier, though Sussex was thought much the more honest man, and far the better souldier."[12]

Naunton is of course guilty of oversimplification for the sake of a clear pattern, as many of the dramatists were. But even the men whom Naunton confines within this pattern saw themselves similarly. Essex wrote to Willoughby protesting that hard as his Irish campaign was, it was more tolerable than having enemies at court "barking at him that is every day venturing his life for his country abroad. . . . The Court is the centre; but methinks it is the fairer choice to commaund armies than humours."[13] Even Sir Philip Sidney, who of Elizabethan soldiers was the least troublesome in court, was aware of the court-war cleavage and of his role in it. According to Fulke Greville, Sidney saw in his native country "greatness of worth, and place, counterpoysed there by the arts of power, and favor. The stirring spirits sent abroad as fewell, to keep the flame far off: and the effeminate made judges of danger which they fear, and honor which they understand not."[14]

This is not to say that the two theaters of action could not merge harmoniously in the well-proportioned individual esteemed by courtly tradition. Most Elizabethans would have disagreed with Greville in placing Sidney on the side of the martialists. Like a few other choice spirits, Sidney came close to the Renaissance ideal of the complete gentleman—learned, courtly, and valorous. Shakespeare recognized that this ideal could become an actuality. Bedford, in *1 Henry VI,* is a soldier who is also a courtier (III.ii.134):

> A brave soldier never couched lance,
> A gentler heart did never sway in court.

Aeneas, in *Troilus and Cressida,* describes the corresponding versatility of ideal courtiers (I.iii.235):

> Courtiers as free, as debonair, unarm'd,
> As bending angels. That's their fame in peace.
> But when they would seem soldiers, they have galls,
> Good arms, strong joints, true swords; ...

And the ideal is most memorably described, though not fully displayed, in the person of Hamlet. Ophelia remembers him, before his falling off, as "the courtier's, scholar's, soldier's, eye, tongue, sword" (III.i.159).

It is perhaps significant that Hamlet is never presented as a soldier, though Fortinbras elegiacally reflects that the Prince would, if tried, have proved a good one. The truth of the matter is probably that outside of instructive works like *The Faerie Queene* and the *Arcadia,* the soldier-courtier ideal is seldom embodied in a major character in Elizabethan literature. Dramatists, especially, seem to have preferred the conflicts available in two imperfect figures rather than the instructiveness of a single exemplary one. The courtier gradually fossilizes into the caricatured dandy of Jacobean drama, and the soldier develops the rough, simple traits that make him either a tragic or comic misfit when he returns from war to society. What is more, the soldier and courtier are not merely separated as types; they frequently are placed in hostile opposition, so that it is the courtier, or his politic equivalent, whose guile leads the plain soldier to disaster.

IV

Since dramatists chose the rough rather than the chivalric soldier for significant dramatic purposes, they were obliged to decide what attitude to take toward the warrior who failed to adapt himself to a peacetime regimen, especially one demanding courtly or political tact. The issue of right and wrong was never clearly drawn in real life—as evidenced by the doubt which long surrounded the criminality of Essex's indiscretion. With simple and passionate men, as these soldiers tended to be, it is not easy to distinguish between crime and impulsiveness; and the Elizabethan drama faithfully reflected this ambiguity. Shakespeare, needless to say, was not untypically clear. Nevertheless his artistry, if not his meaning, becomes more impressive in the light of the Renaissance controversy concerning the proper status of the warrior in court or government.

On one side were the strong advocates of civil government or courtly ideals. Although many of these men had a realistic awareness of the value of war, they distrusted the professional warrior, particularly the kind who, like Coriolanus, was unwilling or unable to lay down his military habits when war was over. Machiavelli was one of the most emphatic spokesmen against this type of warrior. In the first place he warns princes not to allow men to make warfare their profession, "for there is not found more perilous men, then those, whiche make the warre as their arte."[15] From such men the prince faces both the problem of keeping them employed in wars and the threat that if discontented they will usurp the sovereignty. Secondly, Machiavelli deplores the uncivil habits in which soldiers take a professional pride. "Whereby it is often seene, that if any determine in the exercise of that kind of service to prevaile, that incontinent he doth not onely chaunge in apparell, but also in custome and maner, in voyce, and from the fashion of all civill use, he doth alter." In denouncing this attitude, Machiavelli asks the soldier to consider his relation to the state, of which he is not an independent part. "In whome," moreover, "ought ther to be more love of peace, then in him, which onely by the warre may be hurt . . . ?"[16]

In Elizabethan England, Lord Burghley was the most important advocate of civil life. His advice to his son Robert Cecil agrees substantially with Machiavelli's doctrine: "Neither by my consent shall thou train them [Robert's children] up to the wars. For he that setteth up his rest to live by that profession can hardly be an honest man or good Christian. . . . Besides, it is a science no longer in request than in use: soldiers in peace are like chimneys in summer."[17]

The misgivings expressed by both Machiavelli and Burghley concerning the professional warrior's role in peace were shared by many of the wiser Elizabethan military authors. A general, according to Procter, becomes most honorable and most serviceable to his country if, after wars are ended, "he can frame him selfe to peace, good government, and to be as profitable unto the cyvill estate by his industrie and policye, as he was by his valure in the warres."[18] Aptness in civil "policye" was of course the very quality that generals could least be expected to acquire. But they could, other authorities felt, learn to avoid violent indiscretions. Garrard describes the most reprehensible kind of behavior to which the confirmed warrior was addicted. Such a man, "being altogether ignorant in treading the steppes of a stayed life (through the small experience he hath of the world, which by tract of time is obtained, and by long practice, specially in the exercise of Armes) perswades himselfe he shall win credite and commoditie through the meanes of insolent actions, which altogether ought to be abhorred."[19] So gross had become the habits of many Englishmen who made war their profession, according to Sir Henry Knyvett, that they "are not held worthie to come into the company of civill people."[20]

There were conspicuous examples in Elizabethan England of generals who proved incapable of turning from the casque to the cushion. Many of these feared, sometimes rightly, that in peace their stature would suffer. Camden suspected that Norris drew out a campaign in Ireland because he belonged to the type of "military men, who are pleased that warre be drawne out at length, knowing they are no longer esteemed than they are in use."[21] Sir John Perrot afforded a more dramatic example. He encountered difficulty at court, Naunton reports, "out of a desire to be in command at home, as he had beene abroad." Thus he conducted himself with a "freedome and boldness of speech [which] drew him on to a clouded setting, and layd him upon the spleene and advantage of his enemies." His gravest indiscretion grew from his stubborn insistence upon his worth as a warrior and his sense that he was imperfectly valued during peacetime. When, according to Naunton, an invasion from Spain seemed imminent, and the Queen began treating Perrot with unwonted respect, he "sayd publiquely in the great chamber, at Dublin:—Loe, now she is ready to bepisse her selfe, for feare of the Spaniards, I am againe one of her White-boys."[22]

Of Elizabeth's generals who refused to abandon their military carriage and reputation, Essex was of course the most serious example, and we shall see that his fate may have influenced dramatic attitudes toward the unfortunate warrior. It was significant that as early as 1596 his disastrous trend was expertly analyzed by an uncommonly shrewd friend. Sir Francis Bacon wrote him a letter warning him particularly not to maintain his "military dependence." "I cannot sufficiently wonder at your Lordship's course," Bacon declared, "that you say, the wars are your occupation, and go on in that course; whereas, if I mought have advised your Lordship, you should have left that person at Plymouth; more than when in counsel, or in commending fit persons for service in wars, it had been in season." But the politic Bacon did not advise the Earl entirely to abandon his military character: "I say, keep it in substance, but abolish it in shows to the Queen."[23] Bacon erred only in one respect: he expected the General to be capable of the same type of policy that would seem natural to Bacon himself.

A few Elizabethan generals, to be sure, were better fitted for strategy of this sort than was Essex, but they were a small minority. Sir Walter Ralegh, for whom the motto "Tam Marti, Quam Mercuri" was placed above his portrait in the 1650 edition of his *Essayes and Observations,* was noted for his ability to combine the Machiavellian lion and fox, though his career in court was as troubled and tragic as that of Essex. Leicester was also politically astute, but, as Naunton remarked, "he had more of Mercury than he had of Mars," and was only incidentally a military leader, and a bad one at that.[24] Probably of all Elizabeth's generals, Mountjoy displayed the greatest tact in lessening his stature at the appropriate time. Benefiting from the lesson of Essex, he wrote in 1601 to Sir Robert Cecil (who would especially appreciate the statement), "I meane not to make the warres my occupation," and a few months later sent another letter of pious tone: "I beseech God to send me the height of my ambition, which is, with the conscience of having done her Majestie the service I desire, to injoy a quiet, private life, and that her

Majestie may never more have need of men of our profession."[25] Mountjoy had profited from the wisdom, never within the full grasp of Essex, of the Renaissance ideal sententiously expressed by Shakespeare (*Richard II* II.i.173):

> In war was never lion rag'd more fierce,
> In peace was never gentle lamb more mild.

With so much judicious and authoritative sentiment against the self-assertive professional warrior, it would appear unlikely that soldiers of this conviction should ever earn sympathy, let alone approval, in the drama. There would seem to have been little hope for the militaristic point of view, in either literature or life, if we accept the testimony of Henry Cuffe, sentenced to die for his role in the Essex conspiracy. His "last words" apparently are meant to express the plight of the entire military profession: "Scholars and martialists (though learning and valour should have the preeminence yet) in England must die like dogs and be hanged. To mislike this were but folly; to dispute of it but time lost; to alter it impossible, but to endure it manly and to scorn it magnanimity."[26] But Cuffe was speaking from the disillusionment of the year 1601, when the case for soldiers seemed lost. For a period of almost thirty years before 1601, soldiers had not taken the point of view that "to dispute of it" was "time lost." So vehemently, in fact, did they dispute the condemnation of their profession that they acquired a reputation as a hotly defensive group, a reputation which dramatists were to exploit with good effect. What is more, the soldiers' self-defense stood these unfortunates in good stead. As much as any other influence, these defenders of the military profession were responsible for the prevailingly sympathetic role which professional warriors received in Shakespeare until the year 1601, and to a certain extent even beyond that time.

The formal defenses of the military profession began in England early in the 1570's. In 1574 appeared one of the first of such books, Barnaby Rich's *A Right Exelent and Pleasaunt Dialogue Betwene Mercury and an English Souldier.* In this work Mercury speaks so eloquently on behalf of warfare as a career that Rich, as the English soldier, thanks him for having "so earnestly defended the souldiers cause, we want such atturneis in England to pleade in their behalfes where I thinke of all other Countreys they are had in least estimation."[27] Although in 1587 Rich was still complaining that "souldiours must learne of other men to speake for them selves, for there is no body else that will,"[28] not only Rich but others had by that time demonstrated their mastery of the art of self-defense. In 1579 Geoffrey Gates had published *The Defence of Militarie Profession,* and in 1581 William Blandy had upheld the profession in *The Castle, or Picture of Pollicy.*

These defensive works were not, of course, ostensibly devoted to a vindication of the warrior's rudeness in civil life. In fact, most of them contended that soldiers are, or can be, learned men. The Mercury of Rich's *Dialogue* is paired with the soldier to suggest that the two should ideally accompany each other. Even more emphatically, none of these writers overtly attempted to justify the role of the soldier at the expense of the total economy.

But these works signified and accomplished more than their authors acknowledged as their intentions. Generally, they represented a plea for a profession that was not deemed safe or worthy. More particularly, however, they represented a vindication of the soldier *as a soldier* in society. Superficially, their plea might be only for recognition of the soldier's value in defending his country, from which one might draw the exemplary inference that the soldier would become a normal citizen during peacetime. Or again the writers might affirm, as does Blandy, that the soldier deserves only a confined, if comfortable, room in the castle of government. But the military defenders could seldom stop there. In defending, they characteristically—like their unfortunate brethren on the stage—became assertive. Blandy first argues, with model Renaissance esteem for harmony in society, that when any group becomes inordinate, the entire social structure is shaken.[29] But presently he is led by zeal for his profession to a demonstration that the soldier is a worthier part of the state than the judge, and to a contemptuous attack on lawyers, who prove, as other writers evidence, to be one of the most loathed antagonists of the military.[30] Gates, with even more obvious assertiveness, begins his *Defence* by evoking a controversy concerning "what profession of life is most honorable in worldly states." England, he notes, gives preëminence to the lawyer, whereas if it were not an island, but "stood in the continent of the world environed with mightie nations . . . , then should it know the value of the soldier, and lick the dust off the feete of her men of prowesse: then would the lawer and the mercheant humble themselves to the warriers."[31]

The inevitable result of these aggressive defenses was that soldiers, in their own minds and in those of their sympathizers, became still further estranged from the regular orbit of society. Martialists seemed temperamentally incapable of defending their own status without attacking the more artful occupations and thereby displacing themselves further from civil company. It was equally natural that in defending their vocation they should exaggerate rather than conceal the rude traits of which critics had accused them. These traits became, in a way, a badge of their profession. In the idealized version given them by the military defenders, they represented not pointless rudeness but plain honesty.

The manner in which the professional warrior, while vindicating his social worth, reasserted his independent plainness, is best revealed in fictional works presenting the soldier as a defensive character. In Barnaby Rich's fiction, especially, the worth of the warrior is upheld without his having to renounce the rude traits that blemished his profession. Sappho, duke of Mantona, the hero of a tale in *Riche His Farewell to Militarie Profession* (1581), is characterized as a noble general who held the favor of the emperor so long as there was war; "but the warres beyng once finished and broughte to an ende, so that the empire remained in tranquilitie and peace ... suche as had profered them selves to fight for the saftie of their countrey, were now shaken of, and suche were preferred in their roomes as had any facultie in them tendyng to pleasure and delight." Duke Sappho, who "had no skill in courting trade," was ill-equipped for this elegant society. "His voice served hym better to cheare his souldiors in the feeld, then either to fayne or syng ditties in a ladies chamber; his tongue had more used to speake simplie and plaine, then to dissemble with his freend, or to flatter with his foe." Rich thus brightens the soldier's plainness by setting it off against a darkened portrait of the courtier. The soldier's ineptitude in peace is excused by making the courtier's harmony with peace seem blameworthy. The theme is elaborated as the artless Duke is libeled by envious courtiers and, "despite his former service dooen for his countrey," sent into exile.[32] Rich's Sappho thus becomes one of the earliest Elizabethan examples of a plain soldier whose banishment for courtly disabilities is sympathetically interpreted. Robert Greene, whose point of view is often a reliable index of current literary trends, follows Rich's model in *Euphues His Censure to Philautus*. Roxander, an Athenian general of generous but not canny spirit, falls victim to courtly envy, which "brought him as deepe hate with the Senators, as hee was in favour with the souldiers," and he is exiled.[33] Fortunately, as often happened in works sympathetic to the soldier, the pressure of war ultimately returns Roxander into favor.

In neither of these cases, however, is the charge of criminality so clearly associated with the soldier's plainness as in Rich's later novel *The Adventures of Brusanus Prince of Hungaria*. Martianus, a blunt soldier, is arrested on the charge of one Gloriosus, a courtier. Martianus had innocently voiced the soldier's typical complaint about the difficulty met by men of his profession in court, but had unluckily spoken with some acerbity of courtiers: "Many a one hath beene rewarded, and commended by some noble man for his great service, that hath but holpe him off with his hose when hee went to bed at night, or peradventure a ruffesetter, a bottel carier, a newes bringer, a parracide, a flaterer."[34] Gloriosus, informing on Martianus, shapes the soldier's discontent into a treasonable attitude. As a result, Martianus is brought to trial for his life before the Prince.

The trial scene in *Brusanus* is of unusual interest in a study of the civil fate of Shakespeare's soldiers and of those in the Elizabethan drama as a whole. It is, first of all, one of the earliest examples of a soldier on trial for uncivil behavior,[35] and it may have helped commence the vogue for such scenes on the stage. The more general defenses of the military profession had, of course, given dramatists an incentive to highlight the defensive role of the rude warrior. But Rich's innovation was depicting the actual scene of trial. Secondly, Rich supplied the kind of friction that was to be evident in so many of the playwrights' scenes involving the soldier. The accuser is a wily representative of the court, and the defendant is not merely a soldier but a soldier who relies proudly on his plainness of address. What is more, the courtier is made to appear so ridiculously elegant and subtle that the soldier emerges with triumphant righteousness from the contention. Gloriosus professes to "have founde by the art of Logique, learned by the rules of Rhetorique, and gathered by the preceptes of philosophy, what unnecessarie members these souldiers are in a well governed state." So gross is Martianus' language, declares Gloriosus, that he is unable to represent the soldier's treasonable speech before the court. "His sentences, althoughe not artificially couched yet strained after a fulsome manner, to the very full sea marke of reproche, his phrases very harshe, but more spitefull, his wordes unaptly placed, yet according to the literall sense, all applied to a malitious purpose."[36] Gloriosus' speech of accusation is "wonderfully commended" by the "young gallantes of the courte," but the Prince fortunately is of Rich's point of view: "So farre as I can perceive, Gloriosus, your learning is more then the matter where-with you have charged Martianus."[37]

The soldier is then invited to speak in his own defense. He responds in a way that becomes conventional for stage warriors. There is first an acknowledgment of his inability to speak, followed by a dignified, if not eloquent, utterance.

"Most gratious prince," Martianus begins, "if in my words I shall not observe that reverence that I know is apertinente to this presence, I must humbly crave pardon, and the rather for that my bringing up hath not beene so muche to direct my speeches to princes in their pallaces, as to souldiers in the fieldes." He proceeds to a defense of the professional soldier's place in society, affirming with increasing warmth that he is "a more profitable member to his country than any vaine headed courtier."[38]

Martianus' innocence is curiously vindicated by this defense of the military profession, as Gloriosus is told by the Prince "to holde his peace like a foole."[30] The distinction between personal innocence and the virtuousness of one's profession was not an easy one for soldiers to grasp. Rich apparently felt that Martianus had cleared his good name merely by proving that the soldier's calling was a nobler one than the courtier's. Stage warriors were later to use much the same reasoning, but not always with equally happy results.

Still other works of this sort served to prepare the way for the rude soldier as an apologetic but righteous character in drama. The second part of Rich's fictional *Don Simonides* has a section labeled "The Apologie of the Souldiour in his owne defence." Here, the soldier is engaged in upholding his profession against the detractions of men in two other professions. The soldier, like Martianus, is no rhetorician, but he is far from mute: "Although I have no Schoole Rethoricke (Gentlemen) or fine phrases to make my cause more commendable, yet as the naked truth leadeth me . . . , I will make you privie to my little skill."[40] Even more significant, perhaps, is the soldier's proud avowal, contrary to all precepts of such civil spokesmen as Burghley and Machiavelli: "As plainesse is my profession, so plainely have I opened my mynde.'"[41] A similar disputation is Nicholas Breton's *The Scholler and the Souldiour. A Disputation Pithily Passed betweene them.*[42] Here, too, the soldier more than holds his own in the controversy by a stubborn defense of his rightful plainness, although Breton ultimately makes a rather strained reconciliation of the difference between these two miserable occupations.

V

A playwright who chose to find significant friction in the theme of the warrior in society had, in the nondramatic materials so far reviewed, a fairly popular context of argumentation to rely upon. The military profession had established a reputation for being self-conscious and assertively plain. Not only did it meet misfortune in civil life; it took a grim pride in doing so. It not only found itself temperamentally opposed to courtiers, scholars, and lawyers, but boasted of this fact. To the dramatist were available abundant arguments for condemning or defending the soldier for his disabilities and his attitude toward his disabilities. Yet, as already noticed, neither side in the dispute proved itself convincingly right. The Essex affair of 1601 did, as we shall see, place the formidable weight of the government against the professional soldier, but even this did not silence him or his defenders. Before and after 1601, dramatists probably valued the soldiers and their point of view less for any doctrinaire purpose than for the passionate quality of their suffering and self-defense. Even in Samuel Daniel's *Philotas,* a play reflecting the Essex uprising with unusual closeness, there occurs a statement defining the more universal dramatic assets of the soldier—assets that had been public knowledge well before Essex made them freshly troublesome. Philotas, at his trial for treason, speaks for all soldiers:

> For souldiers joy, or wrath, is measurelesse,
> Rapt with an instant motion: and we blame,
> We hate, we prayse, we pity in excesse,
> According as our present passions frame.[43]

Shakespeare was typical of most dramatists in discovering primarily animation and passion rather than right or wrong in his professional soldiers. But he was not ignorant of the controversial issues which shaped the soldiers' passions and speeches.

VI

There was still one other dramatic problem which faced Shakespeare if he wished to give the soldier an important nonmilitary role in his plays. As even the defenders of the profession recognized, a soldier was not likely to be gifted in subtle language or intelligence. From a dramatist's point of view, soldierly limitations of this sort were impediments almost as unfortunate on the stage as they were in society. A plain soldier might provide interesting frictions in a scene or two; he did not, despite his capacity for emotion and sudden action, lend himself to entire plays of poetic drama.

The dramatist had two extreme alternatives if he intended to use the soldier as a major character throughout the play. He could, if he sought consistency and was more interested in types than in full characterization, allow the soldier to maintain his plain role throughout. The soldier so presented would ideally be limited to prose dialogue and to simple ideas with much action. Shakespeare found this alternative used in a few plays by early contemporaries. The clearest example was Robert Wilson's *The Coblers Prophesie,* in which a soldier is shown having difficulties in a peacetime court dominated by a courtier, a scholar, and a country gentleman. Although the soldier is given a name, Sateros, he is but a faintly dramatized version of the defensive soldier found in military tracts and fiction. In court he is accused of being "as rough as he were in the field"; he grows "cholericke" in controversy with his canny antagonists; and he speaks throughout the play with almost uniform plainness. Finally war comes to his kingdom, and he then has the pleasure of inviting courtier, scholar, and gentleman to defend the country. Except for his conventional defense of the profession and his indictment of courtly finesse, he never has an idea or interesting emotion throughout the whole drama. He does nothing not completely expected of him.[44]

In the anonymous play *The Noble Souldier,* there promises at first to be a similar limitation in the soldier's role. The conventionalized types are indicated in the Dramatis Personae:

> Baltazar—The Souldier
> Cockadillo—A foolish Courtier

Baltazar supplies interest through the energy, rather than through any variety or unexpectedness, of his actions. But a slight inconsistency becomes noticeable in that Baltazar develops a kind of righteous cunning. Banished from court because he slays a groom in an attempt to gain access to the King, and then offered a pardon if he will kill the King's unwanted wife, he pretends willingness to do the job but actually manages to bring events to a happy conclusion. He does so, to be sure, without losing his honest nature or plain speech, but nevertheless his later role is not so consistent with his nature as that of Sateros in *The Coblers Prophesie.*

Baltazar's slight defection from the character of the plain soldier suggests the second alternative open to dramatists. This is to characterize the soldier initially, or have him characterize himself, as socially graceless, and then to ignore certain of his limitations as the play progresses and as dramatic needs more pressing than consistent characterization arise. Even in the prose fiction of Rich and Breton there are few scruples against allowing a supposedly inarticulate soldier to defend himself with increasing eloquence. The taciturnity of Martianus, for example, gives way during the passionate moments of the trial to the most sincere utterance of the author himself. And dramatists like Beaumont and Fletcher tend to be no more troubled by changes of this sort. Memnon, the almost illiterate hero of *The Mad Lover,* rises in the final scene to some of Fletcher's most facile poetry.

But Shakespeare, although not innocent of disconcerting changes in characters, was to demonstrate that the discrepancy between verbal characterization and actual performance need not be careless dramaturgy. Occasionally, for instance, the supposed discrepancy is superficial only. Fuller exposure to the soldier makes it clear that what appears to be a change in Shakespeare's intentions was premeditated and artistically advantageous. Above all, few firmly typed soldiers are used as important characters in Shakespeare. They may reveal occasional traits of the rude stereotype, but these seldom dominate the entire portrait. And when they do, they are brought to life in such new and poetic ways that the effect is that of an individual creation.

VII

Titus Andronicus was Shakespeare's first experiment with a play centering about a professional warrior who has returned in triumph to court. Because Shakespeare's concern with Titus' role as a soldier was only incidental, the play interests us primarily as a tentative use of themes and materials that were to be important in later works. We shall not find here, for example, a clearly defined statement of Titus' disabilities in court, but it is apparent that he is more vulnerable there than on the battlefield. And we shall not find the usual scene in which the returned soldier appears in self-defense against courtly disgrace or the law, but there is a comparable scene in which Titus pleads, not for himself, but for two of his sons.

Shakespeare's interest in Titus was, at least initially, in the ironic contrast between what a victorious warrior expects upon returning to court and what he receives. It is the contrast most pointedly stated in a ballad, probably influenced by the play, wherein Titus tells his own tragic story:

> You noble minds and famous martial wights,
> That in defence of native countries fights,
> Give ear to me, that ten years fought for Rome,
> Yet reap'd disgrace at my returning home.[45]

Shakespeare's source for the play, if we can judge from the eighteenth-century chapbook preserved in the Folger Library, did not begin with Titus' return, but with his Gothic wars and the background leading to Tamora's role in the tragedy.[46] By placing Titus' triumph at the beginning of the play and by supplying ironic overtones throughout the scene, the dramatist seems intent on sharpening the tragic contrast between war and court.

In the first scene, character after character acclaims Titus' honorable return; and the General himself announces his happiness as, "bound with laurel boughs," he weeps "tears of true joy for his return to Rome" (I.i.74–76). The tragic irony is underscored by the *requiescat* which Titus speaks at the burial of his sons who died in war (I.i.150):

> In peace and honour rest you here, my sons;
> Rome's readiest champions, repose you here in rest,
> Secure from worldly chances and mishaps!
> Here lurks no treason, here no envy swells,
> Here grow no damned drugs, here are no storms,
> No noise, but silence and eternal sleep.
> In peace and honour rest you here, my sons!

The phrase "peace and honour" is used twice, not without ominous meaning. The blessings of peace and the blessings of honor are seldom to be available to live warriors anywhere in Shakespeare.

Titus is conceivably aware of the mischances like treason and envy which he, unlike his dead sons, may have to reckon with in peace. He does not act, however, with the diffidence of a man who faces an uncongenial way of life—as Coriolanus, for instance, is to act. He refuses the dictatorship, it is true, but he does so only because of extreme age, not because it requires a mentality alien to his. Moreover, Shakespeare does not pursue the returned-soldier theme much beyond the opening act of the play. As Titus changes from hapless victim to fantastically cunning avenger, it is hard to remember that he is fundamentally a noble warrior victimized by intrigue.

Only one speech, occurring in the middle of the play, emphatically reminds us of the opening scenes with their ironic promise. Two of Titus' sons who survived the war are now to pay the penalty of the law for killing in peace. And Titus is placed in the position of the defendant soldier speaking on their behalf before the judges and senators who walk heedlessly past his kneeling figure (III.i.1):

> Hear me, grave fathers—noble Tribunes, stay,
> For pity of mine age, whose youth was spent
> In dangerous wars whilst you securely slept.
> For all my blood in Rome's great quarrel shed,
> For all the frosty nights that I have watch'd,
> And for these bitter tears which now you see
> Filling the aged wrinkles in my cheeks,
> Be pitiful to my condemned sons,
> Whose souls are not corrupted as 'tis thought.
> For two-and-twenty sons I never wept,
> Because they died in honour's lofty bed.

Titus is thus subjected to a dual irony: losing two of his sons not honorably in war but dishonorably in peace, and then finding that his own recently acclaimed services to Rome are irrelevant to civil law. It is significant that both these ironies should be present in so early a play as *Titus*, for their presence indicates that it was not solely the example of Essex which motivated their use in *Timon of Athens*.

One other aspect of *Titus* is notable as a foreshadowing of its more considerate use in both *Timon* and *Coriolanus*. This is the theme of the exiled warrior, a theme prominent in non-dramatic writings but apparently Shakespeare's addition to the Andronicus story. Lucius, another of Titus' sons, is banished, rather than executed, for a civil indiscretion: he had drawn his sword to rescue his two condemned brothers. In exile, he places himself at the disposal of Rome's enemies, the Goths, and becomes the general of their army. Later, when leading this army against Rome, he expresses the conventional grievance of the soldier abused and dishonored by his own country (V.iii.104):

> myself unkindly banished,
> The gates shut on me, and turn'd weeping out
> To beg relief among Rome's enemies;
> Who drown'd their enmity in my true tears
> And op'd their arms to embrace me as a friend.
> I am the turned forth, be it known to you,
> That have preserv'd her welfare in my blood
> And from her bosom took the enemy's point,
> Sheathing the steel in my advent'rous body.
> Alas, you know I am no vaunter, I!
> My scars can witness, dumb although they are,
> That my report is just and full of truth.

In a sense, then, although Titus himself is not persistently represented in terms of the returned conqueror, the theme is finally restated in the person of his son. Like his father, Lucius has fallen afoul of the society for which he fought. Like Titus, in defending himself he pleads the value of his warlike services.

It is especially noteworthy that the military profession, represented by the Andronici, is actually vindicated in this play, and that it is vindicated in opposition to the political body, represented by Saturninus, the dictator, as well as by such embodiments of Machiavellian craft as Aaron and Tamora. Overtly, of course, this soldierly justification is effected only by the soldiers' own tactics—an army and murder. But more basically the warriors are justified because of the context in which they are placed. Their opponents are so criminally wrong that the soldiers by contrast seem unquestionably right. One is not invited to question the rightness of

Titus' headstrong behavior early in the play or of Lucius' essentially treasonable action at the end. In later plays there is not only a more critical awareness of such actions but an awareness more explicitly associated with soldiers as soldiers.

VIII

In *Richard III* Shakespeare at first gives every indication that now he means to construct a play dealing pointedly and persistently with the problem of the returned conqueror. In his famous opening soliloquy, the martially victorious Richard speaks from the vantage point of a confirmed warrior unhappily facing a peaceful world. Like Titus, his brow is "bound with victorious wreaths," but unlike Titus he is consciously critical of the way of life which now confronts him. What is more, he is as much aware as any Elizabethan soldier author of the incompatibility between court and wars:

> Grim-visag'd War hath smooth'd his wrinkled front,
> And now, instead of mounting barbed steeds
> To fright the souls of fearful adversaries,
> He capers nimbly in a lady's chamber
> To the lascivious pleasing of a lute.

Richard states that he is unfit for this transformation. He is not "shap'd for sportive tricks" nor "made to court an amorous looking glass." In "this weak piping time of peace," he cannot hope to prove a lover, and therefore,

> To entertain these fair well-spoken days,
> I am determined to prove a villain
> And hate the idle pleasures of these days.

Except for the villainous resolution, Richard's self-portraiture is not far different from the simple but highly favorable character which Barnaby Rich gives Sappho, duke of Mantona. Sappho too, "the warres beyng once finished," found that he was inferior to those who "had any facultie in them tendyng to pleasure and delight." Also, like Richard, he could not "fayne or syng ditties in a ladies chamber." Except for one important difference, moreover, Richard III's deliberate adoption of villainy and intrigue is curiously related to Barnaby Rich's own cynical advice to his "good companions and fellowe souldiours": "If you will followe myne advice, laie aside your weapons, hang up your armours by the walles, and learne an other while (for your better advauncementes) to pipe, to feddle, to syng, to daunce, to lye, to forge, to flatter, to cary tales, to set ruffe, or to doe any thyng that your appetites beste serve unto, and that is better fittyng for the tyme."[47] The important difference is that Rich recommends, aware of its ridiculous impossibility, that his unfortunate military brotherhood learn the courtier's art; Richard, in dead earnest and with conviction of success, turns effortlessly from a career of war to a career of courtly intrigue—and that of the most criminal sort.

Although there would seem to be a contradiction in character between the hapless Richard of the first part of the soliloquy and the cunning Richard of the second part and of the play as a whole, the contradiction is a superficial one and probably does not indicate either that Richard radically misunderstood his own nature or that Shakespeare needed two Richards for his play. The only courtly failing acknowledged by Richard is that of the lover, and his disability as a lover is due more to his deformed body than to his ungainly manners. He promptly demonstrates, in fact, that he is an extraordinarily gifted wooer. It is natural, however, that Richard should see himself also, in idealized form, as a victim of peace and society as well as of "dissembling Nature." But Shakespeare did not choose to elaborate further in this play upon the theme of the misplaced soldier. If pursued, the theme would do more than motivate his villain; it would win unwanted sympathy for him. Shakespeare therefore used only enough of the formula of the returned conqueror to make of Richard a disaffected but not an unfortunate soldier.

IX

In the Hotspur of *1 Henry IV* we encounter a more complicated example of the misplaced soldier. There is not only a more apparent inconsistency between Hotspur's avowed character as a soldier and his actual behavior, but also a more interesting ambiguity concerning the degree of sympathy he should receive. But Hotspur's role is, for our purposes, most remarkable in that it represents Shakespeare's first considered attempt to depict a self-consciously rough, soldierly behavior and its political consequences, and to employ a soldier as defendant in an important scene.

That Shakespeare intended to enlist his audience's interest in Hotspur as a warrior unlucky in political and domestic affairs, is suggested by the familiar pattern of a triumphant return from war to immediate troubles at court. In the first scene, Percy is repeatedly eulogized for the honor he has won against the Scots. But the scene ends with the King's ominous announcement that the young hero has already been summoned to court to answer the charge of having withheld prisoners. Thus Hotspur's first appearance on the stage is significantly not on the battlefield but in the palace; what is more, he is at once presented in the defensive position habitual to the Elizabethan soldier.

In this appearance the stand taken by Hotspur and by others on his behalf has certain features of the conventional apology of the soldier found in nondramatic works. It is true that Hotspur is not defending the military profession as such. But as a representative of that profession defending himself, he utilizes the role of the early soldier apologists and employs a defensive technique similar to theirs.

Basically, his apology is that he was asked about the prisoners during a military situation that made a civil answer impossible. The battle was just over, and Hotspur was "dry with rage and extreme toil, / Breathless and faint, leaning upon [his] sword" (I.iii.30). "All smarting with [his] wounds being cold," out of grief and impatience he "answer'd neglectingly," he knew not what (I.iii.49–52). The psychology behind this excuse is more fully explained by Samuel Daniel's Philotas at his great trial scene, as he apologizes for his irreverent words about Alexander:

> And God forbid, that ever souldiers words
> Should be made liable unto misdeeds,
> When fainting in their march, tir'd in the fight,
> Sick in their tent, stopping their wounds that bleed,
> Or haut and jolly after conquest got,
> They shall out of their heate use words unkinde.[48]

The basis of conflict in Hotspur's defensive stand is also comparable to that found in the nondramatic works. His unstudied words—so he and his father assert—had been maliciously embellished by the person who reported them to the King. According to Northumberland,

> Either envy, therefore, or misprision
> Is guilty of this fault, and not my son.
>   (I.iii.27)

And Hotspur requests that the informer's words not be held against him (I.iii.67):

> let not his report
> Come current for an accusation
> Betwixt my love and your high majesty.

More specifically, Hotspur conceives his real adversary, the informer, to have been a courtier. And in Hotspur's eyes this courtier has both the foppish elegance and the malice of Rich's Gloriosus, who, it will be remembered, distorted an innocent statement by the honest soldier Martianus and testified against him in court. But Shakespeare departs from the traditional trial scene pattern of courtier vs. soldier by not bringing the former on stage. Instead he both enlivens and complicates the stereotype by presenting the dispute through the observant eyes and picturesque speech of the supposedly plain soldier, Hotspur. The courtier, thus presented by his conventional—but not conventionally inarticulate—adversary, emerges with extraordinary vividness. He appears, moreover, not in court but—a happy innovation—on the battlefield. There, we learn, he had suddenly presented himself to Hotspur, "neat and trimly dress'd, / Fresh as a bridegroom," and "perfumed like a milliner." On the battlefield his speech is as grossly inappropriate as the soldier's would be in court. "With many holiday and lady terms," the courtier questioned Hotspur, and talked about war "like a waiting gentlewoman" (I.iii.33–56).

No exact antecedent for Shakespeare's brilliant scene exists, but a faint suggestion for it may have come from Rich's *Farewell,* a book that Shakespeare demonstrably used for *Twelfth Night* and *The Merry Wives of Windsor,*[40] and probably, as we shall see, for *Henry V*. In his address "To the noble Souldiers, bothe of Englande and Irelande," Rich tells how he met a dandy fantastically dressed and holding a fan of feathers "verie womanly" against his face. Rich was moved to ask one of this fop's followers "what gentlewoman his master was?"[50] But Rich does not clearly place the encounter between soldier and courtier on the battlefield, a setting which gives Shakespeare splendid opportunity for a detailed account of the dandy's discomfiture and the soldier's angry contempt.

Despite the brilliance of this scene, Shakespeare gains much of its picturesqueness by sacrificing, to a degree never found in Rich, the soldier's integrity as a man of simple language. This integrity was of some importance in Hotspur's case, not only because it helped justify the conventional conflict with the courtier, but because elsewhere in the play Hotspur describes himself as a man of few words and plain sentiments: "I, that have not well the gift of tongue" (V.ii.78); "For I profess not talking" (V.ii.92); "By God, I cannot flatter, I defy / The tongues of soothers" (IV.i.6); he winces at poetry (III.i.129-135); and for love he has a soldier's contempt (II.iii.94):

> This is no world
> To play with mammets and to tilt with lips.
> We must have bloody noses and crack'd crowns,
> And pass them current too.

Granted that Hotspur is inclined to be tactless in human relationships and ill-adjusted to civil life; still, laconic speech and a limited emotional capacity are traits that conflict not only with his poetic eloquence in the courtier scene but with the facts of the play as a whole. His claim to taciturnity seems

to have impressed only those who have never known him
well. In fact, Prince Hal alone refers to Hotspur's poverty of
speech. Likening his eloquence to that of Francis the drawer,
who has "fewer words than a parrot," Hal continues (II.-
iv.114):

> I am not yet of Percy's mind, the Hotspur of the North; he that
> kills me some six or seven dozen of Scots at a breakfast, washes his
> hands, and says to his wife, 'Fie upon this quiet life! I want work.'
> 'O my sweet Harry,' says she, 'how many hast thou killed to-day?'
> 'Give my roan horse a drench,' says he, and answers 'Some four-
> teen,' an hour after, 'a trifle, a trifle.'

Hal's burlesque does, of course, aptly catch the formula of
Hotspur's relationship with his wife and his passion for war.
But it does not necessarily mean that young Percy's coldness
of spirit and taciturnity are natural traits. Even Hal's notion
of Hotspur, distantly acquired though it is, may have a per-
ceptiveness characteristic of the Prince in that it hints at
something affected about the youth's behavior. Those who
know Hotspur more intimately are not deceived by what
he says about himself. His wife seems undismayed by his
curt way with her and his attitude toward love. And referring to him eulogistically in Part II, she describes his speech
as defectively "thick," by which she seems to mean that his
words came pell-mell. And she also indicates that he spoke
in a spasmodic manner, with a high pitch; for, she adds,

> those that could speak low and tardily
> Would turn their own perfection to abuse
> To seem like him.
>
> (II.iii.24–28)

Both his father and his uncle have occasion in the palace scene in Part I to regret Hotspur's compulsive and spirited garrulity. As Northumberland tells him,

> Why, what a wasp-stung and impatient fool
> Art thou to break into this woman's mood,
> Tying thine ear to no tongue but thine own!
> (I.iii.236)

It is fairly clear that Hotspur is anything but the strong, silent type he professes to be; and it is equally clear that Shakespeare wrought this situation consciously and successfully. The playwright wanted primarily a high-spirited, poetic, and imaginative youth to give vitality and some beauty to the conspiracy; to embody, in contrast with Falstaff, the strenuous concept of honor;[51] and to provide a general temperamentally ill-matched with Glendower and Worcester. But Shakespeare also recognized an opportunity to deepen this character study psychologically and to enliven it comically by creating a Hotspur who fancied himself in the role of soldier both plain and martyred.

To what extent Hotspur's scene with the courtier is the result of his own imagination, it is difficult to say. No character in Shakespeare is less able to separate fact from make-believe. Probably his colorful narration of Mortimer's heroic stand against Glendower, an engagement he had not seen, is an idealized version which he mistakes for actuality. His own encounter with the courtier is perhaps equally idealized—though not consciously falsified—to fit the artistic design which he has come to recognize as traditional and right for a soldier vilified. The King takes characteristically a more literal view of the situation, dourly noting after Hotspur's long self-defense, "Why, yet he doth deny his prisoners"

(I.iii.77). Hotspur, like Rich's Martianus, had defended himself mainly by damning a courtier.

Since, from the facts unmistakably present, both Hotspur and the King are at fault, it is difficult to decide how the Elizabethan audience would have apportioned its sympathy in the scene. Hotspur errs in his defiance of royal authority. But Henry appears equally unreasonable for refusing to listen to any argument which might lead to the ransom of Mortimer, and what reasons he secretly has for the refusal are not admirable ones. During this scene, at least, the audience's sympathy would probably have gone to the abused General, even though his self-defense proves, upon second thought, to have been more imaginative than logical and relevant. Newsworthy events in England during the 1590's had made the plight of returned commanders like Hotspur especially understandable, and Shakespeare may well have reacted to this situation as his contemporary Spenser had done in 1595. According to Josephine Waters Bennett, Spenser converted in this year the whole of the twelfth canto of Book V of *The Faerie Queene* to fit allegorically the current misfortunes of Sir John Norris. In London, Spenser had heard criticism of Norris' conduct of the Irish campaign and, indignant at this carping attitude, had mirrored Norris' plight in the attack on Artegall by Envy and Detraction. "Contemporary readers," Mrs. Bennett argues, "would undoubtedly understand and relish the scornful satire of the closing stanzas in which the poet foresees for Norris the envy and detraction which met all commanders upon their return from Ireland. That had been the fate of Lord Grey, and more recently Sir John Parrot had died in the Tower after coming home from Ireland to face a trial for treason."[52] There is certainly a similarity between

these instances and the kind of disgrace which Hotspur, as a
returning general, faces at the beginning of *1 Henry IV*. His
sovereign, he complains (IV.iii.92), "disgrac'd me in my
happy victories"; and it is this sense of unmerited disgrace,
rather than any blameworthy conduct that might have justified it, that the audience is apt to feel during the scene in
the palace.

If, however, the audience is at first encouraged to sympathize with Hotspur as the wronged general, it is not permitted
long to dwell upon that aspect of his soldierly character. As
Shakespeare gradually darkens the original brightness of the
conspiracy, showing its leaders as selfish individualists, he
begins to explore Hotspur as the crude rather than unlucky
soldier. The youth's affected plainness may be lightly, even
pleasantly, depicted; but the fierce and unaffected willfulness
of his temper appears in uglier hues. As we saw in the second
chapter, this temper threatens to ruin the conspiracy by alienating Glendower. Shakespeare puts an authoritative rebuke
of Percy's uncivil conduct into the mouth of Worcester
(III.i.177):

> In faith, my lord, you are too wilful-blame,
> And since your coming hither have done enough
> To put him [Glendower] quite besides his patience.
> You must needs learn, lord, to amend this fault.
> Though sometimes it shows greatness, courage, blood—
> And that's the dearest grace it renders you—
> Yet oftentimes it doth present harsh rage,
> Defect of manners, want of government,
> Pride, haughtiness, opinion, and disdain;
> The least of which haunting a nobleman
> Loseth men's hearts, and leaves behind a stain
> Upon the beauty of all parts besides,
> Beguiling them of commendation.

Worcester himself may not be an attractive character, but he has at least a knowledge of civil life that his nephew lacks, or refuses to recognize. Similarly, Francis Bacon, not an entirely engaging human being, had recently been able to give practical advice to Essex on adapting himself to civil situations. This advice, too, went unheeded—with tragic results.

Unlike Essex, and unlike most of Shakespeare's other great soldiers, Hotspur has the good fortune to die in war rather than peace. But before Shakespeare permits his young warrior a final return to his only congenial kind of employment, he has exposed him to the oblique light of civil life sufficiently to show his shortcomings as a citizen and the rightness of civil government under even so doubtful a sovereign as Henry IV.

x

In *Henry V* Shakespeare concentrates during one sustained episode upon a theme developed only slightly in *Richard III* and *1 Henry IV:* the difficulties of the soldier in love.[53] Although Henry's amorous trouble represents, as in the earlier two plays, a turning from war to peace and from battlefield to court, it differs in that it comes at the end of the play and not as an unrestful beginning. Its purpose is a comic and lighthearted aftermath to Henry's solemn business in the war. It restores opportunely—just after the severity of the peace treaty, in fact—the genial Prince Hal of *1 Henry IV*.

By failing to recognize that the courtship scene is meant to depict the distress of a plain soldier in a sophisticated situation, critics have almost uniformly misjudged and undervalued Henry's role in it. To Swinburne, the King's conduct had "the savour rather of a ploughman than a prince"; Mark

Van Doren was reminded of a "hearty undergraduate with enormous initials on his chest"; and to John Palmer the scene unpleasantly suggested the traits which "are most admired in the legendary Englishman."[54] E. E. Stoll correctly perceived that "the wooing scene itself ... must have been enough to float the play,"[55] but he neglected to place the work in the body of popular thought which would explain its appeal to theatergoers.

Probably it is knowledge of the immediate source of Shakespeare's scene, with the implication that Shakespeare felt bound to use it, that has caused critics to overlook the dramatist's enthusiastic recreation of what he inherited. The courtship scene in *The Famous Victories of Henry the Fifth* did indeed suggest to Shakespeare the idea not only of such an episode but also of Henry's difficulties as a wooer. In this early play, Henry proposes to Katherine bluntly:

> Tush Kate, but tell me in plaine termes,
> Canst thou love the King of England?
> I cannot do as these Countries do,
> That spend halfe their time in wooing.[56]

But the scene is brief and perfunctory. No reason is given for Henry's curt directness except lack of the more leisurely European manners. Above all, there is no reference to Henry as a soldier; and this is precisely what we do find, thoroughly elaborated, in Shakespeare; and it is this which becomes the reason for Henry's unhappiness in the French court.

His roughness in courting Katherine is constantly related to the conventional soldierly temperament, as it was denounced by critics and acknowledged by defenders of the profession. "I speak to thee plain soldier," Henry tells the demure French princess (V.ii.157); and again, "take me, take a soldier." The very outset of the wooing stresses the plain soldier's inability to command the niceties of language. "Fair Katherine, and most fair!" the King essays,

> Will you vouchsafe to teach a soldier terms
> Such as will enter at a lady's ear . . . ?
> (V.ii.98)

Henry then proclaims his inability to "mince it in love." He has "neither the voice nor the heart of flattery" about him. And equally characteristic of the professed martialist, he wants the graces of poetry and dancing: "For the one I have neither words nor measure; and for the other I have no strength in measure, yet a reasonable measure of strength."

Besides these conventional disabilities, Henry suffers another handicap often associated with the soldier as lover: he is not handsome, and he confesses the fact at length. His face is "not worth sunburning." He "never looks in his glass for love of anything" he sees there. When he comes to woo ladies he frightens them. But his comfort is, "that old age, that ill layer-up of beauty, can do no more spoil upon [his] face"; and he dares hope that Katherine will love him "notwithstanding the poor and untempering effect of [his] visage." These strictures upon Henry's face are of course Shakespeare's invention. The historical Henry had, according to C. L. Kingsford (and contemporary portraits), "an oval, handsome face with a broad, open forehead and straight nose."[57] But one need merely turn to early comments upon the soldierly type of face to see where Shakespeare got Henry's professed ugliness. Barnaby Rich notes that soldiers were expected to have "a Crab-tree looke, a sowre countenance, and a hard favoured visage."[58] Commenting upon types known to physiognomy, Ben Jonson pays detailed attention to "your souldiers face, a menacing, and astounding face, that lookes broad, and bigge; the grace of this face consisteth much in a beard."[59] This face would obviously frighten ladies; and in Fletcher's *The Captain,* Jacomo's "rusty swarth Complexion" affords women both alarm and merriment.[60]

Grossly handicapped though Henry may be when taken from his native element and placed in the polite company of women, Shakespeare assuredly did not intend his mirror of Christian kings and ideal general to be finally an object of ridicule. Henry himself, as a matter of fact, far from regarding his lack of the polite virtues as a disgrace, proffers his plain traits as credentials for his fitness as a lover. "And while thou liv'st," he advises the Princess (V.ii.160), "take a fellow of plain and uncoined constancy; for he perforce must do thee right, because he hath not the gift to woo in other places."

But the point of view expressed by Henry did not become at all tenable in England without considerable debate. Indeed, the question of whether a soldier might retain without ridicule his plain traits in the company of women was one of the most popular adjuncts of the larger question concerning the status of the soldier in society. It was also connected with the popular debate as to the worth of the soldier as lover.

Courtly tradition had firmly established a contemptuous attitude toward the soldier who was unable or unwilling to forget his soldiership when in female company; and for Elizabethan purposes this attitude was most influentially expressed in Castiglione's *The Courtier.* One of Count Lewis' most felicitous anecdotes is that told in ridicule of the graceless warrior:

For unto such may well be said, that a worthie gentle woman in a noble assemblie spake pleasantly unto one ... whom she to shew him a good countenance, desired to daunce with her, and hee refusing it, and to heare musicke, and many other entertainments offered him, alwaies affirming such trifles not to be his profession, at last the gentlewoman demaunding him, what is then your profession? he answered with a frowning looke, to fight.

Then saide the Gentlewoman: seeing you are not now at the warre nor in place to fight, I would think it best for you to be well besmered and set up in an armory with other implements of warre till time were that you should be occupied, least you waxe more rustier than you are. Thus with much laughing of the standers by, she left him with a mocke in his foolish presumption.[61]

It is appropriate that from so civilized a group the plain soldier should be dismissed with urbane derision and with that most humiliating of weapons, feminine laughter.

In early fiction and drama, likewise, the attitude of Castiglione's soldier is used almost solely to provide derisive comedy. Anaxius, a similar warrior in the *Arcadia,* is absurdly and professedly resistant to love and the social graces.[62] Lyly gives the attitude almost a clownish embodiment in the person of Sir Thopas. In Greene's *Orlando Furioso,* we meet a character who promises at first to approximate the role of Henry V. A confirmed warrior, Sacrepant falls in love with Angelica and proposes accordingly:

> Then know, my love, I cannot paint my grief,
> Nor tell a tale of Venus and her son.
>
> . . . .
>
> It fits not Sacrepant to be effeminate.[63]

But Sacrepant proves to be an unscrupulous individual, and the reader is left in little doubt that Greene approved of neither the wooer nor the wooing.

There was also, in many works, only slight approval of the worth of soldiers as lovers. The young lady in *The Captain* expresses the conventional opinion incisively:

> I had as lieve be courted by a Cannon
> As one of those.[64]

In Marlowe's *Tamburlaine,* a disappointed suitor warns Zeno-crate (incorrectly, as it turns out) that the conqueror will make an unsatisfactory lover:

> How can you fancie one that lookes so fierce,
> Onelie disposed to martiall Stratagems?
> Who when he shall embrace you in his armes,
> Will tell you how many thousand men he slew,
> And when you look for amorous discourse,
> Will rattle foorth his facts of war and blood,
> Too harsh a subject for your dainty ears.[65]

That this amorous technique had become conventionally expected of soldiers is suggested in a typical debate written by Barnaby Rich. Therein a man defends the soldier as lover, but a woman advocates the courtier. The courtier, states the woman, "with seamly personage, with honourable behaviour, with philed phrases, with sweet musicke, and with twentie amorous devices will delude the time so pretely, that we Laidies can not imagine them, but to be the onely ministers to our pleasure." "The Souldiour," on the other hand, "is fed with murthers, delighted in blodshed, the memorie of his pleasures most loothsome."[66] Evidence that Shakespeare was aware of these conventional objections to soldierly strategy in love is found in the complaint of Hotspur's Kate that as she lies beside him at night she hears him

> murmur tales of iron wars,
> Speak terms of manage to thy bounding steed,
> Cry 'Courage! to the field!'
> (*1 Henry IV* II.iii.51)

Similarly, if there is any truth in Hal's impression of the marriage, at breakfast Kate seeks conversation with her strong, silent husband by asking, "How many hast thou kill'd to-day?" (*1 Henry IV* II.iv.119).

If it is asked why, in the light of this derisive attitude toward the plain soldier as wooer and lover, Shakespeare chose to subject King Henry to this humiliation—and at the end of the play, to boot—one might merely answer that here was another example of Hal's play-acting, and that the audience was not expected to take it seriously. This explanation is largely true, but it is also open to one or two questions. Why, if Henry chooses to play a role, does he select one that would impress the audience as churlish? And why would he do so in a scene in which he represents not only a conqueror but an English conqueror? It was surely not Shakespeare's purpose to commend French urbanity at the expense of the English.

As we noticed in the study of Henry as general, his choice of conduct is usually appropriate to each situation. He is a consciously exemplary general in that he knows, as well as performs, the actions befitting a Christian general. It is therefore likely that as he turns from a military to a civilian problem, he should choose his conduct with some awareness of its fitness. He consciously chose, I believe, a role that would vindicate English manhood without conveying also the character of clownish roughness. His choosing the role of the plain soldier as lover was due not only to his actually being in a position of a conqueror, fresh from the battlefield, now in a French court, but to Shakespeare's awareness that this role had, by 1599, begun to acquire dignity and popular approval—enough, at any rate, to warrant using it to animate the stiff and scarcely motivated behavior of Henry in *The Famous Victories*.

No single influence can account for this change in attitude toward the soldier as wooer. It could not have been simply the labors of those who defended the military profession, since they had not been able to elevate and make secure the status of the professional warrior generally. That the soldier as uncouth lover was approved, whereas the soldier as a disruptive force in civil government remained under suspicion, may have been because the uncouth lover could do less harm. Henry V, unlike Hotspur, never allows his rudeness to injure the state or his political relationships.

If, however, any one writer specifically prepared the way for the courtship scene in *Henry V*, it was Barnaby Rich; and the particular book was again the *Farewell to Militarie Profession*, which Shakespeare had but recently used for incidents in *The Merry Wives*. What is more, the story in the *Farewell* which he had used for *The Merry Wives*—"Of Two Brethren and Their Wives"—was precisely the one which would have helped him in *Henry V*.

The major character in this tale is a soldier "lately retourned from the warres, I gesse aboute the same tyme that Kyng Henry the Fift was retourned from the winnyng of Agincourt feelde." Happening to espy a beautiful woman, this ungainly creature is "sodainly stroken into a greate[r] maze to see this lampe of light, then ever he had been in the feelde to see the ensignes of his enemies." He is nevertheless able to make a forthright declaration of his love, at which the woman shows seemly alarm. Disturbed but not routed by her modesty, the soldier confesses his inability to court with due elegance. "Gentlewoman," he announces, "I am not able to encounter you with wordes, because it hath not been my trainyng up, but if you doubte of my love and good likyng, please it you to make triall." The gentlewoman, who "had never been apposed with such a rough heawen fellowe, that was so blunt and plaine, as well in his gesture as in his tearmes, beganne to thinke with herself that he might well bee a Souldiour, for she knewe that thei had little skill in the courting of gentlewomen." The significant, and unusual, aspect of this episode is that the soldier's suit is successful and that he is favored over two more gifted individuals, a doctor and a lawyer. What is even more unusual, the woman accepts the soldier because of his very "plainnesse," for "she perceived by his countenance the vehemencie of the love he bare unto her."[87]

Rich's endorsement of the soldier's behavior in "Two Brethren" owes much of its sincerity to the manner in which this episode parallels the author's own endeavor in the book as a whole. Rich, himself a soldier, is self-consciously trying to win the favor of "the right courteous Gentlewomen, bothe of Englande and Irelande," to whom he dedicates the *Farewell*. In this unwonted venture he is troubled by his social limitations. He finds in himself "no one maner of exercise, that might give me the least hope to win your good likinges." In a passage suggesting Henry V's misgivings about dancing, Rich confesses his awkwardness in "measures": "Although I like the measures verie well, yet I could never treade them aright, nor to use measure in any thyng I went aboute."[88] Again, like Henry, he laments his inability to "discourse

pleasauntly, to drive away the tyme with amourous devises";
nor is he able "to propone pretie questions, or to give readie
aunsweres."[69]

We see, then, in the *Farewell* a significant and remarkably
early reversal of the usual attitude toward the plain soldier as
suitor. He is not brought into the picture merely that we may
deride his ungainly appearance. In Rich the soldier is the
hero. He will obviously make the best husband; and it is to
be regretted that gentlewomen are deceived by accomplished
"love makers, suche as can devise to please women with newe
fangles, straunge fassions, by praisyng of their beauties."[70]

Rich's attitude was gradually adopted by other writers before the turn of the century, and by many writers thereafter.
In Greene's fictional *Tullies Love* (1589), Lentulus, a soldier
fresh from battle, confronts the ladies at court with a proud
rather than shamefaced statement of his limitations. He cannot, he declares, "faine conceited supposes of affection to
proove my selfe lovesicke, by Poetrie. But as a blunt souldier
newe come from the warres, I offer my selfe a devoted servant
to your beauties."[71] His suit is unsuccessful, but his role is a
sympathetic one. In dramatic performances, especially, Shakespeare's Henry had antecedents and contemporaries. In a
formal program of *Speeches Delivered to Her Majestie this
Last Progresse* (1592), "an olde gentleman, sometimes a souldier," pays his devotion to the Queen by claiming a greater
sincerity for his "rough hewen" speech than that found in
courtly addresses. We soldiers, he declares, "use not with
wordes to amplifie our conceites, and to pleade faith by figures, but by deedes to show the loyalty of our harts."[72] A more
comparable dramatic precedent for Henry's courtship was
that of William the Conqueror in *Faire Em* (*ca.* 1590), who

proposes plainly, though without most of the specific disabilities of Shakespeare's hero:

> I cannot, Madam, tell a loving tale,
>
> . . . .
>
> That am a soldier sworn to follow arms—
> But this I bluntly let you understand—
> I honour you with such religious zeal
> As may become an honourable mind.[73]

In *Olde Fortunatus,* a play which followed *Henry V* so closely in time that influence is unlikely, Dekker revealed that he had thoroughly accepted the point of view of the *Farewell.* Orleans, a professedly plain soldier seeking the hand of Agripyne, and maligned as an inept wooer by a rival, is gratifyingly defended by the young lady herself:

Me thinkes a Souldier is the most faithfull lover of all men els: for his affection stands not upon complement: his wooing is plaine home-spun stuffe; theres no outlandish thred in it, no Rhetoricke: a Souldier casts no figures to get his mistris heart, his love is like his valour in the field, when he payes downeright blowes.[74]

By the time Donne wrote his *Paradoxes and Problemes* the successful direction of the soldier as wooer was still considered somewhat of a paradox, but an accepted one nevertheless. Bashfulness in wooing, Donne writes, "is far from men of Valour, and especially from souldiers, for such are ever men (without doubt) forward and confident, losing no time least they should lose opportunity, which is the best Factor for a Lover, and because they know women are given to dissemble, they will never believe them when they deny."[75]

Shakespeare had obviously chosen for his hero a role which proved just as suitable for the late 1590's as it would have proved unsuitable for the 1570's or even the 1580's. It was a role, moreover, harmonious with the lowest, but not the least impressive, patriotic message of the play: French sophistication coming under the heel of English manliness. And despite Henry's assured intelligence in other civil matters, it was a role happily befitting a military hero who prevailed

> without stratagem,
> But in plain shock and even play of battle.
> (IV.viii.113)

XI

The perseverance of the theme of soldier as successful wooer is faintly visible in *Othello,* Shakespeare's next play concerned with the problems of the warrior in society.[76] Othello, who seems to Brabantio a rude, barbarous warrior, and a mercenary at that, has won Desdemona's hand in competition with "the wealthy curled darlings of our nation" (I.ii.68). Othello's success seems to the outraged father so incredible that he suspects the Moor of having used "mixtures pow'rful o'er the blood" to influence the maiden (I.iii.104). Actually, as Othello's "round unvarnish'd" story of his courtship makes clear, he had won Desdemona by recounting "the battles, sieges, fortunes" he had experienced (I.iii.130), and by doing so at her request. If, she had told Othello, a friend who loved her were to tell her this story, "that would woo her."

Although a similar ineptitude underlies both proposals, Othello's solemn, diffident recital is a far cry from Henry V's brusque wooing. Henry talks vigorously about the soldier's courtly troubles; Othello more genuinely illustrates them, and is fated to suffer the consequences of his ignorance of love, women, and courtly ways.

It is not, however, at all clear how far Shakespeare intended to pattern Othello's tragic discomfiture after the soldierly stereotype. That the Moor was meant to be viewed as a soldier unlucky once out of his "occupation" is probable; but that he was also meant, because of rude as well as simple traits, to be significantly responsible for his tragedy, is more questionable. As a Shakespearean tragic hero, Othello defies most attempts at classification; but as the least complex of the major heroes, he is more readily confined than a character like Hamlet. It is at any rate illuminating to find occasional evidence in this play that Shakespeare had in mind the soldier's traditional difficulties in turning from casque to cushion.

It is first of all apparent that, perhaps more than any other Shakespearean general, Othello is a professional soldier. War is his sole occupation, and in his great farewell to it he expresses both devotion to the profession and his pain at leaving it. Once "Othello's occupation's gone," all purpose, all control, seem to go from his life.

Early in the play he gives intimations not merely that war is his sole element but that his personality has been shaped to fit this way of life. If it were not for his love for Desdemona, a rare and strange thing for him, he would not his

> unhoused free condition
> Put into circumscription and confine
> For the sea's worth.
>
> (I.ii.26)

When, just after his marriage, he is dispatched for military duty in Cyprus, he gladly accepts a return to that austerity and barrenness of life that has become natural to him (I.iii.-230):

> The tryant custom, most grave senators,
> Hath made the flinty and steel couch of war

> My thrice-driven bed of down. I do agnize
> A natural and prompt alacrity
> I find in hardness.

It is important to remember that many Renaissance thinkers, including the Machiavelli of Othello's Italy, would have regarded this addiction pessimistically.

Perhaps the clearest evidence of Shakespeare's associating Othello with the plain-soldier convention is in the shaping of the early scenes to place the Moor in a defensive position because of rude conduct. The pattern reminds one of the introduction of Hotspur in *1 Henry IV*. When we first see Othello, he faces the law's penalty because Iago and Roderigo have informed on him. Their accusation proves, as we have seen, to be a distorted and malicious one—a plight common for the soldier.

Othello's mode of defense is also traditional. When Iago warns him that the Duke will

> put upon you what restraint and grievance
> The law, with all his might to enforce it on,
> Will give him cable,

Othello, instead of planning a direct and specific answer to the accusation, proposes to rely upon his military services:

> Let him do his spite.
> My services which I have done the signiory
> Shall outtongue his complaints.
> (I.ii.11–19)

Like Rich's soldier defendants, Othello is ungifted in the sophistries or even in the essential forms of the law, and he proposes that his military worth will prove a sufficient answer to charges involving civil crime. In fact, Othello would seem to prefer not to answer verbally at all.

He does, however, make a long and able speech of self-defense when he is brought before the Duke and senators. This speech begins, in the apologetic manner of soldiers on trial, with a declaration that he is ungifted in the language of peace (I.iii.81):

> Rude am I in my speech,
> And little bless'd with the soft phrase of peace;
> For since these arms of mine had seven years' pith
> Till now some nine moons wasted, they have us'd
> Their dearest action in the tented field;
> And little of this great world can I speak
> More than pertains to feats of broils and battle;
> And therefore little shall I grace my cause
> In speaking for myself.

The contradiction between this introduction and the controlled eloquence of the defense which follows is not the obvious and comic discrepancy found in Hotspur. Percy's "I profess not talking" is plainly an affectation and is absurdly inconsistent with his flamboyant eloquence; but there is nothing absurd or pretentiously simple about Othello's plain statement. It is the undramatized story of his life that he is earnestly summarizing, as he had recounted it more fully for Desdemona. It had been a socially impoverished life, without contact with education, women, or court. And there is nothing in the play generally, except heightened language, to contradict Othello's self-description. Superficially, of course, one might explain the power and skill of Othello's defense in terms of the defendant soldiers of Rich and others. In the trial scene of *Brusanus,* it will be remembered, there is slight connection between the apologetic introduction and the subsequent defense. But more fundamental—and more consonant with Shakespeare's superior artistry—is the explanation that Othello is not necessarily limited in intelligence because he has seen only a barren aspect of the world. And certainly there is no reason why simple language should not be warm and intense language—if it is the language of a noble and sensitive soul—especially when it is translated for the medium of poetic drama.

A similar generalization may be made about Othello's conduct. Reduced to its lowest terms, his behavior resembles that of the rude, graceless soldier type. But Othello is no ordinary soldier. With all his simplicity and social ineptness, he is an impressively enlarged and romanticized warrior. In him, rude traits take on poetic intensity and amplitude. He becomes almost the archetype of soldierly plainness, as Milton's Satan does of criminal genius.

Othello's criminal conflict with society does not come until the latter half of the play. His earlier indiscretion—the sudden and unorthodox marriage—is not interpreted by Shakespeare as seriously blameworthy. Indeed, Othello's early behavior generally, even under the stress of Brabantio's insulting accusation, is disciplined if not urbane. He resists a street brawl and controls both his sword and his temper. It is not until he comes under the influence of Iago that he proves inadequate to the Venetian milieu. It is Iago who complicates that milieu for him, by explaining to him subtleties of women and Venetian society that had never before concerned him. Only when confronted by a social problem that seems too involved for him does he abandon his civil behavior and resume the brutal, direct habits that the battlefield had necessitated." And appropriately he ends both his life and his impossible situation as he had dispatched a problem on the battlefield: he

> took by th' throat the circumcised dog
> And smote him—thus.
>
> (V.ii.355)

Shakespeare surely did not intend to condemn Othello's conduct in Venetian society on the grounds that he was a soldier who had reprehensibly failed to learn the arts of peace. Had Shakespeare intended such an interpretation, he would not have given the Moor an abnormal social predicament to contend with. He would not have wanted an Iago to complicate the issue. No doubt, only a soldier of Othello's social innocence could have fallen victim to Iago, but the blame must rest on the villain, not on the tragic hero.

It is an indication of Shakespeare's design that the relationship of Iago to Othello resembles, with interesting variations, the traditional courtier-soldier relationship. In *The Coblers Prophesie* the courtier is not only a cunning but a criminal character, in opposition to the soldier Sateros; and the criminally scheming aspect of the courtier is increasingly evident in Jacobean plays like Chapman's *Byron* and Fletcher's *The Loyal Subject*. In Iago, however, Shakespeare added a remarkable complication to the stereotype. Iago is ostensibly a soldier and a plain one. It is he, as we saw in an earlier chapter, who professed to have been wronged by a courtier, and perhaps had even convinced himself of some degree of martyrdom. His reputation with Othello and other military personnel is of an honest, plain-dealing, socially inept soldier. He, rather than Othello, is the one who thought to have "yerk'd" Roderigo under the ribs for his slander of the Moor.

It is he, according to Cassio, who "speaks home. . . . You may relish him more in the soldier than in the scholar" (II.i.166). Because of his "plain" reputation, Iago functions with unparalleled effectiveness in misleading a genuinely simple soldier. With all the wiles (and plenty more besides) of the courtier, Iago is especially damaging to soldiers because they think him to be one of them. It is upon Iago, then, the nearest equivalent of the courtier antagonist for the soldier in *Othello,* that Shakespeare places most of the blame for his noble warrior's tragic blunder. To a certain extent, therefore, Shakespeare followed the example of those soldier authors and dramatists who made the courtier and, indirectly, the court responsible for the soldier's indiscretion.

In whatever contact Othello may make *directly* with the court—without Iago as intermediary and interpreter—neither the court nor Othello is one-sidedly blameworthy. The Moor is respectful and modest in the presence of the Duke and senators; and these in turn respect his military services and character. "I have done the state some service, and they know't," he declares (V.ii.339). The tragedy is, then, not simply a conflict between stereotyped versions of war and court. It is a conflict between a simple, but ennobled, soldier and a nonmilitary situation aggravated by a villain who has inside knowledge of the potential weaknesses of the soldierly temperament and the court. This villain manipulates both soldier and court so that each will be of utmost incompatibility with the other.

XII

In turning from *Othello* to the last two plays in which Shakespeare brings a soldier into prolonged friction with society, we enter a social and dramatic world that is different in several ways. *Timon of Athens* and *Coriolanus* are distinct as tragedies from *Othello* in that they belong to the world of Shakespeare's final tragedies, a world that has recently and for the first time been adequately defined. In *Shakespeare's Tragic Frontier,*[78] Professor Farnham shows that the heroes of Shakespeare's final tragedies, like those of Chapman and Webster, are distinguishable from the heroes of his middle tragic period in that they are more deeply flawed and yet, paradoxically, win a measure of sympathy because of their very imperfections. It becomes, therefore, more difficult to separate what is blameworthy from what is admirable. This is true even of characters who are not the tragic protagonists, since the whole ethical atmosphere of this last tragic world is a confusing blend of good and evil. Undoubtedly the problem of the noble soldier in conflict with society is affected by this changed atmosphere and becomes more complicated.

The problem is complicated also by political developments. In the last chapter we noted the possible effect of King James's political views upon Shakespeare's interpretation of war and peace. Although the King's dislike for militarism must certainly have made the cause of the assertive martialists less tenable, it produced also a covert but strong reaction in favor of the soldier who was imperfectly valued in time of peace.

But the political development which most specifically affected and complicated the role of the soldier in society was the ill-fated uprising of the Earl of Essex, with his subsequent trial and execution. No other national event more dramatically displayed both the noble and ignoble traits latent in professional soldiers. Although *Othello* was produced shortly after the execution of Essex, the impact of the event on this play was probably not great. If there is any allegorical relationship between the deception of Othello by Iago and the alleged deception of Essex by Bacon or Henry Cuffe, it is not clear or detailed enough to illuminate the play. But both *Timon of Athens* and *Coriolanus* have been more reasonably associated by recent critics with the fortunes of Essex. And although we shall probably never ascertain the precise influence of the Earl's indiscretion on these plays, it is important to try to recapture those aspects of the event that an audience of the early 1600's would have had painfully fresh in mind. We must review not only the uprising and trial, but also two non-Shakespearean plays which present comparable problems of interpretation.

Immediately following one of his most discontented periods, Essex was in Ireland with the largest army Elizabeth had ever supported. The menace to the government was considerable, since the Earl had chosen devoted followers like Southampton and Mountjoy as his officers and might call upon the military to back him in any forcible assertion of his discontent. He had convinced himself that his enemies at home had come between him and the Queen. From Ireland he complained to the Privy Council that he felt himself "open to the malice and practice of mine enemies in England, who first procured a cloud of disgrace to overshadow me, and now in the dark give me wound upon wound."[79] Finally he left Ireland without authorization and went directly, in unprecedented manner, to the Queen's bedchamber. For his insubordination and for his practice of building up a faction among the military by creating knights in wholesale quantities, he was tried for treason, but escaped with only confinement (ultimately at Essex House) and the loss of power at court. During this confinement, he regarded himself as an exile; he wrote to the Queen, "my soul cries out unto your Majesty for grace, for access, and for an end of this exile."[80] Inopportunely his *Apology,* written two years earlier, was printed in 1600, ostensibly without his permission; and this document, by defending his profession of war and the soldiers who followed him, offended the Queen and the court.

The immediate cause of Essex's downfall was his wild and futile uprising. No one has ever determined what Essex had in mind when he began his descent on the town, with the court as his ultimate objective. Apparently he wanted to repeal his own banishment, get the Queen out of the control of his enemies, and—though this is less certain—make some provision for the succession of James. The statement of purpose which he later made is idealized in its humility, but it is probably as close to the truth within Essex's strange mind as we shall ever get:

My purpose was to have come unto her Majesty with eight or nine honourable persons, who had just cause of discontentment, though not equal with mine, and so prostrating ourselves at her Majesty's feet, to have put ourselves unto her mercy. And the effect of our desires should have been, that she would have been pleased to have severed some from her Majesty, who, by reason of their potency with her, abused her Majesty's ears with false informations.[81]

Underlying the episode in Essex's mind was clearly an irreconcilable conflict between war and court. And this conflict interestingly dominates Essex's subsequent trial for treason. It appears, moreover, not in the prosecution of Essex alone but in that of his followers. His own defensive position, in fact, is more starkly apparent in the stand taken by certain other conspirators. Southampton, for instance, repeatedly declared that his ignorance of the law had made him incur its perils, that he was being condemned "by ye letter of the Lawe," and that he had employed his "whole time in her Majesty's service."[82] Captain Lee, the least clever of the accused, illustrated most clearly the plight of a military man in a court of law. He also illustrated the tendency of all the conspirators to aggravate their offense by asserting their status as soldiers. When the Attorney General avowed that he would prove Lee guilty of treason, the Captain confidently replied: "Nay for all your wit and learning, you shall never do that. I care not what you can say. I have lost a great deal of blood in her Majesty's service, and done good service in Ireland."[83] To virtually every specific accusation his answer was the same. In denying that he had meant any harm when standing at the Privy Chamber door, he declared: "I have spent my blood in her majesty's service, and would do so again."[84] Charged with being "full of cruelty and blood," he answered: "I protest I have been in her majesty's service forward, and indeed in fair fight I would do the worst against her majesty's enemies: but when they submitted to my mercy, I ever used them but as became a soldier and a gentleman, as merciful as any." The last was probably his most expert plea, since it used a military analogy to good advantage. But while making a fair case for mercy, it did not explain the point at issue: his criminality and brutality in peace.

Essex's own defensive stand was considerably more versatile and adept. Until testimony after testimony had made him desperate, he spoke with eloquence and gave a specific answer to charges. But it became progressively clear that his principal defense consisted in vilifying his enemies at court and in exploiting the tragic pattern of the soldier martyred by a cunning antagonist. He deliberately, it would seem, played up his own plainness. When Sir Edward Coke had made a legally erudite statement against him, Essex scornfully answered: "Will your Lordship give us our turne to speake, for he playeth the Orator, and abuseth your Lordships eares, and us with slaunders, and they are but fashions of corrupted states, or the corrupt Instruments of corrupted States."[85] Essex pointedly acknowledged his own inability to speak adequately for the occasion, and begged his judges that "yf anie thinge by the earnestnes of his speeche or default or weaknes of his memorie ... should slipp fourth to his disadvantage which should be contrarie to the truth of his sincere hart that it might not be taken hold of with rigorous severitie."[86]

He managed in some respects to shape his bitter clash with Secretary Cecil so that it became an issue of deserving warrior pitted against courtier. At one point in the trial he spoke directly to Cecil: "You knowe well I hazarded my self and putt my life in adventure in those accions when you weare quiett and saffe at home."[87] Against Bacon, also, Essex called attention to their contrasting professions. Of the legal minds ranged against him, Bacon's was certainly the subtlest and most deadly. The Earl conveniently associated him with the traditional lawyer antagonists of the military profession. When, for example, Bacon insisted that possession of rapier and dagger was sufficient to make one "an armed man," Essex retorted, "Say you soe, Mr. Attorney? By this you proove yourself, to bee a better lawier than a souldier."[88] Even upon being sentenced, Essex maintained nobly his role as a soldier martyred by society. "I think it fit," he declared, "my poor quarters that have done her majesty true service in divers parts of the world, should be sacrificed and disposed of at her majesty's pleasure."[89]

Viewed in the light of the traditional defenses of the military profession, the aspects of Essex's "exile" and trial in which he appears as warrior in court do not seem strikingly new. And possibly they appear familiar because Essex was more or less consciously aware of the role that tradition had prescribed for a noble soldier in his predicament. To a certain extent he was dramatist as well as actor of his own tragedy. As with Shakespeare's Hotspur—who may have owed something to the preconspiracy Essex—there is no way of drawing the line between spontaneous action and self-dramatization. Essex was often passionate, sudden, and tactless. He was also, as Naunton recognized, more the soldier than the courtier; and when it came to a life-and-death fight, with the battleground the court rather than the field, he could not hold his own against men like Cecil and Bacon, whose element was court and law. On the other hand, however naïve he may have been politically, Essex was not without considerable charm and the self-consciousness that often attends it. That he knew when to be plain is evidenced not only by his behavior during the trial, but in an earlier exchange of letters between him and Bacon. When Bacon warned him (July 20, 1600) against flying with "waxen wings" in the manner of Icarus, Essex professed to be confused by this elegant kind of talk: "I am a stranger to all poetical conceits, or else I should say somewhat of your poetical example." Having professed plainness, Essex suddenly proceeds to elaborate the "wings" metaphor with the curiously wrought imagery which he frequently used, especially in addressing the Queen:

But this I must say, that I never flew with other wings than desire to merit, and confidence in my Sovereign's favour; and when one of these wings failed me, I would light nowhere but at my Sovereign's feet, though she suffered me to be bruised with my fall. And till her Majesty, that knows I was never bird of prey, finds it to agree with her will and her service that my wings should be imped again, I have committed myself to the mew.[90]

Even before the conspiracy, Bacon had recognized that Essex's kind of artful innocence might prove dangerously subversive for the Queen if she were ever to bring him to trial. Bacon had advised Elizabeth not to make "publicke question" out of the Earl's behavior in Ireland.

I told her, my Lord was an eloquent and well spoken man, and besides his eloquence of nature or art, he had an eloquence of accident which passed them both, which was the pittie and benevolence of his hearers; and therefore that when he should come to answer for himselfe, I doubted his words should have so unequall passage above theirs that should charge him, as would not be for her Majesties honour.[91]

There was irony in the fact that Bacon was to be principal among those "that should charge him," and that in 1604, even after Essex had been legally condemned and executed, Bacon should still be trying to vindicate the triumph of the law over its soldier victim. Nor was the irony for Bacon appreciably lessened by his having known in advance about Essex's "eloquence of accident."

Whether or not Essex patterned his self-defense after the soldierly stereotype, it was often close enough to that stereotype to present a serious problem in interpreting subsequent drama. The important point is that neither Essex's misconduct nor his defense was original. Behind them were age-old prototypes in real life and recent parallels and models in literature.

The difficulty in separating the Essexian from more universal materials in drama is most instructively evident in Samuel Daniel's *Philotas*. This play, dealing with the treason, trial, and sentencing of Alexander's ambitious general, was performed early in 1605 and promptly resulted in the author's being called before the council to explain parallels—apparently sympathetic—between Philotas and the late Earl. On the basis not only of this occurrence but of a considerable number of detailed resemblances, Professor Michel, the recent editor of *Philotas,* is warranted in declaring that Daniel's play can be shown "to have a closer kinship with Essex than any other piece of writing so far studied."[92] Daniel was a member of the Essex circle, and Essex had patronized him. It was natural that his sympathies should have emerged in his retelling of the classical story. On the other hand, Daniel firmly declared his innocence of any intentional parallels with Essex's troubles. He proved that he had mentioned the subject of his play as early as 1597 and that the first three acts had been written in 1600. In a letter to Mountjoy, he affirmed also the timeless nature of his theme; he had been concerned with "the universall notions of the affayres of men, which in all ages beare the same resemblances, and are measured by one and the same foote of understanding."[93]

That many of the "universall notions" of the unlucky soldier had appeared in England before 1601 and had been given literary formulas, we have already seen. And some of these are to be found, fundamentally placed, in *Philotas*. Although, as Michel has suggested, there is a blurring of at least three points of view in the play, the following statement by the Chorus is an adequate analysis of Philotas' tragic weakness (lines 421–428):

> Some warrs have grac'd, whom peace doth ill become,
> And lustfull ease hath blemisht all their part.
> We see Philotas acts his goodnesse ill,
> And makes his passions to report of him
> Worse than he is: and we do feare he will
> Bring his free nature to b'intrapt by them.
> For sure there is some engin closely laid
> Against his grace and greatnesse with the King.

Philotas demonstrates not only that he is ill-acclimated in peace but that he is vulnerable to courtly "engins." He announces, with a complacency typical of the soldiers already studied (lines 65–66):

> I cannot plaster and disguise m'affaires
> In other colours than my heart doth lay.

Though he attributes his fall from royal favor to malicious men near the King, he resolves to rely upon his "plaine / And open actions" rather than "Baseness and smoothing" (lines 648–650). He typically generalizes his predicament by decrying the contempt in which the military profession is held. Courtiers, he complains (lines 73–82),

> divide the spoyles, and pray of powre,
> And none at all respect the publicke good;
> Those hands that guard and get us what is our,
> The Soldierie ingag'd to vent their blood,
> In worse case seeme then Pallas old-grown Moile.
> . . . .
> And nothing shall bring home of all these warres,
> But empty age, and bodies charged with scarres.

Daniel does not, however, as would the partisan spokesmen for the military profession, go so far as to allow his hero's defense to justify treasonable actions. The wise old Chalistenes exposes the selfish rationalization behind Philotas' lament for public defenders (lines 83–84):

> Philotas, all this publike care, I feare,
> Is but some private touch of your dislike.

Similarly, when Philotas expresses confidence that his warlike services will speak persuasively for him, Chalistenes warns him that those services "will be deem'd, done for your owne availe" (lines 117–125). At the formal trial scene the same arguments with the same refutation recur. In reply to Philotas' confident citation of his services, Ephestion devastatingly draws a line between battlefield and society (lines 1645–1658):

> We blame not what y' have been, but what you are;
> We accuse not here your valour, but your fact,
> Not to have beene a leader in the warre,
> But an ill subject in a wicked act.
> . . . .
> God gives to Kings the honour to command,
> To subjects all their glory to obay;
> Who ought in time of war as rampiers stand,
> In peace as th' ornaments of State aray.

In the light of this large, judicious view, it is difficult to accept Philotas' own explanation of his tragedy (lines 1717–1718):

> Such the rewards of great imployments are,
> Hate kills in peace, whom Fortune spares in warre.

Clearly the martyred soldier is no longer in the same benign political climate as that of *Titus Andronicus* or Rich's *Sappho*. And clearly too, as Michel has demonstrated, the change is due in part to the Essex affair, which even in 1605 would be embarrassing to men like Cecil and Bacon. But the

Essex affair cannot alone account for the defensive tactics used by Philotas or the severe judgment upon them. The tactics, as Daniel implied, were age-old. And the judgment was the same as that recommended by Machiavelli and Burghley; it had merely been given new authority by Essex's vividly dramatized illustration of irresponsible militarism.

A similar influence from older ideas and models, freshly vitalized, is to be found in Chapman's *Byron*. Although this two-part play doubtless owed much of its current interest to the Essex affair and to the well-known and recent tragedy of the Duc de Biron himself, it represented also the culmination in England of years of thought upon the problem of the professional soldier. In Grimestone's translation of De Serres' *Inventorie* (1607), the factual source for the play, Chapman found not only the real-life situations involving the misplaced warrior, but also a moral judgment upon the general problem. In Grimestone, Chapman would have recognized, even if he had not already known it, that the tragic story of Biron was the tragic story of many other warriors. He read in the *Inventorie:*

> It is a great happinesse for an Estate to have great Captaines, but there is nothing so hard to entertaine, for when as they thinke that they have bound their Country unto them, although all they doe bee lesse then their duties, they are easily discontented and like to Pausanias and Themistocles speeke newe allyance and friendship from enemies, if they bee not rewarded to their own wills, and to the heighth of their Ambition.[94]

Like Grimestone, Chapman illustrates this historical truism through the person of Byron. What is more, he emphasizes the universality of his theme by highlighting certain formulas of conflict and defense that had become familiar.

It was noted in the preceding chapter that Chapman puts into Byron's mouth a condemnation of "sensual Peace," which "confounds Valour and cowardice, fame and infamy." It was also noted that Chapman feels obliged to condemn the attitude even though he may give it considerable poetic expression. Chapman probably recognized covertly that a corrupt society might need a military chastisement of the sort intended by Byron:

> I, who through all the dangers that can siege
> The life of man have forc'd my glorious way
> To the repairing of my country's ruins,
> Will ruin it again to re-advance it.[95]

But Chapman also recognized, even without Jacobean pressure, that the issue was more complex than the warrior himself could appreciate. A man of Byron's limited political vision was an unreliable critic of society, however valuable he might be to the state as an agent of political correction. Chapman gives more than due credit to his protagonist's mighty spirit, which sets him apart from the meaner creatures of the court, but Chapman does not endorse Byron's social intelligence or his opinion of himself.

As in *Philotas,* it is in a trial scene that we find Byron's limitations most dramatically revealed. Chapman employs to unusual advantage the established conflict between the soldier and the lawyer and justice. Byron notices that in the very Golden Chamber where he is to be tried, he was wont to be honored "in recompence of my renowned service." The unaccustomed scene of conflict intimidates him:

> Must I be sat on now by petty judges?
> These scarlet robes, that come to sit and fight

> Against my life, dismay my valour more
> Than all the bloody cassocks Spain hath brought
> To field against it.[96]

Later, in the mistaken confidence that he has proved his innocence, he ridicules his legal adversaries, parodying the Chancellor's "most lawyerly delivery" and exclaiming, "Here was lawyer's learning!"[97] The irony of the situation makes clear how ineffectually the soldier has fared in his conflict with civil law.

Typically, the most deadly evidence brought against Byron is produced by a courtier informer, La Fin, and, typically, Byron takes the posture of a noble warrior tricked by perfidy. But although he may denounce La Fin as a "damn'd enchanter," Byron differs from the heroes of Rich, and to a certain extent from Hotspur, in being unable to give any indication that La Fin's testimony is unfounded. Instead, he storms into an assertion of his military value to the state:

> Ye all know, my lords,
> This body, gash'd with five and thirty wounds,
> Whose life and death you have in your award,
> Holds not a vein that hath not open'd been,
> For you and yours.[98]

Then, after a conventional apology for his "intemperate speech," he proceeds to a prodigious statement of his own worth, in which he emerges as the soldier savior of France. "Do ye then return this retribution?" he asks incredulously.

> Can the cruel King,
> The kingdom, laws, and you, all sav'd by me,
> Destroy their saver?[99]

By his psychopathic self-esteem, Byron distorts into absurdity the soldier's traditional tactics of self-justification.[100] Chapman is not ignorant of the case for the professional warrior. Instructed by much the same lessons as those Samuel Daniel had received, he merely places the soldier's point of view in a larger context. There he finds it worthy of a nobly tragic statement, but not worthy of moral or political endorsement. Unlike Rich, Chapman allows the soldier to participate in, but not tell, the story.

As we turn now to Shakespeare's *Timon* and *Coriolanus,* we shall find that the treatment of erring soldiers in these plays is often similar to that in *Philotas* and *Byron.* There is especially noticeable a more explicit criticism of the soldier as soldier than in the earlier plays. The question concerning his proper conduct in society is more pointedly and urgently raised. And the type of soldierly misconduct tends to be treason or an outrage against civil law rather than a general awkwardness in treading a staid path. But if we insist upon looking for instructive political allegory related to Essex, we shall find the going much more hazardous than in *Philotas.* Accordingly, the following discussion acknowledges the presence of Essex somewhere in the background of the play, but makes no attempt to localize that presence beyond reproducing and appraising arguments that have been advanced by others.

XIII

It is perhaps no mere coincidence that one of the ablest "disintegrative" explanations for the rough condition of *Timon of Athens* as a play is based upon a partial identification of Timon with Essex. In "Shakespeare's Purpose in *Timon of Athens*," Dixon Wecter proposed that Shakespeare originally wrote "a full five-act play, probably not much inferior to

Coriolanus, and that this play some time before the publication of the Folio suffered deliberate mutilation."[101] It was mutilated because it bore a close resemblance to Essex's tragedy and thus seemed to Shakespeare's company a dangerous play in the light of Daniel's mishap. Shakespeare probably refused the necessary job of revision, and so the work was turned over to Middleton, who botched it. In the extant play, certain hints of Shakespeare's original design remain, but without any surviving purpose. For example, Shakespeare "plainly intended Timon to be not simply a private citizen, but a public, even a military hero."[102] A remnant of this intention appears in Alcibiades' address to the self-exiled Timon in the forest (IV.iii.92):

> I have heard, and griev'd,
> How cursed Athens, mindless of thy worth,
> Forgetting thy great deeds when neighbour states,
> But for thy sword and fortune, trod upon them.

Another remnant is to be found in the two senators' offer to Timon of "the captainship ... allow'd with absolute power" (V.i.166), if he will defend them against Alcibiades. As Wecter notes, in none of Shakespeare's known sources for the play is there any suggestion of Timon's services as a preserver of the state.[103] Above all, Shakespeare's frustrated purposes are shown in the mutilation of the Ventidius theme. Ventidius, whom Timon had specially befriended early in the play, was apparently meant to be the last and most shocking of the series of ingrates who refuse Timon help. This theme had to be suppressed because of a dangerous parallel with Bacon's treatment of his noble benefactor. One obvious parallel with Essex—the insurrection—Shakespeare himself had transferred to Alcibiades because of its transparent offensiveness, and had rested content with what he found in his sources: Timon's self-exile and renunciation of the world. Yet even this accorded with one of Essex's repeatedly expressed wishes. From the mangled play, Wecter concludes, we may disengage Shakespeare's conception of Timon:

> An impulsive, headstrong, generous nobleman, a distinguished soldier and patron of the arts, who ignoring prudent counsel casts himself unreservedly upon his courtiers, falls upon evil days and is deserted by his host of trencher-friends—even by the man whom he has lifted from debt, is forsaken by the state in whose defense he has so bravely and ineffectually fought; until at last, cherished only by his faithful steward, he passes through a period of bitterest despair to a wretched but welcome death.[104]

In defense of Wecter's contention, it can be said that his reconstruction of Timon's character is closer to Essex's real nature than is to be found in most attempts of this sort. And even in the Timon that survives in the Folio edition there are many convincing resemblances to the Earl. Against Wecter's proposal, however, is the obvious fact that it requires more ingenuity than does E. K. Chambers' explanation that the play as it stands is Shakespeare's, but hastily written and perhaps unfinished.[105] There were possibly some cuts because of the Essex affair, but these may have been Shakespeare's own, and probably they were not so extensive as Wecter's contention requires.

Had Shakespeare's fundamental intention been to show Timon as a military hero abused by the state, he would most likely have followed his usual practice of indicating the fact early and emphatically in the play. Considerable revision would therefore have been needed to remove all the effects of this early pronouncement. An easier conjecture is that the military services theme was never introduced early in the play, but thrown in when it became needed as a means of enhancing Timon's grievances and linking them with Alcibiades. We notice Shakespeare impenitently following this same procedure in *Cymbeline,* a play composed a few years later. There also, since the theme is not of central importance, we must wait until the play is more than half over before we learn of Belarius' background as a military hero maligned by two villains "whose false oaths prevail'd" (III.iii.56):

> O boys, this story
> The world may read in me. My body's mark'd
> With Roman swords, and my report was once
> First with the best of note. Cymbeline lov'd me;
> And when a soldier was the theme, my name
> Was not far off. Then was I as a tree
> Whose boughs did bend with fruit. But in one night,
> A storm or robbery (call it what you will)
> Shook down my mellow hangings, nay, my leaves,
> And left me bare to weather....
> My fault being nothing (as I have told you oft)
> But that two villains, whose false oaths prevail'd
> Before my perfect honour, swore to Cymbeline
> I was confederate with the Romans. So
> Followed my banishment.

Fragmentary expositions of this sort are no guarantee that a fuller characterization once existed. Shakespeare was merely making brief use of a tragic theme which, used long before by Rich, Greene, and others, was familiar to the audience without further dramatization. That he uses it so openly in *Cymbeline* is possibly evidence that he did not fear its being confined in meaning to Essex.

In the printed play at any rate—and this is the play that must be preferred to all unprinted ones—Timon is not convincingly characterized as a military hero, and certainly not as a soldier who because of a military personality meets disaster in peace. But there is in the play another character who meets these specifications. It is not Timon but Alcibiades who runs afoul of the corrupt Athenian government, and he does so with a soldier's personality and a soldier's tactics. In the preceding chapter, I suggested that Alcibiades' role in the play is not so much that of an individual human being as that of an impersonal force bringing the therapy of war to a diseased society. As such, he requires only slight motivation, especially in a play that is abnormally dedicated to a study of society. Nevertheless, Shakespeare does give to Alcibiades what seems to this warrior a valid reason for chastening Athens. This reason, as we shall see, is a limited one, thoroughly in accord with the restricted social horizon of a professional warrior.

The motivation for Alcibiades' turning upon his country is achieved by Shakespeare in a single scene (III.v). The scene is made of maximum dramatic impact and generalized significance by employing the stereotype of the soldier pleading with civil law. Though it is recognizably in the genre of the trial scene, there are enough variations made on the conventional type to make it interestingly new. Alcibiades is pleading not in a court of law, but before the senators, and he is pleading not for his own life, but for that of a soldier friend. His civil indiscretion is not the same as that of his friend—murder—but simply the rough insistence of his pleading, for which he is rewarded by banishment. The irony and special originality of the scene lie in the fact that Alcibiades as a soldier is condemned not for a crime but for using defensive tactics that normally served to clear soldiers of an alleged crime.

In order to determine the degree of sympathy Shakespeare meant to give Alcibiades as opposed to the Senate, we must first inquire as to the rightness of the cause for which he is pleading. He is suitor, he tells the senators, for a friend

> who in hot blood
> Hath stepp'd into the law, which is past depth
> To those that (without heed) do plunge into't.
> He is a man (setting his fault aside)
> Of comely virtues;
> Nor did he soil the fact with cowardice
> (An honour in him which buys out his fault)
> But with a noble fury and fair spirit,
> Seeing his reputation touch'd to death,
> He did oppose his foe.
>
> (III.v.11)

The senators are unimpressed by this pleasant description of murder committed to vindicate one's honor. First Senator ironically commends Alcibiades for dignifying manslaughter and setting "quarrelling upon the head of valour." "He's truly valiant," the senator insists,

> that can wisely suffer
> The worst that man can breathe, and make his wrongs
> His outsides, to wear them like his raiment, carelessly,
> . . . .
> You cannot make gross sins look clear.
> To revenge is no valour, but to bear.

Unsuccessful in reasoning that seems to him irrefutable, and suspecting that his failure may be due to his inability to argue in the form and idiom of the senators, Alcibiades decides that it is necessary to "speak like a captain." This he does—still with civility, but with increasing warmth and with a greater sense of his isolation, as a captain, from the world of the senators (III.v.40):

> My lord, then, under favour, pardon me
> If I speak like a captain.
> Why do fond men expose themselves to battle
> And not endure all threats? sleep upon't,
> And let the foes quietly cut their throats
> Without repugnancy? If there be
> Such valour in the bearing, what make we
> Abroad? Why then, women are more valiant
> That stay at home, if bearing carry it;
> And the ass more captain than the lion.

The distinction is outwardly between heroic action and passive "bearing," but there is also an implication, unsavory to the senators, that the soldiers who go forth and kill are more worthy—certainly subject to diffcrent laws—than the senators who, with the women, "stay at home." "You breathe in vain," Second Senator states with infuriating unreasonableness. Alcibiades then finds it necessary to fall back upon the military services plea, and with a perceptible change toward terse, "soldierly" speech (III.v.63):

> Why, I say, my lords, has done fair service
> And slain in fight many of your enemies.
> How full of valour did he bear himself
> In the last conflict, and made plenteous wounds!

Second Senator, however, insists upon shifting the soldier's crime back from a context of war to where it actually occurred, a situation of peace. He notes that the soldier has made too many wounds--not in battle but as "a sworn rioter."

"He dies," is the verdict of First Senator; and again, "We are for law. He dies." Although Alcibiades pursues his plea beyond this point, his final comment upon the soldier's predicament itself is, "Hard fate! He might have died in war."

Aside from the military services stereotype, Alcibiades' defense of his friend is based upon the assumption that a soldier is obliged—even in defiance of civil law—to vindicate his good name by the sword. The senators, on the other hand, contend that murder in peace is rioting rather than valor, and affirm the jurisdiction of the laws of peace rather than of war. Although the issue is related to the more general Elizabethan controversy about the rightness of revenge, it had special problems of its own in that it concerned soldiers, who were accustomed to place the demands of their profession above the restraints of peace—especially those imposed by the detestable legal profession.

"Military men," wrote John Norden, look upon the vindication of their honor "as a peculiar badge of their profession."[106] De Loque observes sardonically that if two martialists "have anie quarrell or difference betweene them, they must trie and end it by the combat, all justice trodden under foot. If he be a gentleman of a companie, a man at armes, yea but a single souldier, he must not pocket up the least looking in the face awrie, the lye given, or the least injurie that is, but he must crave revenge, to the field they must man to man, to trie their manhood, or else his honour and reputation is lost."[107] It is this military habit to which Shakespeare's Jaques is alluding when he draws the Character of a soldier as "Jealous in honour, sudden and quick in quarrel."[108]

Arguments to justify Alcibiades' defense of his friend may be found in numerous Renaissance nondramatic writings. Sir

Philip Sidney, according to Fulke Greville, observed in England "the effeminate made judges of danger which they fear and honor which they understand not."[109] But it was in Italy, where the subject had first been broached, that the right of the soldier to extralegal procedures was most cogently argued. Gentili, although not asking that soldiers be free of the law, urges that they be tolerated and not imposed upon, because they are simple men unable to grasp legal subtleties.[110] Other Italian authorities, cited by Bryson in *The Point of Honor in Sixteenth-Century Italy,* made more assertive statements on behalf of soldiers. They pointed out that the laws did not consider "the delicate *nuances* of honor," that "soldiers should be subject not to the rigor of the law, but to natural equity," and that "fighting was considered more honorable than going to law."[111] Mora, an officer serving the Polish king, said that if soldiers were as ill-respected in Italy as in Poland, "they themselves would exercise authority, instead of allowing a soldier to be imprisoned by some pedantic ex-shepherd, who had been made judge because in the home of a noble he had learned crudely to sign his name."[112]

In France and England, however, particularly in the later Renaissance, there was mainly condemnation of the soldier who took the law into his own hands. De Loque, as we have seen, ridicules the soldier's justification of such action. La Noue attempts more soberly, and from a soldier's point of view, to show the unreasonableness of the code of honor. He understandingly states the soldier's standard argument, much in the manner of Alcibiades: "Why must I beare wrong and stripes and not revenge my selfe againe?" La Noue supplies the answer: "that my entent tendeth not to will you to suffer all: but rather that you must in no wise commit such injuries."

He then proceeds to ask the meaning of "true honor," and finds that it "consisteth in the possession of vertue." Honor requires good actions rather than bad.[113]

John Norden, whose instructive works for soldiers reflected the opinion approved by Church and state, likewise uses the strategy of inquiring what honor truly is, as opposed to the sort that soldiers mistakenly vaunt. "For that is true honor," he declares, "that proceedeth of wisedome and good government. And hee is onely to bee reckoned excellent, that by the high spirit of inward grace is able to knowe himselfe: and then to subdue what he knoweth in himselfe offensive to God, or prejudiciall to his right rule and government."[114] If, he reasons, in the manner of Shakespeare's senators, "any professour of armes" believes that "refusall of a challenge may argue in him pusillanimitie: let him thinke that the effects of true magnanimitie and valour, is to beare and to endure, with all modestie and patience, the wrongs of private injuries."[115] "Let no man," he warns, "be deceived with vain regard of the preservation, or increase of his honor, by usurping a law unto himselfe, to shed the blood of him, whom the law in every government (yea of armes) hath power to punish."[116]

Such exemplary reasoning was no more likely to persuade the professional soldiers than the senators' stately moralizing was likely to bring the entire social horizon within the ken of Alcibiades. Soldiers in Shakespeare's audience doubtless thrilled to the stirring defense of their representative on the stage. Judicious civilians were possibly sympathetic to its emotional integrity, but recognized that the senators, for all their own blindness, were speaking truth. By what follows in the scene, they would have been made especially aware that there was reason in the senatorial precepts. For the case of the sol-

dier murderer was merely a microcosm of the more comprehensive attack on law to which Alcibiades himself is driven.

Upon being told that his friend must die, Alcibiades tries
once more to translate his own military reasoning into a form
understandable to the pompous, legalistic minds who wield
the law of life and death during peace. A happy thought
occurs to him (III.v.78):

> more to move you,
> Take my deserts to his and join 'em both;
> And, for I know your reverend ages love
> Security, I'll pawn my victories, all
> My honours to you, upon his good returns.

Finding, however, that the senators place no value on his kind
of "security," he is reduced to rude anger. His "wounds ache"
at the Senate. Sentenced to banishment for his conduct, he
cries:

> Banish me?
> Banish your dotage! Banish usury,
> That makes the Senate ugly.

After the senators have left the stage, the outraged General
finds privately the words to express his anger:

> I'm worse than mad. I have kept back their foes
> While they have told their money and let out
> Their coin upon large interest, I myself
> Rich only in large hurts. All those for this?
> Is this the balsam that the usuring Senate
> Pours into captains' wounds? Banishment!

Then with a sudden resolution almost instinctive, he turns to
substantially the same kind of violent redress that his friend

had unluckily used. He will strike, not at an individual, but at Athens:

> It comes not ill. I hate not to be banish'd.
> It is a cause worthy my spleen and fury,
> That I may strike at Athens. I'll cheer up
> My discontented troops and lay for hearts.
> 'Tis honour with most lands to be at odds.
> Soldiers should brook as little wrongs as gods.

Although there is a modicum of valid social criticism in Alcibiades' strictures on senatorial usury, his motivation for revenge is obviously governed by blind passion rather than reason. He is "worse than mad." Banishment is "a cause worthy my spleen and fury." Worst of all, of course, is his statement: "'Tis honour with most lands to be at odds," a statement which contradicts the concepts of "true honor" as defined by the wiser Renaissance spokesmen, and which serves as a bald indication of how limited his sense of his social mission actually is. Athens needs correction, to be sure; but the military instrument of that correction does not, at this stage of the play at any rate, have any clear notion of how discreetly—for the good of Athens rather than the military profession—to apply therapy.

That Shakespeare deliberately gave Alcibiades a limited vision in order not to endorse his type of military discontent, is evident from the simplification which he wrought in the traditional character of the Greek general and politician. In Shakespeare's rude, forthright, and simple Alcibiades one scarcely recognizes the sophisticated, corrupt character found in Plutarch. G. B. Harrison correctly observes that from Plutarch Shakespeare took "little except the general impression that Alcibiades was a young gentleman who turned against his native city of Athens."[117] What is more, Shakespeare's conception of the Athenian youth was remarkable even in the Renaissance. Sir William Cornwallis mentions as one of the types of character to be studied in Plutarch: "Alcibiades an excellent pattern of wisedom to him that will temporize."[118] In *The Courtier,* Castiglione notes that "Alcibiades encreased his good conditions, and made them greater with letters, and with the instructions of books."[119] This is assuredly not the soldier who sits silent and ill at ease during Timon's banquet or who brings about his banishment by rude speech.

A trace of the historical Alcibiades does, however, survive in a curious detail which Shakespeare needed for his plot. Near the end of the play, one of Alcibiades' soldiers comes upon Timon's tomb and, unable to read the inscription, decides to take a wax impression of it to his commander, for

> Our captain hath in every figure skill,
> An ag'd interpreter, though young in days.
> (V.iii.7)

As a stroke of characterization, this is unlucky, but it does make possible the appropriate touch in the final scene when Alcibiades reads Timon's epitaph aloud and manages to merge more securely his own fortunes with those of Timon.

Also justified by this belated characterization is the General's more temperate and enlarged point of view in this scene. He now is willing to forgo personal revenge of the sweeping sort he had contemplated. He listens reasonably to the explanation of the senators that this is a different Athens from the one which offended him. He is no longer of the philosophy that "soldiers should brook as little wrong as gods," but a tolerant statesman who will

> Make war breed peace, make peace stint war, make each
> Prescribe to other, as each other's leech.
> (V.iv.83)

This final transformation is certainly not Shakespeare's plea on behalf of the military as opposed to the state. The dramatist is not attempting to idealize the sort of correction that might be expected from a discontented "exile" like Essex or the French Biron. The issue merely becomes more hopelessly blurred, in the best Shakespearean manner of handling politically touchy material. Political right and wrong are suddenly obscured by the happy expedient of transfiguring, at one stroke, both society and soldier into more pleasant forms. Neither the lawless soldier nor the corrupt society survives to the point where a choice between them becomes necessary.

XIV

Despite his importance to the social message of *Timon of Athens,* Alcibiades does not dominate the play sufficiently to become a full-length study of the professional soldier who, unable to adjust from the casque to the cushion, is exiled and finally seeks redress by the tactics of war rather than peace. In *Coriolanus,* written perhaps soon after *Timon,* Shakespeare gives his full attention to such a study.[120] It is almost as though he conscientiously returned to and fulfilled a theme which he had botched in his earlier play. The progress from Alcibiades to Coriolanus was not, it is true, purely a personal choice for Shakespeare. In Plutarch he had found the two heroes, one Greek and the other Roman, presented as parallel lives. Although the historian did not make the two generals similar enough for a good comparative study, the Renaissance recognized an adequate parallel in that both men were military malcontents in society. Francis Meres, whose *Palladis Tamia* was more a commonplace book than an individual document, wrote as follows: "As Alcibiades being banished by the Athenians, became chiefe Captaine of the army of the Lacedomonians: so Coriolanus was more beloved of the Volscians among whome hee lived in exile, then of the Romanes with whom he was a citizen."[121] But Shakespeare had earlier resisted the lure of other parallel lives, and it is unlikely that Plutarch's hint was enough to suggest twin studies of Alcibiades and Coriolanus.

Although he had perhaps read the two lives together when preparing *Timon,* Shakespeare's need to write about Coriolanus went back in time well before the former play. *Coriolanus* is the culmination of all his earlier, foreshortened attempts to deal significantly with the problem of the professional warrior in society. In no instance had he carried the motif dominantly through the play. In Plutarch's "Coriolanus," for the first time, he recognized a story that with a few critical changes would justify full and central use of the misplaced soldier.

Although this explanation makes unnecessary any detailed connection with the Essex case, possible resemblances deserve at least brief consideration. The strongest argument for associating the fortunes of the two men was made not by a modern scholar but by an Elizabethan divine. William Barlow, in a governmentally encouraged sermon preached shortly after Essex's execution, referred to Plutarch's Coriolanus as "a gallant young, but a discontented Romane, who might make a fit parallel for the late Earle, if you read his life."[122] Probably, however, Barlow was referring not to detailed resemblances in personality but to the common traits of discontent and military valor, and their tragic combination. A present-day attempt by W. T. Conklin to establish resemblances does not cite Dr. Barlow, nor does it go much beyond him in supplying evidence. Conklin writes that Essex "had been about as close to an English counterpart of Coriolanus as one could have required." But the parallels to support this assertion are loosely drawn: "Fiery, indiscreet, unused to flatter—even the necessary flattery of Elizabeth was intermittent and brought trouble almost as often as benefit— Essex had fought for his country, had been accused of mismanagement, had taken arms against the state, and had lost."[123] Essex had not, in point of fact, taken up arms against the state. He had "lost" for a reason quite different from Coriolanus'. And his letters to Elizabeth reveal a whining kind of flattery more obnoxious than that of most other Elizabethan courtiers and diametrically opposed to Coriolanus' deeply felt refusal to flatter even Jove for his power to thunder. It is true, as Conklin goes on to suggest, that Coriolanus shares peculiarities of spasmodic speech with Hotspur, and Hotspur has been likened by critics to Essex; therefore, Coriolanus, who resembles Hotspur, also resembles Essex. But why stop with Hotspur and Coriolanus? Many of Shakespeare's heroes—including Bolingbroke, Henry V, Hamlet, Timon, and Alcibiades—might on occasion have reminded Elizabethans of Essex. Yet all of them are different from one another and from Essex. Moreover, unlike Coriolanus and Hotspur, Essex was considered blameworthy not for an inability to please the people but for a remarkable knack, abhorrent to Elizabeth, of ingratiating himself with the populace. If, indeed, he resembled Hotspur, he also resembled Hotspur's temperamental opposite, Bolingbroke, in his habit of bending the neck and uncapping to throngs; and in *Coriolanus* he would have shared traits not merely with the tragic hero but with that hero's loathed opponents, the tribunes of the people. We shall see, moreover, that Shakespeare's intentions in the play are often best revealed by changes he made in Plutarch's story, and these are not made in the direction of greater resemblance to Essex.

More so than in any of his earlier works, Shakespeare seeks in *Coriolanus* a clear demarcation between war and peace as social areas for exposing the strengths and weaknesses of his soldier hero. In plays like *Titus Andronicus* and *1 Henry IV,* an early part of the action is given to praising the recent military triumphs of the hero. In *Coriolanus,* however, there is an added emphasis on this traditional aspect of the play in that the hero is not merely praised upon his return from war but is seen vividly engaged in battle. The effect of this new emphasis is not only to magnify Coriolanus as a warrior but, through the manner of his fighting, to foreshadow personality traits which will cause him trouble once he returns to the "cushion." As a soldier he proves to be a fierce, individual fighter rather than a deliberate, army-minded general. His youthful impetuosity, as we have seen, contrasts with the cautiousness of his soldier-statesman fellow, Cominius. Shakespeare also increases the dissension between Coriolanus and the common soldiers, thereby affording a parallel in war to the more serious dissension in peace when the General will be forced to sue rather than command.

Nevertheless, Coriolanus proves so successful in the Volscian campaign that he returns a national war hero. The tribune Brutus describes bitterly (II.i.221) the idolatry of the welcoming throngs. A herald announces the great honors that Coriolanus has won, and proclaims—in one of Shakespeare's nicest touches of dramatic irony—"Welcome, /

Welcome to Rome, renowned Coriolanus!" (II.i.182). It seems to be merely *Titus Andronicus,* highly amplified, all over again. But this time Shakespeare is prepared to use more than tragic irony. He is now to demonstrate, detail by detail, the traits in Coriolanus' nature that produce his tragic incompatibility with society. The dramatist does not, as he had done in *Titus,* build all the tragedy incongruously upon a single error in judgment made by the triumphant warrior at the beginning of the play.

In *Titus Andronicus,* it will be recalled, the protagonist refuses the office of dictator, due him for his military services, merely because of old age. Coriolanus also dislikes the idea of standing for consul—an honor which his mother and friends consider incumbent upon him—but he shrinks from the office because his very nature rebels against its political demands. He has, indeed, firmly held convictions about government, and his thinking is by no means limited to the battlefield. But it is only on the battlefield that he is thoroughly at ease. The consulship requires a political skill and, especially, a tactful relationship with the people of which he knows himself incapable. As he tells his mother,

> I had rather be their servant in my way
> Than sway with them in theirs.
>
> (II.i.219)

His disinclination to become a politician represents an apprehension—which he never clearly grasps or expresses—of the Renaissance concept of degree. Professor Phillips has demonstrated how this concept pervades Shakespeare's Greek and Roman plays. In *Coriolanus* it is most notably expressed in Menenius' fable of the belly and the members. But one of the citizens names the distinct parts of the body politic in a form specially applicable to Coriolanus (I.i.119):

> The kingly crowned head, the vigilant eye,
> The counsellor heart, the arm our soldier,
> Our steed the leg, the tongue our trumpeter.

As Phillips points out, Coriolanus is "the arm our soldier," and there is no evidence that his "celebrated service to Rome was ever of anything but a military nature."[124] And the General has rightly a distrust of changing his occupation from war to politics.

The underlying formula for Coriolanus' troubles as a politician is to be found in Plutarch. Nevertheless, Shakespeare gave this formula a Renaissance interpretation not only in a new emphasis on degree but in changes made upon Plutarch's aristocratic warrior so as to bring him closer to the Elizabethan version of the socially inept soldier. The haughty, class-minded patrician is still strongly evident in Shakespeare's interpretation, but his personality and social intelligence suffer a diminution almost comparable to the shrinkage which we observed in Alcibiades.

Although Plutarch states that Coriolanus "lacked the gravity and affability that is gotten with judgment of learning and reason,"[125] the historian does not ascribe this lack of learning to a military background, nor does he show the hero suffering from the conventional soldierly disabilities. Plutarch's Coriolanus is a clever and eloquent, though not a wise or disciplined, character. He is capable, as has been seen, of craft in war on at least two occasions. And he is conspicuously an orator. Addressing Volscian lords, he "spake so excellently in the presence of them all, that he was thought no less eloquent in tongue, than warlike in show: and declared himself both expert in wars, and wise with valiantness."[126] To most Renaissance readers, Plutarch's characterization would suggest the well-rounded-gentleman ideal, blemished only by passion and a lack of affability.

Shakespeare rejected this interpretation in favor of a more clearly defined distinction between warrior and politician. He accepted quite literally Plutarch's statement that Coriolanus lacked education, and he assumed that the lack was due to the limited type of experience which he had described in *Othello*. A man who had spent his "dearest action in the tented field" would be "rude" in speech, "little bless'd with the soft phrase of peace," and unable to speak more of "this great world" than "pertains to feats of broils and battle." The military reason for Coriolanus' uncouth speech is amply commented upon later in the play, but it is first adumbrated in an interesting hint which is generally overlooked. Volumnia says of Coriolanus' young son, "He had rather see the swords and hear a drum than look upon his schoolmaster." Her old family friend, Valeria, adds enthusiastically, "O' my word, the father's son" (I.iii.59–61). The audience would have recognized here the old conflict between scholar and soldier, alluded to in *Othello* in Cassio's comment on Iago, "You may relish him more in the soldier than in the scholar" (II.i.166). In Breton's *The Scholler and the Souldiour,* the soldier acknowledges a childhood similar to that of young Marcius (and of Coriolanus himself): "What shall I say, I loved a Drumme and a Fyfe, better than all the fidling Musicke in the worlde: and growing to some yeeres, I woulde practise now and then a little of warlike exercises, till in the ende, the delight therein, drewe me quite from my Booke."[127]

Shakespeare's hero, who presumably had preferred drum to schoolmaster, vividly demonstrates, as Plutarch's Coriolanus does not, his limited ability in speech.

Shakespeare exposes this limitation most effectively in the two crucial episodes of the candidacy for the consulship and the resultant trial for treason. The first of these episodes is of Shakespeare's own devising. Whereas, as MacCallum observes, Plutarch stresses the political background for the circumstances resulting in Coriolanus' banishment, Shakespeare traces the exile almost exclusively to the hero's inept behavior as a candidate, "and this behaviour ... is altogether a fabrication on Shakespeare's part."[128] In Plutarch, the returning General exhibits no reluctance toward becoming a candidate for consul. He goes unprotestingly to sue for the people's "voices." And he does not demur at the Roman custom of showing his wounds to the people; nor does he address them uncivilly. Although the citizens ultimately revoke their approval of his candidacy, they do so not because of his rude speech but because they see him proceeding proudly to the market place, accompanied by the nobility, and recognize that they can never look to him for justice. In contrast, Shakespeare's hero ruins his fortunes by his surly, reluctant address to the citizens in a scene to which Shakespeare has given full and grim dramatization.

But despite Coriolanus' crude manners, he does not guide himself to ruin. Shakespeare has brought his hero still more closely into the familiar Elizabethan scene by supplying the equivalents of the courtier vilifier. These equivalents, the two tribunes of the people, are, of course, present in Plutarch's story. There, however, although mean-spirited demagogues, they have little of the crafty scheming found in Shakespeare's tribunes. They are directly opposed to Coriolanus the patrician rather than to Coriolanus the soldier, and the contrast in social intelligence is accordingly not so great. In Shakespeare they succeed in producing their enemy's downfall because they understand so thoroughly his soldierly traits and, like Iago in *Othello,* lead the noble warrior into situations impossible for him.

Shakespeare's tribunes are not courtiers; but that he may have had certain traits of the courtier in the back of his mind is suggested by the contrast drawn by an officer of the Capitol. In discussing Coriolanus' qualifications for the consulship, he observes (II.ii.27):

He hath deserved worthily of his country; and his ascent is not by such easy degrees as those who, having been supple and courteous to the people, bonneted, without any further deed to have them at all into their estimation and report; but he hath so planted his honours in their eyes and his actions in their hearts that for their tongues to be silent and not confess so much were a kind of ingrateful injury; to report otherwise were a malice that, giving itself the lie, would pluck reproof and rebuke from every ear that heard it.

It is the tribunes, obviously, who have "been supple and courteous to the people," and it is these politic creatures also who "report otherwise" than the truth about Coriolanus and who therefore show a "malice" suggestive of the conventional invidious antagonist of the soldier.

That these demogogues succeed in public affairs, whereas Coriolanus fails, is due in part to their ability to talk. The contrast between artful speech and heroic action is emphasized in a bitter exchange between the tribune Brutus and the General. Having struck home with a malicious comment,

Brutus notices that Coriolanus is preparing to leave. He inquires, with mock concern (II.ii.74):

> Sir, I hope
> My words disbench'd you not?

Coriolanus replies:

> No, sir. Yet oft,
> When blows have made me stay, I fled from words.

Although the retort is complacently made, the trait of which Coriolanus is proud proves less successful in peace than it had in war. But Coriolanus' lack of appropriate "words" is not, of course, an endorsement of the opposite characteristic, embodied in the tribunes. Volumnia supplies the proper scorn for these talkers when she berates them after her son has been banished (IV.ii.18):

> Hadst thou foxship
> To banish him that struck more blows for Rome
> Than thou hast spoken words?

In Shakespeare's version of the story, it is the "foxship" of these men that leads the people to renounce Coriolanus, whereas in Plutarch the people had done so on their own initiative. It is also Shakespeare's innovation to make the tribunes responsible by their provocative words for Coriolanus' furious outburst against the people. And it is this outburst, together with his resistance of lawful authority, that results in the General's arraignment for treason.

In the tumult which follows Coriolanus' ill-fated candidacy, the conflict between warrior and civil law is revealingly depicted. The tribune Sicinius is at first unwilling to honor Coriolanus with a lawful trial (III.i.266):

> He shall be thrown down the Tarpeian Rock
> With rigorous hands. He hath resisted law,

> And therefore law shall scorn him further trial
> Than the severity of the public power,
> Which he so sets at naught.

Whereupon Menenius, Coriolanus' "humourous" old friend, defends the General by strategy similar to the formal defenses of the military profession (III.i.298):

> What has he done to Rome that's worthy death?
> Killing our enemies, the blood he hath lost
> (Which I dare vouch, is more than that he hath,
> By many an ounce) he dropp'd it for his country;
> And what is left, to lose it by his country
> Were to us all that do't and suffer it
> A brand to th' end o' th' world.

But, like the senators in *Timon,* the tribunes refuse to shift the issue from peace to war. "This is clean kam," they protest. "Merely awry. When he did love his country, / It honour'd him." Menenius, more skillful as an advocate than Alcibiades had been, shows the relevance of his argument by an expert analogy (III.i.305):

> The service of the foot,
> Being once gangren'd, is not then respected
> For what before it was.

The body imagery reminds one of "the arm our soldier." The tribunes, however, are no more cognizant of the whole body politic than is Coriolanus, and they threaten to refuse all further discussion of the matter.

Menenius is thereupon forced to resort to the standard apology for the rude soldier (III.i.320):

> Consider this: he has been bred i' th' wars
> Since 'a could draw a sword, and is ill-school'd
> In bolted language; meal and bran together
> He throws without distinction.

"Give me leave," he continues,

> I'll go to him and undertake to bring him
> Where he shall answer by a lawful form
> (In peace) to his utmost peril.

The tribunes consent. Perhaps they are willing to condone Coriolanus' rude conduct in the light of the defense that Elizabethans had long been asked to accept. But it is more likely that they recognize the difficulty of dealing effectually with Coriolanus by force—his element—and prefer to have him brought by his friends into their own arena, that of words and politics. They further recognize that the General has not the slightest chance of answering them successfully "by a lawful form / (In peace)." Their sinister understanding of their enemy's limitations appears in the advice which Brutus gives his fellow tribune concerning how to disable Coriolanus at the trial (III.iii.25):

> Put him to choler straight. He hath been us'd
> Ever to conquer, and to have his worth
> Of contradiction. Being once chaf'd, he cannot
> Be rein'd again to temperance; then he speaks
> What's in his heart, and that is there which looks
> With us to break his neck.

All that will be necessary is to "chafe" the warrior. Having been accustomed to victory and command in battle, he will be unable to endure contradiction in peace.

Indeed, it proves almost impossible for Coriolanus' friends to induce him even to present himself for trial, let alone do so in a "lawful form." In this respect again Shakespeare has markedly altered his source in the interest of greater friction between warrior and society. Plutarch's hero goes without protest to answer the accusations against him. In fact, it is his patrician friends who demur, and Coriolanus, because he wishes to help them, who insists upon going. In the play, the efforts of the patricians and his mother to make him go to the Forum produce one of the most dramatic episodes. Although there is no single precedent for this scene in earlier literature on soldiers, most of its important details are clearly reminiscent of this literature.

Persuasions by Menenius and the senators, arguing the welfare of Rome, have no discernible effect on the stubborn General. It is his mother, who knows his temperament even better than the tribunes do, who prevails upon him. Sensing his deep feeling of wounded honor, she refrains from asking him to abandon revenge, and merely insists that he direct his anger "to better vantage" (III.ii.29–31). What she must persuade him to do is to use "policy," a quality distasteful to him. With a strategy worthy of the tribunes, she phrases her argument in the form of a military analogy (III.ii.41):

> I have heard you say,
> Honour and policy, like unsever'd friends,
> I' th' war do grow together. Grant that, and tell me,
> In peace what each of them by th' other lose,
> That they combine not there.

Hearing his own military pronouncement thus strangely translated into the language of peace, Coriolanus can answer only, "Tush, tush!" Menenius expresses the approval of the bystanders, "A good demand." She then proceeds to apply the military parallel specifically to her son's present situation (III.ii.52):

> now it lies you on to speak
> To th' people, not by your own instruction,

> Nor by th' matter which your heart prompts you,
> But with such words that are but roted in
> Your tongue, though but bastards and syllables
> Of no allowance to your bosom's truth.
> Now, this no more dishonours you at all
> Than to take in a town with gentle words
> Which else would put you to your fortune and
> The hazard of much blood.

Coriolanus is significantly silent. Perhaps he is trying, as his mother instructs him, to think of this incredible situation in terms of a military campaign. Perhaps he is perplexed by her reasoning—though recognizing its military soundness—because he has never, at least in the play, been known to use policy or to "take in a town with gentle words." But Menenius recognizes jubilantly that the shaft has found a mark. "Noble lady!" he exclaims. Volumnia is wise enough not to stop here. She knows that her son must be thoroughly briefed not merely in the need for policy but in all details of the necessary strategy (III.ii.72):

> I prithee now, my son,
> Go to them, with this bonnet in thy hand;
> And thus far having stretch'd it (here be with them),
> Thy knee bussing the stones (for in such business
> Action is eloquence, and the eyes of th' ignorant
> More learned than the ears), waving thy head,
> Which often, thus, correcting thy stout heart,
> Now humble as the ripest mulberry
> That will not hold the handling—say to them
> Thou art their soldier, and, being bred in broils,
> Hast not the soft way which, thou dost confess,
> Were fit for thee to use, as they to claim,
> In asking their good loves.

Still he is silent. What she asks of him, except the plea based on having been "bred in broils" and lacking the appropriate "soft way," is utterly repugnant to him. That he considers acquiescing at all may be not merely because of her strong hold over him but also because the soldierly apology had acquired, in Elizabethan times, a manly sort of dignity. The playwright surely recognizes this fact when he has her stress it in her detailed directions. In the same line of strategy is Volumnia's next plea, for it penetrates understandingly to Coriolanus' fundamental incompatibility with peacetime tactics (III.ii.89):

> Prithee now,
> Go, and be rul'd; although I know thou hadst rather
> Follow thine enemy in a fiery gulf
> Than flatter him in a bower.

Although Coriolanus is not asked to become, strictly speaking, a courtier, Volumnia's imagery shows that Shakespeare had in mind the conventional antithesis of court and wars. Volumnia further acknowledges the sharp antithesis when she pleads with him that, as her "praises make thee first a soldier," so

> To have my praise for this, perform a part
> Thou hast not done before.
>
> (III.ii.108)

In consenting, Coriolanus painfully pictures to himself "a part which never / I shall discharge to th' life." "Well, I must do't," he announces miserably.

> Away, my disposition, and possess me
> Some harlot's spirit! My throat of war be turn'd,
> Which quier'd with my drum, into a pipe
> Small as an eunuch or the virgin voice
> That babies lulls asleep!
>
> . . . .

                    A beggar's tongue
        Make motion through my lips, and my arm'd knees,
        Who bow'd but in my stirrup, bend like his
        That hath receiv'd an alms!

                                        (III.ii.111)

One of his most intense utterances, this speech derives its
power ultimately from the same source as Othello's great
"Farewell." It is consciously a farewell to his occupation, but
unlike Othello's speech it expresses not only the glorious
aspects of war that he is renouncing but the meaner, courtier-
like arts of peace that he must try to "discharge to th' life."
As it turns out, his farewell to the military profession is of
short duration. In fact, it scarcely lasts through the trial scene
which follows.

    This scene is one of the three great episodes toward which
Shakespeare is building in this play. In Plutarch's version it
is scarcely a scene at all, but merely a summary statement.
That Shakespeare built toward a trial scene as the first great
crisis in the play is evidence of the strong convention governing the construction of stories and plays dealing with the
misplaced soldier.

    Coriolanus proceeds stoically to the Forum, the "words
that are but roted in" held resolutely in mind. In response to
Menenius' "Calmly, I do beseech you," he promises to take
insults meekly. He seems almost to be rehearsing his "bastard"
words as he makes a grim prayer for peace (III.iii.33):

                    Th' honour'd gods
        Keep Rome in safety, and the chairs of justice
        Supplied with worthy men! plant love among's!
        Throng our large temples with the shows of peace
        And not our streets with war!

The mechanical tone of the prayer is amplified in the meaningless repetition of the word "peace" throughout the scene. It is harshly echoed by an Aedile's cry, "Peace, I say"; by the tribunes' clamorous "Peace, ho!"; and, after the people begin to riot, by Sicinius' command, "Peace!" Repetition of this inappropriate word, in a scene leading from civil trial to war, is an ironic accompaniment to Coriolanus' inability to "answer by a lawful form / (In peace) to his utmost peril."

Upon Menenius and Cominius falls the task of guiding their difficult charge through the trial. They wait uneasily for him to recite the soldier's apology that his mother had taught him. As the scene progresses, and Coriolanus begins to show the effect of being "chaf'd," the two patricians recognize with dismay that the apology is not forthcoming. Anxiously Menenius attempts to make it for him, taking advantage of Coriolanus' single agreeable utterance, that he is "content" to stand for trial. "Lo, citizens, he says he is content"; Menenius relays the curt statement to the throng, elaborating it in his own manner (III.iii.49):

> The warlike service he has done, consider.
>   Think
> Upon the wounds his body bears, which show
> Like graves i' th' holy churchyard.

But possibly Menenius senses the unpleasant truth that the citizens can only "think" of these wounds, since the General has refused to show them. Nor is his plea helped by Coriolanus' sardonic attempt at humility (reminiscent of his behavior as a candidate):

> Scratches with briers,
> Scars to move laughter only.

Menenius hastens to the agreed-upon apology for Coriolanus'
soldierly speech (III.iii.52):

> Consider further,
> That when he speaks not like a citizen,
> You find him like a soldier. Do not take
> His rougher accents for malicious sounds,
> But, as I say, such as become a soldier
> Rather than envy you.

Menenius' apology is not helped by Coriolanus' prompt illustration of the need for it. Forgetting that it is he who is on
trial, he turns angrily upon the people and tries to make
them the defendants in the scene. It now requires only
Sicinius' pointedly worded charge of treason to move Coriolanus "to choler straight," and the rest of the scene is mainly
his mighty vituperation against citizens and tribunes.

Although he fails in this scene to utilize any of the humble
aspects of the soldier's traditional apology, Coriolanus takes
advantage of its more assertive features by denouncing the
people's ingratitude toward the military profession. Upon
being banished, he cries out, much in the manner of Alcibiades (III.iii.123):

> I banish you!
> And here remain with your uncertainty.
> Let every feeble rumour shake your hearts!
> Your enemies with nodding of their plumes
> Fan you into despair! Have the power still
> To banish your defenders, till at length
> Your ignorance (which finds not till it feels,
> Making not reservation of yourselves,
> Still your own foes) deliver you, as most
> Abated captives, to some nation
> That won you without blows!

Coriolanus is thus untutored by his failure to live harmoniously in a peaceful Rome. His instinctive solution to his personal problem is not to correct himself but to correct Rome, and to do so by blows rather than words. The composure that he exhibits in the next scene is not so strange as readers have occasionally felt it to be. It is merely the result of his returning to his occupation after a miserable attempt to measure up to the code of civil government. Already he has made up his mind to offer his services to the enemy. There is, accordingly, an appropriateness, which he alone recognizes, in his parting assurance to his friends (IV.i.51):

> While I remain above the ground, you shall
> Hear from me still, and never of me aught
> But what is like me formerly.

In giving up Rome for Antium, Coriolanus is not, therefore, giving up the fatal limitations that Menenius had recently acknowledged:

> Consider further,
> That when he speaks not like a citizen,
> You find him like a soldier.

It is as a soldier that he approaches Antium. To him, the city is a military area (IV.iv.1):

> A goodly city is this Antium. City,
> 'Tis I that made thy widows. Many an heir
> Of these fair edifices fore my wars
> Have I heard groan and drop.

And it is only as a soldier that he can serve this city, just as he had been of use to Rome only during war.

As a prospective military savior of Antium, he is idolized by his former enemies (IV.v.202): "Why he is so made on here within as if he were son and heir to Mars; set at upper end o' th' table; no question ask'd him by any of the senators but they stand bald before him." And his triumphant reëntry parallels his earlier reception in Rome. He "returns splitting the air with noise,"

> And patient fools,
> Whose children he hath slain, their base throats tear
> With giving him glory.
>   (V.vi.50)

But once again it is his misfortune that the end of the war will leave him not only useless but vulnerable in his new country. He seems to be aware of this fact, and his awareness of it gives an added poignancy to his sacrifice in obeying his mother. When Volumnia prevails upon him to give up his attack on Rome, he speaks what are probably his most connotative lines in the play (V.iii.185):

> O my mother, mother! O!
> You have won a happy victory to Rome;
> But for your son—believe it, O believe it!—
> Most dangerously you have with him prevail'd,
> If not most mortal to him. But let it come.

Then he turns to Aufidius (V.iii.190):

> Aufidius, though I cannot make true wars,
> I'll frame convenient peace.

Of all men, he is the least capable of exchanging "true wars" for "convenient peace." This fact Aufidius thoroughly understands. It was he who had made the analysis of Coriolanus' tragic flaw that was quoted early in this chapter: that Coriolanus' nature could be only one thing,

> not moving
> From th' casque to th' cushion, but commanding peace
> Even with the same austerity and garb
> As he controll'd the war.

But in the Volscian situation, as in the Roman, Coriolanus does not go unescorted to disaster. Aufidius himself serves now as the cunning adversary who will misrepresent the Roman's actions to the populace and move him "to choler straight." It is partially to achieve this end that Shakespeare debases Aufidius in the final episode almost to the level of the Roman tribunes.

This final episode is clearly designed as a restatement of the theme expressed in Coriolanus' Roman ordeal. Here, once more, he returns from wars to brief acclaim at home. Once more, when charges are brought against him, he is compelled to justify himself to the people, and he again fails because he thinks in terms of blows rather than words. He reminds the people how "like an eagle in a dovecoat," he had "flutter'd your Volscians in Corioles." "Alone I did it," he roars, just before he is killed, longing in this crisis again for a chance to use his "lawful sword."

These parallels with the first trial scene are not accidental. In achieving this reiteration of theme, Shakespeare was forced not only to debase Aufidius but also to contradict Plutarch's express interpretation of the tragedy. In the historian's version, Aufidius so respects the Roman's command of oratory that he does not give Coriolanus a chance to speak in his own defense, but has him cut down instantly.[129] For Plutarch, the crisis in Coriolanus' career was the episode in which he allows his mother to dissuade him from "true wars." In Shakespeare, the scene is still supremely moving—in fact, it is transcribed almost verbatim from North's language—but in the context of the play it is not in itself disastrous. Consistent in a way that Plutarch seldom is, and rare even for himself, Shakespeare carries to the play's end his distinctive reason for Coriolanus' failure. Twice the Roman has tried to move from the casque to the cushion, and twice he has failed.

In *Timon of Athens,* we recall, Shakespeare prevented a clear-cut judgment upon Alcibiades as a rude warrior by failing to keep the same warrior and the same society to the end of the play. Coriolanus, on the other hand, is the same person at the finish as at the start; and although the social scene shifts from Rome to Antium, there is no substantial difference in Shakespeare's depiction of the two cities. But the dramatist, while repeatedly stressing the fact of his hero's failure, again finds ways of baffling any attempt to assess the exact extent of his blame.

Changes from Plutarch's version indicate that Shakespeare intended both to worsen certain of Coriolanus' unsocial traits and to find new ways to defend them. By lessening the warrior's social intelligence and by utilizing the historian's hint about meager education, he created a citizen more convincingly troublesome and vulnerable than the original. But these changes also tended to diminish those flaws in Plutarch's hero that derived from his greater cleverness. Plutarch's Coriolanus, having more of a brain to guide his actions, comes closer to being a villain. In Shakespeare's interpretation of the story, much of the villainy is transferred from the character of the protagonist to external agents, notably the tribunes and Aufidius. Had the dramatist's primary intention been to censure Coriolanus' character, he would not have highlighted the criminal cunning of his adversaries.

Shakespeare's reasons for giving a greater simplicity to Coriolanus seem to have been friendly ones on the whole, for the transformation permitted him to bring the harsh Roman aristocrat into a context wherein the Elizabethan audience would understand, if not fully condone, his difficulties. In this context—that of the noble soldier who fails as a citizen—the soldier still commanded much of the respect as a tragic hero that Rich had once given him. Jacobean pacifism and the reaction to Essex's rebellion had indeed made the soldier's place in the story a less comfortable one. But, as Chapman's Byron and Daniel's Philotas had proved, the position was by no means indefensible and certainly not ignoble. Soldier citizens of this caliber could no longer claim a political endorsement, but they still exhibited an integrity and largeness of spirit that lifted them above their meaner adversaries as subjects for tragic drama.

Notes

NOTES TO CHAPTER I

"A Fearful Battle Rend'red You in Music"

[1] In addition to the scholars mentioned in the preface, the principal students of Shakespeare's war and soldiers have been Sir John Fortescue, J. R. Moore, F. S. Boas, and G. B. Harrison. Miss Lily B. Campbell's study of *Henry V* in *Shakespeare's "Histories": Mirrors of Elizabethan Policy* (San Marino, California, 1947), chapter xv, perhaps comes closest to a thorough examination of battle within a single play; but the real achievement of her investigation is a central and entire illumination of *Henry V* as a political play dealing with war.

[2] *Henry V* III.ii.3–4. All Shakespeare references are to *The Complete Works of Shakespeare*, ed. G. L. Kittredge (Boston, 1936).

[3] Quoted by Sir John Fortescue in *Shakespeare's England* (Oxford, 1916), II, 284.

[4] Edited by Richard Simpson, *School of Shakespeare* (London, 1878), I, 202.

[5] John Pikering, *The Historye of Horestes* (1567), sig. D 1, Tudor Facsimile Texts, Vol. LIX.

[6] *Henry V* IV.Chorus.50–51.

[7] *Ibid.*, III.Chorus.35.

[8] *The Arte of Warre*, tr. Peter Whitehorne (1560), in The Tudor Translations (London, 1905), p. 93. Cf. Louis Le Roy, *Of the Interchangeable Course, or Variety of Things*, tr. Robert Ashley (1594), fol. 116. For the titles of Elizabethan military books, I have followed, except for capitalization, the form given in Maurice J. D. Cockle's *A Bibliography of English Military Books up to 1642 and of Contemporary Foreign Works* (London, 1900).

[9] "Orchestra," stanza 87, in *The Complete Poems of Sir John Davies*, ed. A. B. Grosart (The Fuller Worthies' Library, 1869), p. 211.

[10] *Histriomastix* V.i, in *The Plays of John Marston,* ed. Geoffrey Bullough (Edinburgh, 1949), Vol. III.

[11] Thomas Heywood, *2 Edward IV,* in *The Dramatic Works of Thomas Heywood* (London, 1874), I, 102.

[12] *The Tragedie of Caesar and Pompey. Or Caesars Revenge* (1607), sig. H 4ᵛ, Tudor Facsimile Texts, Vol. XI.

[13] Gretchen L. Finney has suggestively described the origins and some of the features of that frame in a recent article: "A World of Instruments," *ELH,* XX (1953), 87–120. She has not, however, included war in her study.

[14] II.i.38, in *The Shakespeare Apocrypha,* ed. C. F. Tucker Brooke (Oxford, 1929).

[15] The Stationers' Register entry is of 1631. See E. K. Chambers, *The Elizabethan Stage* (Oxford, 1923), III, 300.

[16] Signature C 2ᵛ, Tudor Facsimile Texts, Vol. LXXVI.

[17] *The Complete Works of Shakespeare,* p. 1113.

[18] "The Bleeding Captain Scene in *Macbeth,*" *Review of English Studies,* XXII (1946), 127.

[19] *The xiii Bookes of Æneidoes* (1584), sig. O 4ᵛ (Book IX, lines 503–504, in the Loeb edition, 1922). Phaer's translation was completed by Thomas Twyne.

[20] *Ibid.,* sig. D 2 (lines 486–488 in the Loeb edition).

[21] Thomas Nashe is possibly mocking the genre when, in a declamation, he promises to omit "encomiasticall Orations, and mercuriall and martiall discourses of the terribilitie of war;" *Have with You to Saffron-Walden* (1596), in *The Works of Thomas Nashe,* ed. R. B. McKerrow (London, 1904), III, 45.

[22] I.ii.16, in *The Works of Thomas Kyd,* ed. F. S. Boas (Oxford, 1901). Subsequent references to Kyd are to this edition.

[23] IV.ii.104. References are to J. W. Cunliffe's edition in *Early English Classical Tragedies* (Oxford, 1912).

[24] See D. C. Collins, *A Handlist of News Pamphlets, 1590–1610* (London, 1943); and for a specific discussion of the military newsbooks, H. J. Webb, "Military Newsbooks during the Age of Elizabeth," *English Studies,* XXXIII (1952), 241–251. Many of these books can be viewed, in an expertly supplied contemporary context, in G. B. Harrison's *The Elizabethan Journals* (London, 1938).

[25] For evidence that Hotspur was using the very best and latest vocabulary of Elizabethan warfare, read almost any section of Sir Roger Williams' *A Briefe Discourse of Warre* (1590). Between pages 48 and 50, this professional soldier uses the following terms: *casamat, counterskarf, mines, bulwarke, trenches, sallie, cavalero, culvering,* and *rampir.* Through them, Williams succeeds in giving "all the currents of a heady fight."

[26] Edition cited, sig. H 4ᵛ.

[27] *The Noble Spanish Soldier,* sig. C 2ᵛ. Here the intention is comic, as it is in *Edward III* when young Phillip exclaims (III.i.123):

> O Father, how this echoing Cannon shot,
> Like sweete hermonie, disgests my cates!

But most uses are serious. Peele, in his "A Farewell," typically orchestrates cannon with musical instruments, human screams, and horses' neighing (lines 13–15, in *The Works of George Peele,* ed. A. H. Bullen [London, 1887]).

[28] The best account of Elizabethan achievement in gunnery is to be found in H. J. Webb, "The Science of Gunnery in Elizabethan England," *Isis,* XLV (1954),

Notes † 317

10–21. The kindred science of fortification is ably examined by P. H. Kocher in "Marlowe's Art of War," *Studies in Philology*, XXXIX (1942), 207–225.

[29] See W. G. Stone's introduction to his edition of *Henry V*, The New Shakspere Society Publications, no. 10, ser. 2 (London, 1880), p. xx.

[30] *The Miracle of the Peace in Fraunce*, tr. Joshua Sylvester (1599), p. 30.

[31] *The Spanish Tragedy* I.ii.48.

[32] *Edward III* V.147.

[33] Presenter's speech at beginning of Act V, line 23, in Bullen's edition.

[34] Paul Hentzner's observations may be found in W. B. Rye, *England as Seen by Foreigners in the Days of Elizabeth* (London, 1865), p. 111.

[35] See the chapter "How Passions are mooved with musicke and instruments" in Thomas Wright's *The Passions of the Minde in Generall* (1604), pp. 159–172.

[36] Jacobus, comes Purliliarum [Porcia, Giacomo, Count], *The Preceptes of Warre*, tr. Peter Betham (1544), sigs. B 7ᵛ–B 8. For Renaissance instances of strategic clamor, particularly in the Spanish army, see Sir Roger Williams, *The Actions of the Lowe Countries* (1618), pp. 28, 93.

[37] *The Spanish Tragedy* I.ii.28. See also Kyd's *Cornelia* V.v.151–153.

[38] *Five Decades of Epistles of Warre* (1622), pp. 57–58.

[39] *Orchésographie* (1588). Cited by H. G. Farmer, *The Rise and Development of Military Music* (London, 1912), p. 33.

[40] Most contemporary sketches of armies on the march show both fife and drum. The military funeral for Sidney portrayed in T. Lant's *Celebritas et pompa funeris* [1587] shows two drums and one fife. One drum and one fife are apparent in the army of Sir Henry Sidney setting out on an expedition, as it is pictured in T. Derricke's *Image of Ireland* (reproduced in Cyril Falls, *Elizabeth's Irish Wars* [London, 1950], facing page 64).

[41] Markham does so in the passage just cited (note 38). Grose (*Military Antiquities* [London, 1786–1788], I, 314) notes that the fife was occasionally called the "Allamane whistle."

[42] *Of the Interchangeable Course, or Variety of Things*, fol. 116.

[43] See Markham, *op. cit.*, p. 60; Le Roy, *op. cit.*, p. 116.

[44] Markham, p. 83. See also J[ohn] C[ruso], *Militarie Instructions for the Cavallerie* (Cambridge, 1632), p. 55.

[45] *Shakespeare and Music* (new edition; London, 1931), p. 174.

[46] For the retreat see *1 Henry IV* V.iv.163; *Henry V* III.ii.89. The drum predominantly sounded the alarum, possibly indicative of the scarcity of cavalry action in Shakespeare. Naylor (*op. cit.*, p. 160) finds that of seventy-two alarums in stage directions, seventy usually mean a call to battle by drums. The trumpet alarum is restricted mainly to tournaments. See G. H. Cowling, *Music on the Shakespearean Stage* (Cambridge, 1913), pp. 50–51.

[47] See also *Richard II* III.iii.32, 61; *1 Henry IV* IV.iii.29; *1 Henry VI* III.iii.35; and *3 Henry VI* V.i.16.

[48] For the musical aspects of these signals, see Cowling, *op. cit.*, pp. 45–48.

[49] Grose, *Military Antiquities*, I, 315.

[50] Markham, *op. cit.*, p. 59.

[51] Sir Charles Oman, *A History of the Art of War in the Sixteenth Century* (New York, 1937), p. 61.

[52] In his *Military Discipline* (2d ed.; 1639), William Barriffe devotes a full chapter to the drum, though he does select six beats which every soldier should

learn (p. 12): Call, Troop, March, Preparative, Battaile, and Retreat. Du Praissac's *Art of Warre,* tr. John Cruso (1639), mentions (p. 131): "the march, the alarm, the troop, the chamadoes, and answers thereunto, reveille, and proclamations." Earlier writers, like Smith and Le Roy, although simpler, are apt to include unique items or phrase traditional items in an original manner.

[53] V.i, in *The Works of Francis Beaumont and John Fletcher,* ed. A. R. Waller and A. Glover (Cambridge, 1905–1912).

[54] Quoted by H. G. Farmer, *op. cit.,* pp. 22–23.

[55] *An Itinerary* (1617), III, 267.

[56] "Mars His Triumph," in Barriffe's *Military Discipline,* pp. 2, 6.

[57] Besides the English and French marches, Shakespeare also on one occasion (*Hamlet* III.ii.96) calls for a "Danish march."

[58] Markham, *op. cit.,* p. 59.

[59] A dead march for the funeral of Henry V occurs at the beginning of *1 Henry VI,* an imaginative and effective usage in that it sets the mood for the entire historical series to come.

[60] In contemporary plays, likewise, he observed and imitated the convention of using the alarum for rallying during a battle, as well as for calling to an attack. In *Edward III* IV.iv, as Cowling has noted (*op. cit.,* p. 43), "drums beat not only before but during the fight." Shakespeare does not, however, depict the important strategic employment of the alarum as a feinting maneuver. In *A True Historie of the Memorable Siege of Ostend* (1604), for example, the enemy are reported (p. 17) as intending "to give the Towne an alarme upon the East, and to give an assault upon the West part."

[61] The direction "Alarum, as in battle," beginning the eighth scene of *Coriolanus,* Act I, is apparently unique.

[62] Markham, *op. cit.,* p. 58.

[63] The function of waking the sleepers had also, of course, a religious connotation; and the soldier Gascoigne had used it effectively in his treatise *The Droome of Domes Day* (1576).

[64] *The Battle of Alcazar* II.13.

NOTES TO CHAPTER II

Major Discords

[1] *A Myrrour for English Souldiers* (1595), sig. C 1.

[2] *1 Edward IV,* in *The Dramatic Works of Thomas Heywood* (London, 1874), I, 17.

[3] Sir Robert Dallington, *Aphorismes Civill and Militarie* (1613), p. 186.

[4] "The Life of Alexander the Great," in *The Lives of the Noble Grecians and Romans,* tr. Thomas North (Stratford-upon-Avon, 1928), V, 165 (henceforth cited as *Lives*). This section of the chapter is drawn from my article "Divided Command in Shakespeare," *Publications of the Modern Language Association of America,* LXX (1955), 750–761.

[5] *Lives,* II, 256.

[6] "The Life of Fabius Maximus," *Lives,* II, 88.

[7] Thomas Procter, *Of the Knowledge and Conducte of Warres* (1578), fol. 12ᵛ.

[8] Jean Bodin, *The Six Bookes of a Commonweale*, tr. Richard Knolles (1606), p. 420.

[9] *The Works of Sir Walter Ralegh*, ed. W. Oldys and T. Birch (Oxford, 1829), VI, 267–268. In *The Cabinet-Council* (*Works*, VIII, 136) Ralegh draws upon another segment of Roman history, that of the creation of the four *tribuni militares*, to enforce his opinion that "the plurality of commanders in equal authority is for the most part occasion of slow proceeding in the war."

[10] Jaques Hurault, *Politicke, Moral, and Martial Discourses*, tr. Arthur Golding (1595), p. 379.

[11] Clement Edmonds, *Observations upon Caesars Commentaries* (1604), p. 121; Henri, Duc de Rohan, *The Complete Captain, or, An Abbridgement of Caesars Warres, with Observations upon Them . . . Englished by J. C.* (1640), p. 164. For the importance of the *Commentaries* in England, see H. J. Webb, "English Translations of Caesar's *Commentaries* in the Sixteenth Century," *Philological Quarterly*, XXVIII (1949), 490–495.

[12] Matthew Sutcliffe, *The Practice, Proceedings, and Lawes of Armes* (1593), p. 51.

[13] Antonio de Guevara, *The Dial of Princes*, tr. Thomas North (1582), fol. 54; Barnaby Rich, *A Souldiers Wishe to Britons Welfare* (1604), p. 12.

[14] Hurault, *op. cit.*, p. 380.

[15] *Machiavels Discourses upon the First Decade of T. Livius*, tr. Edward Dacres (1636), pp. 525–527.

[16] Sutcliffe, *op. cit.*, sig. B 2.

[17] William Camden, *The Historie of . . . Princesse Elizabeth* (1630), Book IV, p. 91.

[18] *Ibid.*, Book IV, p. 95.

[19] See, e.g., the following accounts: Sir William Slyngisbie, "Relation of the Voyage to Cadiz, 1596," ed. J. S. Corbett, in *The Naval Miscellany* (Navy Records Society, 1902); *The Naval Tracts of Sir William Monson*, ed. M. Oppenheim (Navy Records Society, 1902); Sir Francis Vere, "The Calis Journey," in *The Commentaries of Sir Francis Vere* (Cambridge, 1657); "A Briefe and True Report of the Honorable Voyage unto Cadiz, 1596," in *Purchas His Pilgrimes* (Glasgow, 1907), Vol. XX; and the longer version of the "Report" in Richard Hakluyt, *The Principal Navigations* (Glasgow, 1904), Vol. IV.

[20] *A Second and Third Blast of Retrait from Plaies and Theaters* (1580), p. 105.

[21] *Shakespeare's Plutarch*, ed. C. F. Tucker Brooke (London, 1909), I, 168.

[22] This important change has been noticed by Virgil K. Whitaker, *Shakespeare's Use of Learning* (San Marino, California, 1953), p. 236.

[23] *Shakespeare's Plutarch*, I, 171.

[24] James E. Phillips, *The State in Shakespeare's Greek and Roman Plays* (New York, 1940), pp. 48–49.

[25] Besides the works by Phillips and Whitaker already cited, special mention should be made of O. J. Campbell's *Comicall Satyre and Shakespeare's Troilus and Cressida* (San Marino, California, 1938). Although my remarks on *Troilus* do not stress the satirical function of the play, I assume throughout the justness of Professor Campbell's argument for interpreting it as "comical satire."

[26] *The Castle, or Picture of Pollicy* (1581), fol. 24.

[27] Sutcliffe, *op. cit.*, p. 36.

[28] *The Arte of Warre*, tr. Peter Whitehorne (1560), in The Tudor Translations (London, 1905), p. 197.

[29] *A True Copie of a Discourse* (1589), p. 102.

[30] *Calendar of State Papers (Foreign)*, XXI, 210–211.

[31] See O. J. Campbell, *op. cit.*, p. 228.

[32] Camden, *op. cit.*, Book IV, p. 105.

[33] *Ibid.*, Book IV, p. 418.

[34] M. W. MacCallum, *Shakespeare's Roman Plays and Their Background* (London, 1925), p. 349.

[35] Letter of May 8, 1596, to E. Reynolds, his secretary; printed in W. B. Devereux, *Lives and Letters of the Devereux, Earls of Essex* (London, 1853), I, 342.

[36] Vere, *op. cit.*, p. 26.

NOTES TO CHAPTER III

Military Rank

[1] According to Draper, Shakespeare "knew little of army organization and of the ranks and grades of officers"; J. W. Draper, " 'Othello' and Elizabethan Army Life," *Revue Anglo-Américaine*, IX (1931–1932), 319. For Fortescue's argument, see *Shakespeare's England* (Oxford, 1916), I, 117–121; and for Webb's, "The Military Background in *Othello*," *Philological Quarterly*, XXX (1951), 40–52. Many of my own ideas in this chapter are restated (though with considerable revision to take account of Webb's article) from "Military Rank in Shakespeare," *Huntington Library Quarterly*, XIV (1950), 17–41.

[2] *Sergeant Shakespeare* (London, 1949), p. 60.

[3] See, e.g., *Comedy of Errors* IV.iii.30.

[4] My account of Falstaff as captain is indebted to that of Lily B. Campbell in *Shakespeare's "Histories"* (San Marino, California, 1947), pp. 245–254, and to the pioneering study by J. W. Draper, "Sir John Falstaff," *Review of English Studies*, VIII (1932), 414–424.

[5] Humfrey Barwick, *A Breefe Discourse, Concerning the Force and Effect of All Manuall Weapons of Fire* (1594?), sig. F 1ᵛ.

[6] Matthew Sutcliffe, *The Practice, Proceedings, and Lawes of Armes* (1593), p. 60. Thomas Styward likewise stresses "hardie, and valiant of courage"; *The Pathwaie to Martiall Discipline* (1581), p. 34.

[7] *The Castle, or Picture of Pollicy* (1581), sig. F 4. See also Styward, *op. cit.*, p. 34.

[8] *The Approved Order of Martiall Discipline* (1591), p. 11.

[9] For Rich's career, see T. M. Cranfill and D. H. Bruce, *Barnaby Rich: A Short Biography* (Austin, Texas, 1953).

[10] *A Path-way to Military Practise* (1587), sig. C 2.

[11] Elizabethan records showing how captains got their notoriety are discussed by H. J. Webb in "Elizabethan Soldiers: A Study in the Ideal and the Real," *The Western Humanities Review*, IV (1950), 144–149.

[12] "Proeme Dedicatorie," in *Certain Discourses* (1590).

[13] *Ibid.*

[14] *The Fortunes of Falstaff* (New York, 1944), p. 91.

[15] *Foure Paradoxes, or Politique Discourses* (1604), pp. 10–11.

[16] H. J. Webb, "Falstaff's 'Tardy Tricks,'" *Modern Language Notes,* LVIII (1943), 377–379.

[17] *Shakespeare's "Histories,"* chapter xv.

[18] Robert Barret, *The Theorike and Practike of Moderne Warres* (1598), p. 5.

[19] *A Souldiers Wishe to Britons Welfare* (1604), p. 67.

[20] Sutcliffe, *op. cit.,* sig. A 4ᵛ.

[21] Sir John Smythe, "Proeme Dedicatorie," in *Certain Discourses.*

[22] Thomas Procter, *Of the Knowledge and Conducte of Warres* (1578), preface.

[23] *Martial Books and Tudor Verse* (New York, 1951), p. 61.

[24] Sig. A 4ᵛ.

[25] *Ibid.,* sig. B 1.

[26] *Ibid.,* sig. B 1ᵛ.

[27] "The Politics of Shakspere's Historical Plays," *The New Shakspere Society's Transactions* (London, 1874), p. 417.

[28] The theory is attributed to Nicholson by W. G. Stone in his edition of *The Life of Henry the Fifth* (London, 1880), p. lxxxi.

[29] D. H. Madden does so momentarily, but he is surely wrong in saying, "Captain Macmorris falls into a rage at a remark of Fluellen, which if he had been allowed to finish it, would probably have proved inoffensive enough"; Madden, "Shakespeare and Ireland," in *A Book of Homage to Shakespeare,* ed. I. Gollancz (Oxford, 1916), p. 271.

[30] William Camden, *The Historie of . . . Elizabeth* (1630), Book IV, p. 54.

[31] *Shakespeare's Europe. Unpublished Chapters of Fynes Moryson's Itinerary,* ed. Charles Hughes (London, 1903), pp. 238–239.

[32] John Stow, *The Annales of England* (1605), p. 1228.

[33] Printed in *Letters of Queen Elizabeth,* ed. G. B. Harrison (London, 1935), p. 262.

[34] Included in Fynes Moryson, *An Itinerary* (Glasgow, 1907–1908), III, 130.

[35] *Ibid.,* II, 284.

[36] Arthur Collins, *Letters and Memorials of State* (London, 1746), II, 137–138.

[37] William Garrard, *The Arte of Warre* (1591), p. 68. See also Thomas Trussell, *The Souldier Pleading His Owne Cause* (1619), p. 52.

[38] See Leslie Hotson, "Ancient Pistol," *Yale Review,* XXXVIII (1948), 51–66. For Corporal Nym, see J. W. Draper, "The Humor of Corporal Nym," *Shakespeare Association Bulletin,* XIII (1938), 131–138.

[39] *A Souldiers Wishe to Britons Welfare,* pp. 32–33.

[40] *Calendar of State Papers (Foreign),* Oct. ?, 1588, p. 294.

[41] Quoted in C. G. Cruickshank, *Elizabeth's Army* (London, 1946), p. 142. Sir William Segar, authority on honor, would absolutely deny these entrepreneurs the dignities of soldiers, "because such negotiants be occupied in their owne commodities, and therefore, as men of base sort, unworthy to be numbred among men of warre"; Segar, *Honor Military, and Civill* (1602), p. 8.

[42] *Calendar of State Papers (Foreign),* Aug. 30, 1588, p. 168.

[43] *Ibid.,* Sept. 14, 1588, p. 202.

[44] *The Castle or Picture of Pollicy,* fol. 18ᵛ. For a fuller description of these offices, see Cruickshank, *op. cit.,* pp. 36–39.

[45] "The Colonel and His Command," *American Historical Review,* II (1896), 10.

[46] H. J. Webb, "The Military Background of *Othello*," *Philological Quarterly*, XXX (1951), 43.

[47] Sutcliffe, *op. cit.*, p. 12.

[48] Page 225. A facsimile of the first edition (1548) of the French original, *Instructions sur le faict de la Guerre* (Paris, 1548), has recently (1954) been published by the Athlone Press of the University of London.

[49] See Lily B. Campbell, *Shakespeare's "Histories*," p. 287; Holinshed's *Chronicles* (London, 1807–1808), III, 73.

[50] Garrard, *op. cit.*, p. 304.

[51] IV.viii.89; V.Chorus.17.

[52] *An Arithmeticall Militare Treatise, Named Stratioticos* (1579), sig. S 1.

[53] *The Mirror of Honor* (1597), p. 73.

[54] Holinshed, *op. cit.*, III, 99.

[55] Barret, *op. cit.*, p. 175; Sutcliffe, *op. cit.*, p. 39.

[56] Sir Charles Oman, *A History of the Art of War in the Middle Ages* (2d ed.; London, 1924), II, 379.

[57] IV.ii.152, in *Early English Classical Tragedies*, ed. J. W. Cunliffe (Oxford, 1912).

[58] *Foure Books of Offices* (1606), p. 191.

[59] Holinshed, *op. cit.*, III, 67.

[60] Procter, *op. cit.*, fol. 37.

[61] Styward, *op. cit.*, p. 3. See also Machiavelli, *The Arte of Warre*, tr. Peter Whitehorne (1560), in The Tudor Translations (London, 1905), XXXIX, 146.

[62] *Shakespeare's "Histories*," p. 288.

[63] Stow, *op. cit.*, p. 1226; Blandy, *op. cit.*, sig. G 3ᵛ.

[64] *Onosandro Platonico, Of the Generall Captaine and of His Office*, tr. Peter Whitehorne (1563), fol. 67. See also Garrard, *op. cit.*, p. 306.

[65] Sig. C 1.

[66] Procter, *op. cit.*, fol. 10ᵛ.

[67] Sutcliffe, *op. cit.*, p. 148.

[68] George Whetstone, *The Honorable Reputation of a Souldier* (1585), sig. B 1.

[69] *Ibid.*, sig. B 1.

[70] *The Preceptes of Warre*, tr. P. Betham (1544), sig. G 2.

[71] *A Myrrour for English Souldiers* (1595), sig E 1ᵛ.

[72] Edition cited, p. 197.

[73] J. W. Fortescue, *op. cit.*, I, 117–118; J. W. Draper, "Captain General Othello," *Anglia*, XLIII (1931), 296–310.

[74] Barret, *op. cit.*, p. 15.

[75] *A Path-way to Military Practise*, sig. E 4ᵛ.

[76] Garrard, *op. cit.*, p. 139; Styward, *op. cit.*, p. 36.

[77] *The Moor of Venice. Cinthio's Tale and Shakespeare's Tragedy* (London, 1855), p. 18.

[78] Barret, *op. cit.*, p. 248.

[79] Sir Charles Oman, *A History of the Art of War in the Sixteenth Century* (New York, 1937), p. 377. As late as 1639, the corporal's charge is still defined as "the command of his squadron," by Du Praissac in *The Art of Warre*, tr. John Cruso (Cambridge, 1639), p. 124. By 1618, however, and possibly earlier, *squadron* was also applied to cavalry organization. See Sir Roger Williams, *The Actions of the Lowe Countries* (1618), p. 38.

[80] Edition cited, p. 81.

[81] Garrard, *op. cit.*, p. 70. Among the requirements for the captaincy, Garrard lists (p. 141) a "special and particular knowledge of al those things that appertaine to the office of a Lieutenant, and the office of an Alfierus, which if hee thinke good, hee may linke."

[82] *An Arithmeticall Militare Treatise, Named Stratioticos*, p. 90.

[83] Garrard, *op. cit.*, pp. 68–69. Similar specifications are made by Trussell, *op. cit.*, p. 52, and Barret, *op. cit.*, p. 22.

[84] *A History of the Art of War in the Sixteenth Century*, p. 377.

[85] Francis Markham's *Five Decades of Epistles of Warre*, published in 1622, mentions the ensign as "the guard of his Captaines Colours" (p. 73).

[86] See Barret, *op. cit.*, p. 19; Garrard, *op. cit.*, pp. 67–68; Clayton, *op. cit.*, p. 14.

[87] Barret, *op. cit.*, p. 20.

[88] Markham, *Five Decades*, p. 73.

[89] Garrard, *op. cit.*, p. 64.

[90] *Ibid.*, pp. 62–63.

[91] *An Arithmeticall Militare Treatise, Named Stratioticos*, p. 89. The authors deemed this requirement so important that they repeat it three pages later. One also wonders if Shakespeare could have read another part of this same work (p. 88): "so ought especiallye this Officer to whom the charge of the Ensigne is committed, above al other to have honorable respect of his charge, and to be no lesse careful and jealous therof, than every honest and honorable Gentleman should be of his wife." Leslie Hotson suggests that Shakespeare knew Thomas Digges personally, and possibly his treatise, before drawing the portrait of Fluellen; see *I, William Shakespeare* (New York, 1938), pp. 118–122; and Lily B. Campbell, *Shakespeare's "Histories,"* pp. 299–300.

[92] Garrard, *op. cit.*, p. 67.

[93] *Five Decades*, p. 73.

[94] "The Military Background in *Othello*," pp. 51–52.

[95] For Smythe's complaint, see *Annals of the Reformation and Establishment of Religion . . . in the Church of England during Queen Elizabeth's Happy Reign*, ed. John Strype (Oxford, 1824), IV, 65.

[96] *Historical Manuscripts Commission. Calendar of the Manuscripts of the Most Hon. the Marquis of Salisbury* (London, 1883–1940), XVI, 130.

[97] *Calendar of State Papers (Foreign)*, July 13, 1588, p. 45.

[98] Sir Henry Knyvett, *The Defence of the Realme* (1596), ed. Charles Hughes (Oxford, 1906), pp. 60–61.

[99] *A View of the Present State of Ireland* (1596), ed. W. L. Renwick (London, 1934), p. 156.

[100] Barret, *op. cit.*, p. 7. See also two works close in date to *Othello*: Rich, *A Souldiers Wishe to Britons Welfare* (1604), p. 33; Robert Pricket, *A Souldiers Wish unto His Soveraigne Lord King James* (1603), sig. C 1ᵛ.

[101] "Thomas Hood's Inaugural Address as Mathematical Lecturer of the City of London, 1588," *Journal of the History of Ideas*, III (1942), 96–97.

[102] Barret, *op. cit.*, pp. 5–6.

[103] *The Art of Gunnery* (1600), sig. A 2.

[104] "Preface to the Reader," in *An Arithmeticall Militare Treatise, Named Stratioticos*.

[105] Camden, *op. cit.*, Book IV, p. 137.

[106] Renaissance Italy's military studies which revolutionized the art of war and, consequently, the qualities needed in an officer, are discussed by F. L. Taylor in *The Art of War in Italy 1494–1529* (Cambridge, 1921).

[107] J. R. Moore, "Othello, Iago, and Cassio as Soldiers," *Philological Quarterly*, XXXI (1952), 189–194.

[108] *The Complete Works of Shakespeare* (Boston, 1936), p. 1242.

[109] V. K. Whitaker, *Shakespeare's Use of Learning* (San Marino, California, 1953); see page 325 for a summary statement.

NOTES TO CHAPTER IV

The Common Soldier: Food for Powder

[1] *Newes from Brest* (1594), sig. B 1.

[2] *The Countesse of Pembrokes Arcadia* (1590), ed. Albert Feuillerat (Cambridge, 1939), p. 390.

[3] *Sir Thomas More's Utopia,* ed. J. C. Collins (Oxford, 1904), p. 114.

[4] *The Letters of Queen Elizabeth,* ed. G. B. Harrison (London, 1935), pp. 178–179.

[5] C. G., *A Watch-Worde for Warre* (1596), sig. E 3.

[6] William Blandy, *The Castle* (1581), fol. 25ᵛ.

[7] *The Mirror of Honor* (1597), p. 36.

[8] *Ibid.,* p. 53.

[9] *The Trumpet of Warre* (1598), sig. C 1ᵛ.

[10] Sir John Smythe, "Proeme Dedicatorie," in *Certain Discourses* (1590).

[11] John Pikering, *The Historye of Horestes* (1567), sig. C 1, Tudor Facsimile Texts, Vol. LIX.

[12] *Edmond Ironside,* Malone Society Reprints, ed. Eleanor Boswell (1927), lines 334–337.

[13] *The Wars of Cyrus,* ed. J. P. Brawner (Urbana, Illinois, 1942), lines 47–48.

[14] *2 Tamburlaine,* in *The Works of Christopher Marlowe,* ed. C. F. Tucker Brooke (Oxford, 1910), IV.iii.4049–4054.

[15] *The Historye of Horestes,* sigs. B 2ᵛ–B 4.

[16] *Ibid.,* sigs. C 3ᵛ–C 4.

[17] G. G. Langsam has made an excellent statement of those traits of blustering soldiers which, in any century, betray their kinship with the *miles gloriosus.* See his *Martial Books and Tudor Verse* (New York, 1951), pp. 95–97.

[18] *Calendar of State Papers (Domestic),* Aug. 9, 1595.

[19] *Ibid.,* Sept. 7, 1595.

[20] *Ibid.,* June, 1599 (p. 227).

[21] John Stow, *The Annales of England* (1605), pp. 1281–1282.

[22] C. G. Cruickshank, *Elizabeth's Army* (Oxford, 1946), p. 15.

[23] *Foure Paradoxes, or Politique Discourses* (1604), pp. 47–48

[24] *The Theorike and Practike of Moderne Warres,* p. 7.

[25] *Acts of the Privy Council. New Series,* ed. J. R. Dasent (London, 1890–), July 26, 1596, XXVI, 59; Sept. 10, 1586, XXVI, 162.

[26] *The Foure Bookes of Flavius Vegetius Ranatus,* tr. John Sadler (1572), sig. A 3.

Notes † 325

[27] *Of the Knowledge and Conducte of Warres* (1598), fol. 21^v.

[28] *The Practice, Proceedings, and Lawes of Armes* (1593), pp. 65–66.

[29] *Acts of the Privy Council*, Apr. 14, 1597, XXVII, 41.

[30] *Calendar of State Papers (Domestic)*, Mar., 1598 (p. 38). See also Gervase Markham, *The Souldiers Accidence* (1643), pp. 1–2.

[31] *Certain Discourses*, sig. H 1^v.

[32] *Instructions, Observations, and Orders Militarie* (1594), p. 188. (Maurice J. D. Cockle had seen only the second edition, 1595, of this work.)

[33] *Ibid.*, p. 180.

[34] William Phillips, *Papers Relating to the Trained Soldiers of Shropshire in the Reign of Elizabeth*, in *Shropshire Archaeological and Natural History Society Transactions, Second Series*, II (1890), 246.

[35] *Acts of the Privy Council*, Jan. 8, 1592, XXIV, 15.

[36] Richard Bagwell, *Ireland under the Tudors* (London, 1885–1890), III, 249.

[37] Vegetius, *op. cit.*, sig. A 3.

[38] Sutcliffe, *op. cit.*, p. 67.

[39] *A Right Exelent and Pleasaunt Dialogue, betwene Mercury and an English Souldier* (1574), sig. G 8.

[40] See, e.g., Anthony Martin, *An Exhortation, To Stirre up the Mindes of All Her Majesties Faithfull Subjects, To Defend Their Countrey in This Daungerous Time, from the Invasion, of Enemies* (1588); *An Oration Militarie to All Natural Englishmen . . . To Move Resolution in These Dangerous Times . . . Written by a Zealous Affected Subject* (1588).

[41] William Bullein, *Bulleins Bulwarke of Defence Againste All Sicknes, Sornes, and Woundes* (1562), fol. lxxiii.

[42] *Correspondence of Robert Dudley, Earl of Leycester*, ed. John Bruce for the Camden Society (London, 1844), p. 87.

[43] *Acts of the Privy Council*, Apr. 14, 1597, XXVII, 41–42.

[44] *Ibid.*, June 14, 1597, XXVII, 197–198.

[45] As did John Norden in *The Mirror of Honor*, p. 49.

[46] *A Souldiers Wishe to Britons Welfare* (1604), pp. 61–63.

[47] *Ibid.*, pp. 63–64.

[48] Quoted by Richard Bagwell, *op. cit.*, III, 249. Another mayor complained that the last levies arrived "in very naked sort, some taken upon the highway and some out of their beds"; *Calendar of State Papers (Ireland)*, July 19, 1595.

[49] *Acts of the Privy Council*, XXVII, 300.

[50] *Ibid.*, XXIX, 43–44.

[51] Lily B. Campbell, *Shakespeare's "Histories"* (San Marino, California, 1947), p. 252.

[52] Sir Henry Knyvett, *The Defence of the Realme*, ed. Charles Hughes (Oxford, 1906), p. 61.

[53] *A Souldiers Wishe to Britons Welfare*, p. 65.

[54] *De Maisse; A Journal of All That Was Accomplished by Monsieur de Maisse, Ambassador in England*, ed. G. B. Harrison and R. A. Jones (London, 1931), p. 109.

[55] *Calendar of State Papers (Foreign)*, before Aug. 28, 1588 (p. 166).

[56] *Calendar of State Papers (Ireland)*, Aug. 2, 1598.

[57] *The Letters of Queen Elizabeth*, p. 178.

[58] *The Populace in Shakespeare* (New York, 1949), pp. 126–128.

[59] "Proeme Dedicatorie," in *Certain Discourses.*

[60] Humphrey Barwick, *A Breefe Discourse* (1594?), sig. I 3.

[61] De Maisse, *op. cit.*, pp. 93–94.

[62] Barret, *op. cit.*, p. 11.

[63] Blandy, *op. cit.*, sig. F 3.

[64] William Camden, *The Historie of . . . Elizabeth* (1630), Book IV, p. 41.

[65] *A Relation of Cadiz Action in the Year 1596*, in *The Works of Sir Walter Ralegh*, ed. W. Oldys and T. Birch (Oxford, 1829), VIII, 673–674.

[66] *The Annales of England*, pp. 1230–2131.

[67] *Shakespeare's Plutarch*, ed. C. F. Tucker Brooke (London, 1909), II, 149.

[68] *Calendar of State Papers (Spanish)*, Nov. 5, 1588.

[69] Willard Farnham, *The Medieval Heritage of Elizabethan Tragedy* (Berkeley, California, 1936), pp. 428–432.

[70] *A Souldiers Wishe to Britons Welfare*, p. 65.

[71] *Calendar of State Papers (Foreign)*, July 12, 1588.

[72] Camden, *op. cit.*, Book IV, p. 135.

[73] *Shakespeare's Plutarch*, II, 148.

[74] *The Dramatic Works of Thomas Heywood* (London, 1874), I, 20.

[75] See *The True Reporte of the Service in Britanie Performed by the Honorable Knight Sir John Norreys* (1591), sigs. A 4ᵛ–B 1.

[76] Letter of Aug. 31, 1599; in *The Letters and Epigrams of Sir John Harington*, ed. N. E. McClure (Philadelphia, 1930), pp. 72–73.

[77] Letter of Nov. 2, 1596; in Thomas Birch, *Memoirs of the Reign of Queen Elizabeth* (London, 1754), II, 189.

[78] By Mountjoy's "extraordinarie forwardnesse to put himselfe into danger," reported Fynes Moryson, his army was moved to do the same; *An Itinerary* (Glasgow, 1907–1908), II, 268.

[79] Birch, *op. cit.*, II, 404.

[80] *Arcadia*, p. 390.

[81] Sutcliffe, *op. cit.*, p. 2.

[82] Peter de la Primaudaye, *The French Academie* (1618), fol. 472.

[83] "The Politics of Shakspere's Historical Plays," in *The New Shakspere Society's Transactions* (London, 1874), p. 419.

[84] *Calendar of State Papers (Domestic)*, Apr. 24, 1596.

[85] A[lexander] L[eighton], *Speculum Belli Sacri* (1624), p. 20.

[86] *The Mirror of Honor*, sig. A 3.

[87] Barret, *op. cit.*, p. 11.

[88] *Instructions for the Warres*, tr. Paul Ive (1589), sig. B 2.

[89] Sutcliffe, *op. cit.*, p. 12.

[90] Stirling, *op. cit.*, p. 56.

NOTES TO CHAPTER V

War and Peace

[1] Lily B. Campbell, *Shakespeare's "Histories"* (San Marino, California, 1947), chapter xv.

[2] A political explanation for some of these is suggested near the end of this

chapter, but a long, separate study would be required to do justice to the tradition behind Shakespeare's rather stylized descriptions of an ideal peace. Chelidonius' "Treatise of Peace and Warre" is, as Miss Campbell points out (*ibid.*, pp. 281–282), a good example of the nondramatic works detailing conventionally the blessings of peace.

³ Most of these are listed by Maurice J. D. Cockle in *A Bibliography of English Military Books up to 1642 and of Contemporary Foreign Works* (London, 1900).

⁴ Commendatory verses to Barnaby Rich's *Allarme to England* (1578).

⁵ *Foure Paradoxes, or Politique Discourses* (1604), pp. 96–98.

⁶ *An Apologie of the Earl of Essex* (1603), sig. F 3.

⁷ Signature A 2ᵛ, Malone Society Reprints (1913), ed. W. W. Greg.

⁸ See also Robert Wilson's *The Three Lords and Three Ladies of London.*

⁹ See my "Moral Guidance and Religious Encouragement for the Elizabethan Soldier," *Huntington Library Quarterly*, XIII (1950), 241–259.

¹⁰ C. G., *A Watch-worde for Warre* (1596), sig. A 4ᵛ.

¹¹ The following titles are typical: John Udall, *The True Remedie against Famine and Warres* (1586?); Stephen Gosson, *The Trumpet of Warre* (1598); Edmond Harris, *A Sermon Preached at Brocket Hall . . . [before] the Gentlemen There Assembled for the Trayning of Souldiers* (1588); William Yanger, *A Sermon Preached at Great Yarmouth* (1600); John Stockwood, *A Very Fruitfull and Necessarye Sermon of the Moste Lamentable Destruction of Jerusalem* (1584); Thomas Nun, *A Comfort Against the Spaniard* (1596).

¹² *Allarme to England*, sig. B 1ᵛ.

¹³ *The Defence of Militarie Profession* (1579), p. 20.

¹⁴ *A Larum for London*, sigs. A 4ᵛ–B 1.

¹⁵ *Liturgies and Occasional Forms of Prayer Set Forth in the Reign of Queen Elizabeth*, ed. W. K. Clay (Cambridge, 1847), p. 619.

¹⁶ C. G., *A Watch-worde for Warre*, sig. A 3.

¹⁷ V.i.49. Kittredge expresses general scholarly opinion in pronouncing this scene "certainly Shakespeare's"; *The Complete Works of Shakespeare* (Boston, 1936), p. 1409.

¹⁸ For the paganism of the sonnets, see Sir Sidney Lee, "Ovid and Shakespeare's Sonnets," *Quarterly Review*, CCX (1909), 455–476.

¹⁹ *Chronicles* (London, 1807–1808), III, 104.

²⁰ *A Discourse of War*, in *The Works of Sir Walter Ralegh*, ed. W. Oldys and T. Birch (Oxford, 1829), VIII, 259.

²¹ "Proeme Dedicatorie," in *Certain Discourses* (1590).

²² *The Politicke and Militarie Discourses* (1597), p. 124.

²³ *A Discourse of War*, in *Works*, VIII, 293.

²⁴ See V. Luciani, "Ralegh's *Discourse of War* and Machiavelli's *Discorsi*," *Modern Philology*, XLVII (1950), 217–221.

²⁵ C. G. Cruickshank, *Elizabeth's Army* (Oxford, 1946), pp. 9–10.

²⁶ See *Acts of the Privy Council. New Series*, ed. J. R. Dasent (London, 1890–), XXVII, 290; XXIX, 62.

²⁷ *Foure Paradoxes, or Politique Discourses*, pp. 105–106. The first two "Discourses" had been the work of Dudley Digges's father, Thomas.

²⁸ *Ibid.*, pp. 104–105.

²⁹ *1 Henry IV* IV.ii.27.

[30] The importance of the "Idea of Rome" is affirmed by M. W. MacCallum, *Shakespeare's Roman Plays and Their Background* (London, 1925), p. 547.

[31] "Proeme Dedicatorie," in *Certain Discourses.*

[32] "Caelica," Sonnet CVIII, in *Poems and Dramas of Fulke Greville*, ed. Geoffrey Bullough (Edinburgh, 1938), I, 151.

[33] *Shakespeare's "Histories,"* p. 285.

[34] *The Defence of Militarie Profession*, p. 21.

[35] Sir Laurence Olivier's film version effectively gives the churchmen and their evidence a comic role, though Sir Laurence is thereby left with no better motive for Henry's war than personal revenge on the Dauphin.

[36] *Foure Bookes of Offices* (1606), p. 161.

[37] *The Works in Verse and Prose Complete of the Right Honourable Fulke Greville, Lord Brooke*, ed. A. B. Grosart (The Fuller Worthies' Library [Blackburn], 1870), I, 203.

[38] Commendatory verses to Rich's *Allarme.*

[39] *A Christian Familiar Comfort and Encouragement* (1596), sig. B 4.

[40] *Discourses upon Seneca the Tragedian* (1601), sig. H 1.

[41] *Civil Wars*, Book IV, line 46, in *The Complete Works in Verse and Prose of Samuel Daniel*, ed. A. B. Grosart (1885–1896).

[42] *The Two Noble Kinsmen* I.ii.23.

[43] C. G., *A Watch-worde for Warre*, sig. C 2.

[44] R. W. Battenhouse, "Tamburlaine, the 'Scourge of God,'" *Publications of the Modern Language Association of America*, LVI (1941), 337–348.

[45] Critics who have significantly reëvaluated him include O. J. Campbell, Willard Farnham, and James E. Phillips.

[46] Thomas Fenne, *Fennes Frutes* (1590), fol. 53ᵛ.

[47] I have used the H. H. Wood edition: *The Plays of John Marston* (Edinburgh, 1949), Vol. III.

[48] The Tudor Translations (London, 1905), p. 6.

[49] Fulke Greville, *The Life of the Renowned Sr. Philip Sidney* (1652), p. 92. See also John Norden, *Vicissitudo Rerum* (1600), sigs. D 4ᵛ–E 1; Essex's letter to the Earl of Rutland, in W. B. Devereux, *Lives and Letters of the Devereux, Earls of Essex* (London, 1853), I, 328; and Francis Bacon's essay "Of the True Greatness of Kingdoms and Estates."

[50] Roger Cotton, *An Armor of Proof* (1596), sig. A 2. See also C. G., *A Watch-worde for Warre*, sigs. D 4ᵛ–E 1; and *Fennes Frutes*, fols. 53ᵛ–54. Though not a divine, George Gascoigne also preferred the Christian interpretation of war to the cyclical one, which he attributed to "the common voice"; "Dulce Bellum Inexpertis," in *The Complete Works of George Gascoigne*, ed. J. W. Cunliffe (Cambridge, 1907–1910), I, 142–143.

[51] *The Political Works of James I* (Cambridge, Massachusetts, 1918), p. 270.

[52] *Ibid.*, p. 273.

[53] Arber's English Reprints (1869), pp. 96–97.

[54] See especially H. N. Paul, *The Royal Play of Macbeth* (New York, 1950); and Lily B. Campbell, "Political Ideas in *Macbeth* IV.iii," *Shakespeare Quarterly*, II (1951), 281–286.

[55] *Honour in His Perfection* (1624), p. 24.

[56] "To the Most High and Mightie Lord, James . . . King of Great Britaine," in *Foure Bookes of Offices.* For other tributes to James's "peace and plenty" see

Gilbert Dugdale, *The Time Triumphant* (1604), sig. A 2; and George Owen Harry, *The Genealogy of the High and Mighty Monarch, James . . . King of Great Brittayne* (1604), p. 39.

[57] This tract is included by A. H. Bullen in his edition of Middleton's *Works* (Boston, 1886), Vol. VIII.

[58] *The Political Works of James I*, p. 297.

[59] "Cloten with Caius Lucius," *Studies in Philology*, XLIX (1952), 188.

[60] *The Life of the Renowned Sr. Philip Sidney*, pp. 209–210.

[61] *Historical Manuscripts Commission. Calendar of the Manuscripts of the Most Hon. the Marquis of Salisbury* (London, 1883–1940), XVI, 269.

[62] See L. B. Wright, "Propaganda against James I's 'Appeasement' of Spain," *Huntington Library Quarterly*, VI (1942), 149–172.

[63] *The Conspiracy and Tragedy of Charles Duke of Byron* I.i.130. Chapman references are to *The Plays and Poems of George Chapman. The Tragedies*, ed. T. M. Parrott (London, 1910).

[64] *Ibid.*, I.i.151.

[65] *The Revenge of Bussy D'Ambois* I.i.32.

[66] *The Atheist's Tragedy* I.i, in *The Plays and Poems of Cyril Tourneur*, ed. J. C. Collins (London, 1878), Vol. I. See also Webster's *The White Devil* V.i.

[67] *The Tragedy of Charles Duke of Byron* I.ii.7.

[68] *The Mirror of Honor* (1597), p. 77.

[69] See H. T. Swedenberg, *The Theory of the Epic in England 1650–1800* (Berkeley and Los Angeles, 1944), pp. 9–10.

[70] *The Contemporary Review*, CXIV (1918), 576.

[71] *Troilus and Cressida* II.iii.78.

NOTES TO CHAPTER VI

The Soldier in Society: From Casque to Cushion

[1] See C. G. Cruickshank, *Elizabeth's Army* (Oxford, 1946), p. 19.

[2] Close parallels to Henry's advice may be found in many works. See, e.g., George Whetstone, *The Honorable Reputation of a Souldier* (1585), sig. C 3ᵛ; John Norden, *The Mirror of Honor* (1597), p. 58; and E. Topsell, *Times Lamentation* (1599), pp. 415–416.

[3] *The Pathwaie to Martiall Discipline* (1581), p. 42.

[4] *Acts of the Privy Council. New Series,* ed. J. R. Dasent (London, 1890–), XXV, 249.

[5] *Ibid.*, XXII, 534.

[6] *Ibid.*, XVIII, 420–421.

[7] *Calendar of State Papers (Domestic)*, Nov. 28 (?), 1599.

[8] *A Souldiers Wishe to Britons Welfare* (1604), p. 28.

[9] Sir Thomas Overbury, *New Characters*, ed. W. J. Paylor (Oxford, 1936), pp. 47–48.

[10] Sir Robert Naunton, *Fragmenta Regalia, Memoirs of Elizabeth, Her Court and Favourites* (London, 1824), p. 146.

[11] *Ibid.*, pp. 73–74.

[12] *Ibid.*, p. 48.

[13] Letter of Jan. 4, 1599, quoted by G. B. Harrison, *The Life and Death of Robert Devereux, Earl of Essex* (New York, 1937), pp. 212–213.

[14] *The Life of the Renowned Sr. Philip Sidney* (1652), pp. 91–92.

[15] *The Arte of Warre*, tr. Peter Whitehorne (1560), in The Tudor Translations (London, 1905), pp. 35–38.

[16] *Ibid.*, p. 14.

[17] Dated 1598. Printed in *Annals of the Reformation and Establishment of Religion . . . in the Church of England during Queen Elizabeth's Happy Reign*, ed. John Strype (Oxford, 1824), IV, 477.

[18] Thomas Procter, *Of the Knowledge and Conducte of Warres* (1578), fol. 18.

[19] William Garrard, *The Arte of Warre* (1591), p. 17.

[20] *Defense of the Realme* (1596), ed. Charles Hughes (Oxford, 1906), p. 32.

[21] William Camden, *The Historie of . . . Elizabeth* (1630), Book IV, p. 83.

[22] Naunton, *op. cit.*, pp. 86–90.

[23] Letter of Oct. 4, 1596. Printed in James Spedding, *The Letters and the Life of Francis Bacon* (London, 1862), II, 43. See also an anonymous letter to Essex dated Nov. 16, 1597, printed in *Calendar of State Papers (Domestic)*.

[24] Naunton, *op. cit.*, pp. 45–46.

[25] Letters of Aug. 9, 1601, and Dec. 13, 1601. Both letters printed in Fynes Moryson, *An Itinerary* (Glasgow, 1907), III, 72, and II, 427.

[26] *Calendar of State Papers (Domestic)*, Mar. 13, 1601.

[27] Signature C 2.

[28] *A Path-way to Military Practise*, sig. B 2ᵛ.

[29] William Blandy, *The Castle, or Picture of Pollicy* (1581), sig. B 3ᵛ.

[30] *Ibid.*, sigs. E 3–F 1.

[31] Geoffrey Gates, *The Defence of Militarie Profession* (1579), pp. 9–18.

[32] *Riche His Farewell to Militarie Profession* (1581), ed. J. P. Collier (London, 1846), pp. 22–23.

[33] "Achilles Tragedie," in *Euphues His Censure to Philautus* (1587), sig L 3ᵛ.

[34] *The Adventures of Brusanus Prince of Hungaria* (1592), p. 22.

[35] Though published in 1592, *Brusanus* had been written, according to Rich, seven or eight years before, and had been printed "by the great intreaty of divers of his freendes" (Title page).

[36] *The Adventures of Brusanus*, p. 29.

[37] *Ibid.*, p. 30.

[38] *Ibid.*, pp. 30–31.

[39] *Ibid.*, p. 31.

[40] *The Second Tome of the Travailes and Adventures of Don Simonides* (1584), sig. D 1ᵛ.

[41] *Ibid.*, sig. D 4.

[42] Included in *The Wil of Wit* (1597), the unique copy of which is in the Huntington Library.

[43] *The Tragedy of Philotas*, ed. Laurence Michel (New Haven, 1949), lines 1595–1598.

[44] *The Coblers Prophesie* (1594), Malone Society Reprints, no. 37 (1914), ed. A. C. Wood and W. W. Greg.

[45] "The Lamentable and Tragical History of Titus Andronicus," in *The Roxburghe Ballads* (Hertford, 1874), II, 544.

[46] The chapbook version is summarized and commented upon by J. C. Maxwell, in the Arden edition of *Titus Andronicus* (London, 1953), pp. xxxiv–xxxvii.

[47] *Riche His Farewell to Militarie Profession*, p. 10.

[48] *The Tragedy of Philotas*, lines 1587–1592.

[49] See Dorothy Hart Bruce, "*The Merry Wives* and *Two Brethren*," *Studies in Philology*, XXXIX (1942), 278.

[50] *Riche His Farewell to Militarie Profession*, pp. 8–9.

[51] The theme of honor in this play has now become a commonplace of criticism. It is succinctly described by E. M. W. Tillyard, *Shakespeare's History Plays* (New York, 1946), pp. 265 ff. See also W. Gordon Zeeveld, " 'Food for Powder'—'Food for Worms,' " *Shakespeare Quarterly*, III (1952), 249–253.

[52] Josephine Waters Bennett, *The Evolution of "The Faerie Queen"* (Chicago, 1942), pp. 204–205.

[53] Most of what I say here about Henry as a suitor is a revised statement of my article "The Courtship Scene in *Henry V*," *Modern Language Quarterly*, XI (1950), 180–188.

[54] *A Study of Shakespeare* (3d ed.; London, 1895), p. 105; *Shakespeare* (New York, 1939), p. 176; *Political Characters in Shakespeare* (London, 1945), p. 245.

[55] *Poets and Playwrights* (Minneapolis, 1930), p. 45.

[56] *Shakespeare's Library*, ed. W. C. Hazlitt (2d ed.; London, 1875), V, 371.

[57] *Henry V: The Typical Medieval Hero* (New York, 1903), p. 81.

[58] *A Souldiers Wishe to Britons Welfare*, p. 52.

[59] *Cynthias Revells* II.iii.26–29, in *Ben Jonson*, ed. C. H. Herford and P. Simpson (Oxford, 1925–1952), IV, 70.

[60] II.i and II.ii, in *The Works of Francis Beaumont and John Fletcher*, ed. A. R. Waller and A. Glover (Cambridge, 1905–1912).

[61] Translated by Sir Thomas Hoby, Everyman edition (London, 1937), pp. 36–37.

[62] *The Countesse of Pembrokes Arcadia* (1590), ed. Albert Feuillerat (Cambridge, 1939), pp. 441–442.

[63] II.i.443–446, in *Plays and Poems of Robert Greene*, ed. J. C. Collins (Oxford, 1905).

[64] *The Captain* I.ii.

[65] *1 Tamburlaine* III.ii.1025–1032, in *The Works of Christopher Marlowe*, ed. C. F. Tucker Brooke (Oxford, 1953).

[66] *The Second Tome of . . . Don Simonides*, sig. S 1ᵛ.

[67] *Riche His Farewell to Militarie Profession*, pp. 134–136.

[68] *Ibid.*, p. 4.

[69] *Ibid.*, p. 5.

[70] *Ibid.*, p. 22.

[71] Robert Greene, *Tullies Love* (1589), pp. 127–128.

[72] Attributed to Lyly by R. W. Bond, and included in *The Complete Works of John Lyly* (Oxford, 1902), I, 485.

[73] *A Pleasaunt Comedie of Faire Em*, lines 721–726, in *The School of Shakespeare*, ed. Richard Simpson (New York, 1878).

[74] *Olde Fortunatus*, in *The Dramatic Works of Thomas Dekker* (London, 1873), I, 130.

[75] *Paradoxes and Problemes* (Soho, 1923), p. 77.

[76] In *Julius Caesar* there is, of course, friction between the returning hero and

the state, but it is not a friction explicitly involving Caesar as a soldier. The same explanation accounts for the omission of *Macbeth* from the ensuing discussion.

[77] See A. H. R. Fairchild, *Shakespeare and the Tragic Theme* (Columbia, Missouri, 1944), p. 33.

[78] Willard Farnham, *Shakespeare's Tragic Frontier: The World of His Final Tragedies* (Berkeley and Los Angeles, 1950).

[79] Quoted by G. B. Harrison, *op. cit.*, p. 228.

[80] Letter of Oct. 18, 1600, quoted by Harrison, *op. cit.*, p. 273.

[81] Quoted by Harrison, *op. cit.*, pp. 304–305.

[82] *State Trials*, ed. H. L. Stephen (2d ser.; London, 1902), III, 77.

[83] *Ibid.*, p. 93.

[84] *Ibid.*, p. 97.

[85] *Ibid.*, p. 31.

[86] *Ibid.*, p. 32.

[87] *Ibid.*, p. 54.

[88] *Ibid.*, p. 68.

[89] T. B. Howell, *A Complete Collection of State Trials* (London, 1812–1826), I, 1358.

[90] Quoted by Spedding, *op. cit.*, II, 190, 192.

[91] *Sir Francis Bacon His Apologie, in Certaine Imputations Concerning the Late Earle of Essex* (1604), pp. 39–40.

[92] Michel, *op. cit.*, p. 45.

[93] Quoted by Michel, *op. cit.*, p. 38.

[94] J. de Serres, *A General Inventorie of the History of France*, tr. Edward Grimestone (1607), pp. 959–960.

[95] *The Tragedy of Charles Duke of Byron* I.ii.13, in *The Plays and Poems of George Chapman. The Tragedies*, ed. T. M. Parrott (London, 1910).

[96] *Ibid.*, V.ii.38.

[97] *Ibid.*, V.iii.22,32.

[98] *Ibid.*, V.ii.206.

[99] *Ibid.*, V.ii.259.

[100] The absurdity found even in Byron's greatness is significant, and is explained by Professor Farnham, *op. cit.*, p. 22.

[101] *Publications of the Modern Language Association of America*, XLIII (1928), 703.

[102] *Ibid.*, p. 704.

[103] *Ibid.*, p. 705.

[104] *Ibid.*, p. 707.

[105] E. K. Chambers, *William Shakespeare: A Study of Facts and Problems* (Oxford, 1930), I, 462.

[106] *The Mirror of Honor* (1597), p. 22.

[107] Bertrand de Loque, *Discourses of Warre and Single Combat*, tr. I. Eliot (1591), sig. A 3ᵛ. For an example of this behavior between two captains (Maltby and Allen) see *Calendar of State Papers (Domestic)*, Feb. 4, 1601.

[108] *As You Like It* II.vii.151. See *Politeuphuia. Wits Common-wealth* (1598), fols. 100ᵛ–101: "The talke of a souldiour, ought to hang at the poynt of his sword."

[109] *The Life of . . . Sidney*, p. 79.

[110] Alberico Gentili, *De Iure Belli Libri Tres* (Oxford, 1935), Book II, chap. iv, p. 145.

[111] F. R. Bryson, *The Point of Honor in Sixteenth-Century Italy* (New York, 1935), pp. 79–80.

[112] *Ibid.*, p. 80.

[113] *The Politicke and Militarie Discourses* (1587), p. 164.

[114] *The Mirror of Honor*, p. 20.

[115] *Ibid.*, p. 25.

[116] *Ibid.*, p. 26.

[117] *Shakespeare: The Complete Works* (New York, 1952), p. 1316. Plutarch refers to the oratorical skill of Alcibiades and his shrewdness as a politician; see M. B. Kennedy, *The Oration in Shakespeare* (Chapel Hill, 1942), p. 85.

[118] *Essayes* (1600), p. 52.

[119] *The Courtier*, p. 69.

[120] Part of what I have to say about Coriolanus in this chapter appeared in my essay "Shakespeare's Coriolanus: Elizabethan Soldier," *Publications of the Modern Language Association of America*, LXIV (1949), 221–235.

[121] *Palladis Tamia* (1598), p. 236.

[122] *A Sermon Preached at Paules Crosse* (1601), sig. C 3ᵛ.

[123] "Shakespeare, 'Coriolanus,' and Essex," *The University of Texas Bulletin*, no. 3133 (1931), p. 44.

[124] James E. Phillips, *The State in Shakespeare's Greek and Roman Plays* (New York, 1940), p. 162.

[125] *Shakespeare's Plutarch*, ed. C. F. Tucker Brooke (London, 1909), II, 162.

[126] *Ibid.*, p. 184.

[127] In *The Wil of Wit* (1597), sig. I 1ᵛ.

[128] M. W. MacCallum, *Shakespeare's Roman Plays and Their Background* (London, 1925), p. 510.

[129] *Shakespeare's Plutarch*, II, 206.

Index

335